THE 50-GUN SHIP

THE 50-GUN SHIP
A Complete History

Rif Winfield

Plans and cutaway drawings by John McKay

MERCURY BOOKS

Frontispiece:
This fully-rigged, and superbly detailed, model of a ship from the early 1740s illustrates the basic ambiguity of the 50-gun Fourth Rate. With two tiers of ordnance and a full range of upper stern lights, the design exhibits the layout and main features of a ship of the line; yet the fittings expose her relatively small size – no greater in length and tonnage than the frigates of forty years later. Small size meant small building and running costs, which were particular attractions to economy-minded Admiralties trying to maximise the number of units in the fleet, while in terms of role they could equally function as heavy cruiser or emergency addition to the battlefleet. Like many a 'jack of all trades' they were possibly 'master of none', but their flexibility ensured that substantial numbers were constructed down to the 1770s, and examples were being added to the Navy List almost to the end of the Napoleonic War. (Science Museum photo B001653)

Copyright © Rif Winfield 1997

First published in Great Britain in 1997 by Chatham Publishing.

This soft back edition published in 2005 by Mercury Books,
20 Bloomsbury Street, London WC1B 3JH
ISBN 1 845600 09 6

British Library Cataloguing in Publication Data
A catalogue record for this book is available from the British Library.

Cutaway drawings and plans by John McKay

Designed by Roger Lightfoot

Typeset by Dorwyn Ltd, Rowland's Castle, Hants
Cover Design by Open Door Limited
Printed and bound by C.T.P.S. Hong Kong

Contents

Acknowledgements and Glossary   6

Part I: Development

1. The Earliest Frigates   7

2. The Commonwealth Period   12

3. The Fourth Rate in the   18
   Restoration Navy

4. The 12pdr Fifties   25

5. The 18pdr Fifties   37

6. The 24pdr Fifties   46

7. The Last of the Two-Decker 50s   63

Part II: The Ships

8. General Arrangement and Layout   69

9. Manpower and Accommodation   77

10. Masting and Rigging   84

Cutaway drawings of HMS *Leopard 1790:*
Orlop deck and Lower deck   88-9

11. Fittings   98

12. Armament   103

Cutaway drawings of HMS *Leopard 1790:*
Upper deck, Forecastle and Quarterdeck
and Poop deck   104-5

13. Stores   114

14. Costs and Funding   117

15. Aspects of Service   119

Appendices   123

Bibliography   123

Notes   126

Index   127

Acknowledgements

Much of the source material in this book, and the bulk of its illustration, comes from the archives of the National Maritime Museum at Greenwich – in particular its vast compilation of Admiralty prints and draughts – and I am grateful to staff of the Museum and its Library for their kind assistance in my research. Most of the rest of the prime material was located at the Public Records Office at Kew, whose staff were as always helpful. As with virtually every book on the sailing navy, the detailed records of ship dimensions, armaments and histories contained in the Dimensions and Progress Books at Greenwich, and in the ADM/180 series of records at Kew, formed an essential starting point for research, while the lists of notes referred to at the close of this book indicates some of the other source material used – both primary and secondary.

I am deeply grateful to David Lyon for suggesting the idea of this book to me. It would have been much less complete without the invaluable help rendered by Fred Dittmar and David Hepper, who contributed data from their own records and constructive thoughts on early drafts. In particular, David Hepper researched for me the sailing performance records given herein, while Rob Gardiner undertook and wrote most of the analysis of these performances. Research on foreign contemporaries has been much helped by conversations and correspondence with David Roberts and Frank Lecalvé, and with Lieuwe Bouma at the Maritiem Museum Prins Hendrik at Rotterdam. Adrian Caruana has helped in clearing up matters relating to ordnance. Certainly, no modern book on the sailing navy would be honest if it failed to mention the tremendous debt owed to Brian Lavery, without whose unrivalled research, comprehensive writings and cogent advice our understanding of the whole subject matter would be much poorer.

This book has benefited from the masterly cutaway drawings of the *Leopard* prepared by John McKay that form such a valuable feature. The Annapolis photographs and much useful comment has been provided by Grant Walker at the United States Naval Museum. Most of all, an enormous debt is due to Rob Gardiner for his constant encouragement and expert advice, and to his editorial team at Chatham Publishing, Julian Mannering and Stephen Chumbley; between them they turned my typescript into a coherent and comprehensive presentation. To all the above and to others who I may have neglected to mention, I owe thanks for their kind help and expertise. All errors within the resulting work are mine alone.

Finally, this work would not have been completed without the patience and help of my wife Ann, whose tolerance and co-operation were essential in coping with the extra workload through domestic crises, election campaigns and a host of other time-consuming distractions during the progress of this book.

Rif Winfield
August 1997

Glossary

The following alphabetical list excludes modern nautical terms with which the reader is presumed conversant; it also excludes terms defined within the text of this book to which reference is obtainable via the Index.

Beakhead. The forwardmost part of the upper deck, from the stempost as far back as the transverse bulkhead that formed the forward side of the forecastle structure (the *beakhead bulkhead*).

Belfry. An ornately carved housing, usually located amidships at the break in the forecastle, from which the ship's bell was suspended.

Burthen. A measure of the internal capacity of a ship, calculated as a factor of its keel length and widest breadth.

Calibre. The diameter of the bored-out chamber of a gun.

Carronades. A design of short-barrelled gun developed by the Carron Ironworks in Scotland in the early 1770s. It fired projectiles on a flat trajectory at relatively low velocity, and was thus a short-range weapon.

Channels (originally *chainwales*). Pieces of timber projecting from the upper wales along the hull's sides in order to spread the feet of the shrouds.

Clews. The lower corners of a square sail, or the aft corner of a fore-and-aft sail. *Clewlines* were the ropes used to haul these up to the yards.

Courses. The sails set on the lower masts, square shaped for the fore and main masts and fore-and-aft on the mizzen.

Crank. Unstable, liable to lean over or capsize.

Culverin. 16th and 17th century name for a whole family of medium calibre long-barrelled gun, although eventually applied to a version firing a shot of about 17 or 18lbs. It formed the principal piece of ordnance for many 17th century Fourth Rates. The name became disused about 1710 when guns were named after their weight of shot, *eg* 18-pounder.

Cutwater. The part of the ship's stem which actually cleaves the surface of the water.

Establishment. Literally, a set of Regulations governing the construction, fitting and organisation of the ship. Most frequently refers to the specific Regulations governing construction requirements – before 1719 these only specified the principal dimensions of each Class of ship, from 1719 was more precise in defining the scantlings of every piece of timber, but it was not until 1745 that all aspects of ship design were laid down in the Establishment – and this quickly proved so rigid that the Establishments governing hull construction were abandoned within a few years.

Flûte. French term for a large naval storeship. Warships converted for storeship or troop transport by removing their lower deck (or other gun deck) weapons were described as *en flûte*.

Frame. The (approximately) U-shaped ribs of a ship's construction, mounted vertically and at right angles to the keel upon which it is fastened.

Girdling. Adding strakes of timber to the outside of the underwater body of a ship in order to improve its stability.

Knees. Curved timbers linking the deck beams to the side frames of the ship.

Knightheads. Bollards supporting the weight of a bowsprit, their tops originally carved in the form of an armed knight.

Martingale. Stay which secured the forward end of the jibboom from below.

Rasée or *razée*. A warship (usually an elderly one) cut down structurally, usually by the equivalent of a complete gun deck. While losing some of its guns – and thus lowering its Rating – the raséed ship usually retained its main battery and therefore carried heavier guns on its main deck than other ships of its newly-acquired Rate.

Round bow. Design where the stempost and other bow construction continued upwards to the forecastle deck level, eliminating the beakhead bulkhead and extending the forecastle to the bow.

Saker. A small culverin-type gun firing a projectile of about 5¼lbs.

Scantlings. The dimensions of individual pieces of timber and other constructional materials (especially the width, usually constant throughout the length of the timber).

Scarph. The overlapping of adjacent timbers in a ship's frame in order to secure continuity of strength at the joints.

Top. Platform at the summit of a lower mast, useful as a firing position for sharpshooters in battle, but designed principally for its edges to spread the shrouds.

Topgallant. The *third* tier of a ship's top hamper, comprising the mast, yard, sail and rigging above the topmast.

Tumblehome. The inwards curving of the upper part of a ship's side.

Upperworks. The superstructure of a ship rising above its upper deck, encompassing the forecastle, quarterdeck and any roundhouse built on the quarterdeck, together with bulwarks around them. The French term *gaillards* is useful as an alternative.

Waist. The uncovered space on the upper deck of a ship, lying amidships between the forecastle and the quarterdeck.

Wale. A longitudinal strake (strip) of timber stretching the length of the hull and thicker than normal planking, intended to give extra strength to the hull.

Windage. The percentage difference between the diameter of shot designed to be fired by any gun and the diameter of the bore of the gun.

Part I: Development

1. The Earliest Frigates

The 50-gun ship in the Royal Navy derived directly, like the majority of eighteenth-century British warships, from the lines and principles of the early frigates copied from Flemish (generally known as 'Dunkirker') privateers during the first half of the seventeenth century. The introduction of the frigate itself was one phase in an oscillating preference in warship design which swung between the twin but competitive demands of strength (ordnance capacity and structural sturdiness) on the one hand and flexibility (speed and manoeuvrability) on the other.

The importance of firepower during the Henrician period, as the introduction of heavy cannon meant that the relative importance of warships came to be judged by their weight of guns, was historically reinforced by the design of the traditional carrack with its high castles built both forward and aft, joined by a low waist into which small arms fire could be poured from the castles if the ship was boarded. The introduction of the low, 'race-built' galleon of the Elizabethan era was a reaction against these high, unwieldy ships with their poor speed and sailing qualities. The race-built galleon provided a fast and manoeuvrable vessel with which the Elizabethan captains harried the Armada.

But in the closing years of Queen Elizabeth's reign, the pendulum was already swinging back. The forecastles and quarterdecks of the English galleons again rose while their sailing qualities declined. In part this resulted from a natural tendency of the master shipwrights to enlarge their successful designs beyond the point where these were effective, and in part a continued attempt to increase the firepower that could be carried.

Across the Channel, a different design philosophy was being pursued. The many small privateers, hunting for prey in the English narrow seas, particularly those based on Dunkirk and other ports on the Flemish coast, had evolved a lean, low design well suited to brief raiding voyages where their speed enabled them to pounce on merchantmen and return to their base ahead of the slow, lumbering English guard vessels. Blockade was attempted – at least the English ships had the robustness to maintain station outside the Flemish ports – but realisation gradually dawned

that the problem could only be solved by commissioning English warships capable of out-sailing the 'Dunkirkers'.

While it is commonly held that the Jacobean navy made little attempt until the mid 1640s to produce vessels of the same 'frigate' design as the Dunkirkers, a few such vessels were added to the fleet as early as 1612, when the 1590-built hoy *Primrose* was apparently rebuilt along frigate lines. Four years later, a similar-sized vessel – the *Desire* – was built from scratch. These two small frigates provide the earliest evidence of the navy's response to the challenge of the Dunkirkers. Each was of about 80 tons (the *Desire* measured just 66ft on the keel with a beam of 16ft). Yet the virtues of the new design were clearly not universally appreciated, as the *Primrose* was discarded in 1618 and the *Desire* converted to a pinnace – to the detriment of her sailing qualities.

The passage of time makes precise interpretation of the ship-type terminology unclear, but it seems that contemporary use of the word 'frigate' indicated a narrow hull with moderate superstructure compared with the pinnace's broader hull form and lofty upperworks. Technically, the new hull shapes had greatly reduced sheer, a lighter V-shaped beakhead as opposed to the flat cross-section of earlier designs, a more rounded underwater section to increase buoyancy, and a bluffer entry to improve seaworthiness, while the reduced superstructure aft increased stability and made the ship less leewardly. In essence, the new lines improved seakeeping qualities as well as speed, increasing sailing qualities all round. These changes were perhaps a part of more general improvements in hull form during the seventeenth century, but the way the terminology was used suggests a value-judgement rather than an objective technical description.

Although these two small vessels were too limited to qualify as significant contributions to naval design, the principles were not lost during the next two decades. Several attempts were made to introduce a number of frigate-built vessels intended specifically to counter the menace of the Dunkirkers – William Burrell, who had built ten new additions to the fleet in the early 1620s, made several proposals for a squadron of

single-deck, low-built warships. But both difficulties of finance, and the conservatism of the king, who had to be convinced of any radical redesign for the navy, meant that few new frigates were actually put into service. The *Desire* was rebuilt a second time, reinstating her frigate qualities, and several prize vessels were fitted for the navy during the 1620s, yet the only application of frigate design to new-building was for small vessels – Burrell's *Spy* and *Fly*, and Peter Pett's *Henrietta* and *Maria*.

In November 1635 the navy captured a Dutch privateer frigate, the *Swan*, which was based on Dunkirker designs although built at Flushing. Admiral Sir John Pennington successfully urged her incorporation into the navy, and the king soon ordered Phineas Pett at Woolwich to build two vessels which Pett indicated were to be of similar design. Completed in 1636, these two vessels – *Roebuck* and *Greyhound* (the very names indicate they were designed for speed) – proved disappointing, although the evidence suggests that Pett departed from the design principles that were essential features of the Dunkirker type. Another frigate of similar design to the *Swan* fell into the navy's hands in October 1636; this was the *Nicodemus* – this time an actual Dunkirker.

While the *Swan* was wrecked (off Guernsey) in October 1638, the *Nicodemus* lasted until 1657 – and her sailing qualities were undoubtedly a factor in the introduction of the frigate in some quantities into the navy in the mid 1640s. A pair of larger vessels – the *Expedition* and *Providence* – were built on the Thames in 1637, and while never described as frigates their known details indicate that they had many frigate characteristics. Their keel-to-beam ratio of 3.46 to 1, greater even than the *Nicodemus*'s 3.32 to 1, ensured they proved as swift as most Dunkirkers, while at 300 tons apiece they carried a fair armament of 30 guns, enabling them to take their place in the Fourth Rate.

These ratios invite comparison with the more 'conventional' 34-gun ships of 1634, the *Leopard* and *Swallow*. The dimensions specified for these two ships – the specification being dictated personally by the king to the shipwrights – was for the keel to be 93ft and the breadth inside the plank to be 31ft, thus providing a 3 to 1 proportion. In practice, both vessels turned out to be slightly larger and fuller.

Further Dunkirkers were added about 1643 – bought in as the *Warwick* (renamed *Old Warwick* in 1650 to distinguish her from the *Constant Warwick*), *Cygnet* and *Star*. Like all frigates of the period, they had a keel-to-beam ratio of between 3.25 and 3.5 to 1. The sailing qualities of these and the earlier acquisitions began finally to overcome the prejudices of the Commissioners. In 1645 the Navy Board hired the privateer frigate *Constant Warwick* of 32 guns, built by Peter Pett at Ratcliffe as a private venture; his backers included the Earl of Warwick, who commanded the Parliamentary fleet, and Sir William Batten, then Surveyor of the Navy from 1638 to 1648. Although the *Constant Warwick* is traditionally described as the first English frigate, in fact the navy had three decades – albeit intermittently – of operating such vessels, and this ship can better be viewed as the end of a period of experimentation and the start of a period in which frigate characteristics were rapidly adopted for the design of a wide range of warship types and sizes.

Table 1: The early frigates, 1635–47 – construction history

Vessel	Builder	Launched	Fate
Swan (prize)	(Taken from Dunkirkers 1635)		Sunk 10.1638
Roebuck	Phineas Pett, Woolwich	28.3.1636	Sunk in collision 1641
Greyhound	Phineas Pett, Woolwich	28.3.1636	Blown up in action 14.6.1656
Nicodemus (prize)	(Taken from Dunkirkers 1636)		Sold 1657
Expedition	Franckmore, Bermondsey	1637	Fireship 6.1667; sold 10.1667
Providence	Matthew Graves, Bermondsey	1637	Fireship 6.1667; wrecked 31.10.1668
Constant Warwick	Peter Pett II, Ratcliffe	1645	BU 1666 to rebuild
Assurance	Peter Pett II, Deptford	1646	Sold 1698
Adventure	Peter Pett I, Woolwich	1646	BU 1688 to rebuild
Nonsuch	Peter Pett II, Deptford	1646	Wrecked 3.12.1664
Dragon	Henry Goddard, Chatham Dyd	1647	BU 1690 to rebuild
Phoenix	Peter Pett I, Woolwich	1647	Wrecked 3.12.1664
Tiger	Peter Pett II, Deptford	1647	BU 1681 to rebuild
Elizabeth	Peter Pett II, Deptford	1647	Burnt by the Dutch 5.6.1667

Table 2: The early frigates, 1635–47 – dimensions in feet and inches

Vessel	Guns	Keel*	Beam	Depth	Tons**	Keel/Beam Ratio
Roebuck	10	57 0	18 1	6 8	99 ^{14}/94	3.15 : 1
Greyhound	12	60 0	20 3	7 8	130 ^{82}/94	2.96 : 1
Nicodemus (prize)	6	63 0	19 0	9 6	121	3.32 : 1
Expedition	30	90 0	26 0	9 8	323 ^{58}/94 (228)	3.46 : 1
Providence	30	90 0	26 0	9 9	323 ^{58}/94 (228)	3.46 : 1
Constant Warwick	30	85 0	26 5	13 2	315 ^{48}/94 (305)	3.22 : 1
by 1660 listed as:	32	88 0	27 0		341 ^{22}/94	3.26 : 1
Assurance	32	89 0	26 10	13 6	340 ^{81}/94 (337)	3.32 : 1
Adventure	32	94 0	27 9	13 10	385 ^{3}/94 (374)	3.39 : 1
Nonsuch	34	98 0	28 4	14 2	418 ^{4}/94 (389)	3.46 : 1
Dragon	32	96 0	28 6	14 3	414 ^{72}/94 (422)	3.37 : 1
Phoenix	32	96 0	28 6	14 3	414 ^{72}/94	3.37 : 1
Tiger	32	99 0	29 4	14 8	453 ^{19}/94 (448)	3.38 : 1
Elizabeth	32	101 6	29 8	14 10	475 ^{16}/94 (471)	3.42 : 1

* length on the gundeck was not usually quoted at this date; a few figures are known (eg the Adventure had a gundeck length of 116ft 2in), but are of uncertain reliability and the relevant column is thus omitted from Tables 2 and 7.

** during the Commonwealth years, a new rule for measuring the tonnage was introduced, whereby the tons (burthen) were found by the formula $KB^2/188$ (where K and B indicate the keel length and beam in feet), a system which lasted until the early nineteenth century. For comparative purposes, ships built prior to 1660 are shown with their tonnage recalculated on this basis; there are thus discrepancies with seventeenth-century records which show the tons (or 'tons and tonnage') calculated according to the former 'Baker's Rules', using the formula $KBD/100$ (where D indicates the depth in the hold measured from the upper edge of the keel to the point where the widest breadth is found). These original tonnages, on which the price paid to the builder of the ship was calculated, appear in parenthesis after the burthen.

In the same year the Board began construction of a trio of similar vessels at the royal dockyards at Deptford and Woolwich, which were all completed in 1646. Two of these – the Assurance and the Nonsuch – were built at Deptford by Peter Pett, Jnr, while his father (Peter Pett, Snr) undertook the construction of the Adventure at Woolwich. That the Navy Board was finally convinced of the need for this type of vessel is demonstrated by the fact that within the same year orders were placed for another four frigates, slightly broader in the beam but still of essentially Dunkirker design. Following their completion, the navy purchased the Constant Warwick on 20 January 1649 to complete a fairly homogenous group of eight ships.

All eight vessels initially shared the same characteristics as the earlier frigates – a single low-placed gundeck probably carrying a score of demi-culverins, no forecastle, and a quarterdeck upon which a few lighter guns, usually sakers, could be carried. While the Constant Warwick was of blunter design than the 1637 pair (being 5ft shorter on the same breadth), the other seven were built with a similar keel-to-beam ratio of between 3.3 and 3.5 to 1.

No plans survive from this period, so much must be gleaned from the portraits by the Van de Veldes and other marine artists of the period – most of which depict the frigates after their original quarterdecks were extended forward to turn them into full two-decked vessels. The small poops which had been added about 1649 (at around the same time that forecastles were built) became the new quarterdecks.

The contemporary portraits of the Adventure and Tiger, for example, both show two-decked vessels with eleven ports a side on each of the lower and upper decks, with a further two ports a side on the quarterdeck. This – with the later addition of a pair of chase guns on the forecastle – is so precisely the configuration of the 48-gun ship that was the classic Fourth Rate of the close of the century that one must wonder why all the frigates of 1646 and 1647 were not so armed. Isaac Sailmaker's portrait of the Assurance similarly shows the vessels with a second row of guns along the upper deck (the painting can be dated by reference to the other ships depicted, the Elizabeth being launched in 1679 and the Fairfax being lost in 1682).

A more useful guide comes from contemporary models, although the date and precise identity of ships depicted by these are often doubtful. The National Maritime Museum has, among others, a model purportedly of a 'Fifth Rate' of about 1660, which is for several reasons more likely to depict a small Fourth Rate of the late 1640s.[1] The twenty-two ports on the lower deck, its low and narrow design, and the very low rake of the stem all suggest a Fourth Rate as built or modified about 1649, with a forecastle (not fitted to bear guns) and a quarterdeck (fitted for four small guns) and poop above, but with only fourteen ports on the upper deck – six forwards, eight aft, and none in the waist.

It seems probable that all the 1646–47 frigates were built with eleven ports a side on the lower (gun) deck and two pairs on the quarterdeck, but that the upper

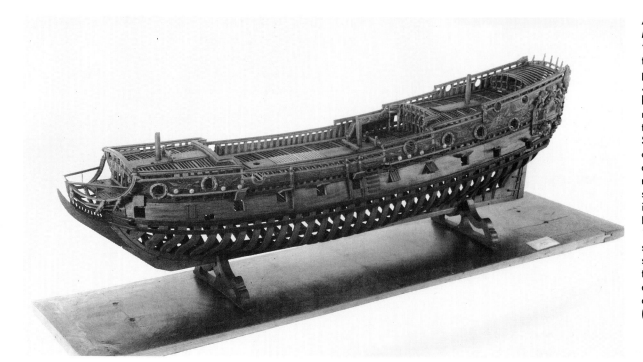

Although this National Maritime Museum model has the word 'Shearnes' carved on a panel on the upper counter, it clearly predates the earliest ship named *Sheerness* (the Fifth Rate of 1691) by several decades; it may be the name of an unknown shipwright or the place the model was built. The Stuart Arms on the stern and circular port wreaths date from after the Restoration in 1660, but might have been added subsequently; other indications including the gun layout suggest a Fourth Rate from the end of the 1640s, and the dimensions would seem to agree with this. It has been suggested that the model represents the *Adventure* of 1646, after the addition of the forecastle deck during the following decade. (NMM: A264)

deck was initially limited to about six or eight ports below the quarterdeck, and that these last were supplemented during the 1650s and 1660s by additional ports firstly below the forecastle and subsequently in the waist. Of course, the gun establishment for all seventeenth-century warships, as we now know, rarely matched the gunport configuration. The gun establishments of the period, and the rare lists of weaponry actually carried, provide some evidence (see Table 3). From the portraits, the 1681 rebuilt *Tiger* retained eleven ports a side on the lower deck and the same on the upper deck, but her quarterdeck ports were increased from two to five. However, it appears that no more than two pairs of guns were ever carried on the quarterdeck.

While the *Dragon* and *Tiger* – following their rebuilds in 1690 and 1681 respectively as 46-gun ships – were eventually armed as 50-gun ships and merged into that class, the original vessels, and their six contemporaries, never carried more than 42 guns and should be seen as progenitors of the 40-gun Fifth Rate. Indeed, the new *Nonsuch* (built 1668) and *Phoenix* (built 1671) were, with their half-sisters of 1666 (*Falcon* and *Sweepstakes*) were built as 36-gun Fifth Rates and only later uprated to 42-gun Fourth Rates; their re-classification as Fifth Rates in 1691 marked the removal of the 44/40-gun vessel from the Fourth Rates and all the frigates of 1645–47 should clearly be considered in the same classification.[2]

The 1685 Proposed Ordnance Establishment – while undoubtedly conforming more closely to what guns were actually carried by individual ships – represented a wartime establishment, whereas most vessels were actually carrying a peacetime armament at this date. The State and Remains of Ships, private

Table 3: Ordnance and manning establishments for the 1645–47 group of frigates

1652 Navy List

Constant Warwick	32 guns	140 men	Dragon	32 guns	150 men
Assurance	32 guns	150 men	Elizabeth	32 guns	150 men
Adventure	32 guns	150 men	Phoenix	32 guns	150 men
Nonsuch	34 guns	150 men	Tiger	32 guns	150 men

1660 Restoration

Constant Warwick	32 guns	115 men	Dragon	38 guns	130 men
Assurance	32 guns	115 men	Elizabeth	38 guns	130 men
Adventure	34 guns	120 men	Phoenix	38 guns	130 men
Nonsuch	34 guns	120 men	Tiger	38 guns	130 men

1666 Ordnance Establishment:

Constant Warwick	34 guns:	12 × culverins, 12 × demi-culverins, 10 × sakers
Assurance	38 guns:	10 × culverins, 24 × demi-culverins, 4 × sakers
Adventure	38 guns:	10 × culverins, 13 × demi-culverins, 14 × sakers
Dragon	40 guns:	12 × culverins, 20 × demi-culverins, 8 × sakers
Tiger	40 guns:	12 × culverins, 16 × demi-culverins, 12 × sakers
Elizabeth	42 guns:	12 × culverins, 20 × demi-culverins, 10 × sakers

Note the first three had a complement of 150 and the second three a complement of 160.

1677 Ordnance Establishment:

Constant Warwick	42 guns:	20 × demi-culverins (GD), 18 × 6pdrs (UD), 4 × sakers (QD)
Assurance	42 guns:	20 × demi-culverins (GD), 18 × 6pdrs (UD), 4 × sakers (QD)
Adventure	44 guns:	22 × demi-culverins (GD), 18 × 6pdrs (UD), 4 × sakers (QD)
Dragon	46 guns:	22 × culverins (GD), 20 × 6pdrs (UD), 4 × sakers (QD)
Tiger	44 guns:	22 × demi-culverins (GD), 18 × 6pdrs (UD), 4 × sakers (QD)

Note the new 42-gun ships recently upgraded from 36-gun Fifth Rates – *Falcon*, *Sweepstakes*, *Nonsuch* and *Phoenix* – had an identical establishment in 1677 to the *Constant Warwick* and *Assurance* above.

1685 Proposed Ordnance Establishment:

Constant Warwick	40 guns:	18 × demi-culverin (drakes), 18 × 6pdrs, 4 × 3pdrs
Assurance	42 guns:	10 × culverin (drakes), 12 × demi-culverin (drakes), 16 × 6pdrs, 4 × 3pdrs
Adventure	40 guns:	12 × culverin (drakes), 6 × demi-culverin (drakes), 16 × 6pdrs, 6 × saker cutts
Dragon	44 guns:	16 × culverin (11 drakes), 20 × demi-culverin (drakes), 6 × sakers (4 drakes, 2 cutts), 2 × 3pdrs
Tiger (rebuilt)	46 guns:	20 × demi-culverin (drakes), 18 × sakers, 8 × saker cutts

Constant Warwick	36 guns:	18 × demi-culverin, 14 × 6pdrs, 4 × 3pdrs
Assurance	36 guns:	8 × culverin, 12 × demi-culverin, 14 × 6pdrs, 2 × 3pdrs
Adventure	42 guns:	12 × culverin (drakes), 8 × demi-culverin, 1 × 8pdr, 15 × 6pdr, 6 × saker cutts
Dragon	40 guns:	16 × culverin (drakes), 18 × demi-culverin (drakes), 4 × sakers, 2 × saker cutts

papers which have survived for the (Julian) calendar years 25 March 1681 to 25 March 1683,[3] list the weaponry opposite in late 1682, and the similarities reveal that this actual disposition is what the 1685 Establishment was based on.

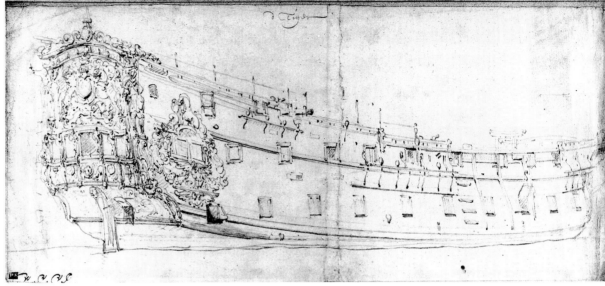

This Van de Velde sketch of the *Tiger* supposedly shows her 'as built', but the complete two-decker layout is a considerable development of the original single-deck frigate design of 1646. Comparison with the later drawing (see Chapter 3) shows few changes except in dimensions. (NMM: VV1106)

Isaac Sailmaker's portrait shows the *Assurance* to the left of the picture, still basically a single-deck ship with only light guns along the upper deck; to the right the *Elizabeth* has clearly become a two-decker – the two ships are partially obscured by the Third Rate *Fairfax* in the foreground. (NMM: BHC3334)

2. The Commonwealth Period

Following the execution of Charles I, the new Commonwealth moved swiftly to augment the navy. The new Navy Commissioners were appointed on 16 February 1649, and in April orders were placed for five frigates; of these the *Speaker* and (original) *Fairfax* were to have two full gundecks and carry 52 guns, in order to serve as flagships for the Winter Guard, and with a dozen similar vessels which followed over the next few years these were to become the ancestors of the Third Rate ship of the line. The other three were to be 'of the same rate with the new frigates lately built' (the 1647 quartet) with a single gundeck and a quarterdeck.

By the close of the year the need for further additions was apparent, and orders for ten more frigates were placed around Christmas. One was an even larger Third Rate – the *Antelope*, while the others were Fourth Rates – four to have single gundecks and five to be two-deckers. Initially, like their predecessors, they were to be built without a forecastle, but by late 1650 a decision was taken to add this to all ships building, to prevent a head sea washing over the length of their decks, to facilitate handling the headsails, and to augment their structural strength (forecastles were not to carry guns until much later). Contracts for all ships on order (above the Fifth Rate) were amended, and within a few years forecastles were added to the earlier frigates. By the end of the First Dutch War, the deficiencies in firepower of single-deck ships were also apparent, and within a few years virtually all were given a second gundeck, while the larger vessels also added a roundhouse, or poop.

A further thirty frigates were ordered in September 1652, ten to be Third Rates similar to the *Speaker* and twenty to be Fourth or Fifth Rates. All but three took to the water within two years, the remaining trio being delayed until the end of the decade. While five of the new frigates were lost – all by accident – during the Commonwealth period, there were forty-eight (including the still-building *Princess* but excluding a few captured vessels) at the Restoration, of which fourteen were Third Rates.

The *Portsmouth* group

The seven frigates ordered in 1649 to have a single continuous gundeck (the smaller three ordered in April and four more ordered at the close of the year), although instructed to follow the pattern of the 1647 group, were eventually to carry a heavier armament than the preceding seven. While all were completed as

Table 4: Commonwealth Fourth Rates, 1649 batch – construction history

Vessel	Builder	Begun	Launched	Fate
34-gun type:				
Portsmouth	Eastwood, Portsmouth Dyd	6.1649	1649	Taken by the French 31.7.1689
Sapphire	Peter Pett I, Ratcliffe		1651	Wrecked 31.3.1671
President*	Peter Pett, Deptford Dyd		1650	Rebuilt 1663
Pelican	John Taylor, Wapping		1650	Burnt 13.2.1656
Reserve	Peter Pett I, Woodbridge		1650	Rebuilt 1701
Advice	Peter Pett I, Woodbridge		1650	Rebuilt 1698
Foresight	Jonas Shish, Deptford Dyd		1650	Wrecked 4.7.1698
Assistance	Henry Johnson, Deptford		1650	Rebuilt 1687
Laurel	Portsmouth Dyd		1651	Wrecked 30.5.1657
Centurion	Peter Pett I, Ratcliffe		1650	Wrecked 25.12.1689
40-gun type:				
Diamond	Peter Pett II, Deptford Dyd		15.3.1651	Taken by the French 20.9.1693
Ruby	Peter Pett II, Deptford Dyd		15.3.1651	Rebuilt 1687

* renamed *Bonaventure* at the Restoration in 1660.

Table 5: Commonwealth Fourth Rates, 1649 batch – dimensions in feet and inches

Vessel	Gundeck	Keel	Beam	Depth	Tons	Keel/Beam Ratio
Portsmouth		99 0	28 4	14 2	422 $^{70}/_{94}$	3.49 : 1
Sapphire		100 0	28 10	14 5	442 $^{20}/_{94}$	3.47 : 1
President		100 9	29 0	14 9	450 $^{65}/_{94}$	3.47 : 1
Pelican		100 0	30 8	15 4	500 $^{22}/_{94}$	3.26 : 1
Reserve	118 4	100 0	31 1	15 6½	513 $^{87}/_{94}$	3.21 : 1
Advice	118 6	100 0	31 2	15 7	516 $^{64}/_{94}$	3.21 : 1
Foresight	121 2	102 0	31 1	15 5	524 $^{19}/_{94}$	3.29 : 1
Assistance	121 5½	102 0	31 0	15 5	521 $^{37}/_{94}$	3.29 : 1
Laurel		102 0	30 1	15 0	489	3.39 : 1
Centurion		104 0	31 0	15 6	531 $^{58}/_{94}$	3.35 : 1
Diamond	127 4	105 4	31 3	15 7½	547 $^{14}/_{94}$	3.37 : 1
Ruby	125 7	105 6	31 6	15 9	556 $^{77}/_{94}$	3.35 : 1

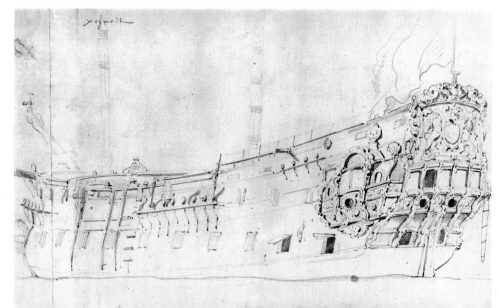

Table 6: Commonwealth Fourth Rates in English fleet at the Gabbard, 2 June 1653

(with launch or acquisition date in parenthesis, plus establishment in men and guns at the date of battle; extracted from Laird Clowes, *The Royal Navy*, Vol 2)

Red Squadron	Men	Guns	White Squadron	Men	Guns	Blue Squadron	Men	Guns
Providence (1637)	140	33	*Expedition* (1637)	140	32			
Adventure (1646)	160	40	*Assurance* (1646)	160	36	*Nonsuch* (1646)	170	40
Tiger (1647)	170	40				*Dragon* (1647)	260?	38
Phoenix (1647)	120	34						
Guinea (1649)	150	34	*Portsmouth* (1649)	170	38			
			Centurion (1650)	200	42			
Pelican (1650)	180	40	*Assistance* (1650)	180	40	*President* (1650)	180	40
Advice (1650)	180	42	*Foresight* (1650)	180	42	*Amity* (1650)	150	36
Diamond (1651)	180	42	*Ruby* (1651)	180	42	*Convertine* (1651)	210	44
Sapphire (1651)	140	38						
Laurel (1651)	200	48						
Bear (1652)	200	46						
Sussex (1652)	180	46				*Kentish* (1652)	180	50
Marmaduke (1652)	160	42						
Violet (1652)	180	40				*Welcome* (1652)	200	40

ordered, established in wartime with 36 guns (two more than when ordered) and 150 men, by the end of the decade all (except *Pelican*, lost in 1656) had their half-deck extended forward to provide a second complete gundeck, and by 1660 the first three (*Portsmouth*, *Sapphire* and *President*) had a peacetime establishment of 38 guns and 130 men, while the other four each had 40 guns and 140 men. Their construction and armament were now seemingly indistinguishable from the three vessels built with full-length upper decks discussed below, and they can be considered along with these.

The *Foresight* group

Of the five vessels ordered in December 1649 which were to have a full-length upper deck, three were of similar size to the *Portsmouth* and six similar vessels mentioned above. By 1660, when the seven 'single-decker' type had been modified, there remained no essential differences from the *Foresight* type, so the survivors formed a relatively homogeneous group.

However, the *Laurel* had by January 1652 been armed with 40 guns and had a complement of 180, and was reclassed as a Third Rate; by her loss in 1657 she carried 46 guns.

The *Ruby* and *Diamond*

Two slightly larger frigates were ordered from Peter Pett at the same time (end of 1649). Like the *Foresight* and her two half-sisters, these were to have two full decks and a forecastle. Laid down at Deptford in 1650, the *Diamond* and *Ruby* were both launched on 15 March 1651. Both were initially recorded as carrying 40 guns, with a complement of 150, and seemingly maintained this level throughout the Commonwealth period. The Van de Velde portrait of the *Diamond* (there is none of the *Ruby*) shows twelve ports per side on the lower deck, eleven on the upper deck and three on the quarterdeck – but there is no evidence that more than twenty-two lower deck guns were ever mounted.

By the 1666 Establishment, the armament had been raised to 48 guns (comprising 22 culverins, 20 demi-culverins and 6 sakers) and 180 men[4] – and the 1677 Establishment confirms similar details, with the demi-culverins replaced by 6pdrs and the sakers by minions, and with the complement raised to 230 men.[5] By the end of 1688 both carried 12pdrs on the lower deck and had reinstated 9pdrs on the upper deck, with saker cutts on the quarterdeck.

The *Ruby* was rebuilt from 1687 on by Sir Henry Johnson at Blackwall[6] but had only the lightest form of rebuild possible (in a 35-year-old ship), with most of the underwater planking left intact and the frames left unaltered (no change occurred to her principal dimensions, as evidenced by continued reference to her being of 556 tons in the 1703 Establishment). The *Diamond* would presumably have undergone similar treatment had she not been taken by the French on 20 September 1693. The *Ruby* soldiered on throughout King William's War and into Queen Anne's before undergoing a second rebuild in 1706 (see below).

Left: The *Portsmouth* was one of the first and certainly the smallest of the new Fourth Rates ordered by the young Commonwealth. She took part in every major battle of the three Anglo-Dutch wars, and was finally captured (and then burnt) after a long duel with a French ship – *Le Marquis* of 58 guns – in the Channel in 1689. (NMM: VV493)

Right: The *Portland* of 1653 as drawn by Van de Velde. She was finally lost in 1692 when she ran ashore near Malaga while trying to evade capture by a French squadron, and burnt. (NMM: VV854)

The First Dutch War

England's Rump Parliament made an offer to the Dutch States General in March 1651 of a 'close union'. Such an alliance, perhaps leading to an eventual merger of the two young Republics (the Netherlands had abolished the office of Stadtholder following Willem II's death), may have seemed a natural development for two nations with very similar economies, although the security of the new Commonwealth regime was certainly the prime English motive. But suspicion and misunderstanding, coupled with a cut-throat rivalry over the maritime trade that was the basis of economic similarities, led inexorably to war, in particular given the threat posed to Dutch shipping by the enforcement of the English Navigation Act of October 1651, and the brutal searches made of Dutch shipping in the Channel by the Commonwealth navy.

War was declared on 31 July 1652, after a couple of minor skirmishes in May. The first significant action between Michiel de Ruyter's fleet and Sir George Ayscue's squadron off Plymouth in August proved disappointing to both sides, but after the commanders were replaced by Witte de With and Robert Blake respectively, the two fleets met in action off the Downs at the end of September, in the battle which became known as the Kentish Knock. De With lost three ships, and the States General replaced him by Maarten Tromp, whose more resolute approach off Dungeness on 30 November resulted in a strategic victory over Blake.

On 18 February 1653, Blake attacked Tromp's fleet off Portland while the Dutch were escorting a huge convoy through from the Mediterranean. The English lost the *Sampson* (a prize), but their superior gunpower caused the loss of eight Dutch vessels in the running battle over the next two days. The major action of the war took place on 2 June near the Gabbard shoal, east of Felixstowe, resulting in the capture of eleven Dutch prizes. A further decisive English victory at Scheveningen on 31 July resulted in the death of Tromp and the rout of the Dutch fleet. The table of Fourth Rates present at the Gabbard illustrates that individual vessels varied frequently from the allocation of guns and men set out initially for them.

While the war's main actions were played out in the Channel and the North Sea, the Mediterranean provided a notable side-show. On 28 August 1652 Johan van Galen's squadron defeated a British squadron under Richard Badiley off Elba; the *Phoenix* (then 38 guns) was taken by the Dutch *Eendracht*, but was retaken on 20 November 1652 at Livorno (Leghorn), when 82 volunteers in boats boarded her at anchor among the Dutch fleet. On 4 March 1653 van Galen avenged this recapture when he destroyed Henry Appleton's smaller squadron at Leghorn. The surviving English ships withdrew from the

Table 7: Fourth Rates acquired by capture/purchase 1649–54

Vessel	Formerly	Captured	Purchased	Fate
Guinea (30 guns)	Royalist (Stuart) Charles[1]		25.4.1649	Sold 27.11.1667
Amity (30 guns)	(mercantile)	–	1650	Sold 27.11.1667
Convertine (40 guns)	Portuguese		1651	Taken by the Dutch 4.6.1666
Violet (44 guns)	Dutch	1652		Hulked 1654; BU 1672
Bear (36 guns)	Dutch Beer	1652		Given to Ordnance Office 1665
Welcome (36 guns)	Dutch	1652		Sunk as blockship 13.6.1667; raised 10.1667 and fitted as fireship, expended 4.6.1673
Marmaduke (32 guns)	Royalist (Stuart) Revenge[1]	31.5.1652	5.6.1652	Sunk as blockship 11.6.1667; wreck sold 22.9.1699
Stork	Dutch Ooievaar	1652		Hulked 1653; sold 11.1663
Estridge (Ostrich)	Dutch Vogelstruys[2]	19.5.1653		Hulked 1653; sunk as a foundation 1679
Elias (36 guns)	Dutch Elias	1653		Wrecked 19.10.1664
Mathias (38 guns)	Dutch Sint Mattheus	1653		Burnt by the Dutch 12.6.1667
Great Charity (38 guns)	Dutch Liefde	1653		Retaken by the Dutch 3.6.1665
Indian (44 guns)	Dutch Roos[2]	14.4.1654		Sold 6.11.1660

Vessel	Keel	Beam	Depth	Tons	Keel/Beam Ratio
Guinea	90 0	28 0	11 4	375	3.21 : 1
Amity	90 0	28 0	12 0	375	3.21 : 1
Convertine	103 0	30 0	13 6	493 8/94	3.43 : 1
Violet	98 0	28 0	12 6	409	3.50 : 1
Bear	106 0	26 6	12 0	396	4.00 : 1
Welcome	82 0	29 0	10 7	367	2.83 : 1
Marmaduke	87 0	31 5	15 2	456 70/94	2.77 : 1
Stork	97 0	27 9	12 6	397	3.50 : 1
Estridge (Ostrich)	116 0	36 3	17 0	811	3.20 : 1
Elias	101 0	27 6	11 6	406	3.67 : 1
Mathias	108 0	32 0	15 0	588	3.38 : 1
Great Charity	106 0	28 4	11 0	453	3.74 : 1
Indian	114 0	33 8	14 0	687	3.39 : 1

Note: various other vessels with fewer than 40 guns were added to the navy by capture – the majority being taken from the Dutch. Although several were added to the Navy and classed as Fourth Rates, all had gone by the end of the Commonwealth, and few details other than names are recorded. The number of guns quoted above for each ship is the number carried at the Restoration in 1660, or during the First Dutch War for ships hulked by 1660. [1] these ships were originally the mercantile *Guinea Frigate* and *Marmaduke*, and thus reverted to original names when taken from the Royalists. [2] both former Dutch East Indiamen, built at Amsterdam (the former in 1640).

The *Dover* was launched by William Castle at Shoreham in 1654 under the 1652 programme which added thirty new frigates to the Commonwealth Navy. Castle's designs were unusual among the frigates in providing one more gunport per side on the upper deck than on the gundeck (13 and 12 respectively). This Van de Velde drawing of about 1675 can be compared with the photographs of the Annapolis model No 50. (NMM: VV504)

This model of a small Fourth Rate of around 1660 is unidentified. It is also damaged and/or incomplete, but an interesting feature is the provision of pairs of sweep ports between gunports on the lower deck, to allow the ship to be manoeuvred under oars in a calm – a feature more usually confined to smaller rates. (NMM: 9262)

The *Newcastle* was the first of the broad-beam Fourth Rates designed to carry 44 guns instead of the 40 guns of earlier frigates. (NMM: VV1190)

Left: The *Maidstone* was one of two Fourth Rates built at Woodbridge in Suffolk; she was renamed *Mary Rose* in 1660 and the Van de Velde drawing reflects her appearance in later life. (NMM: VV491)

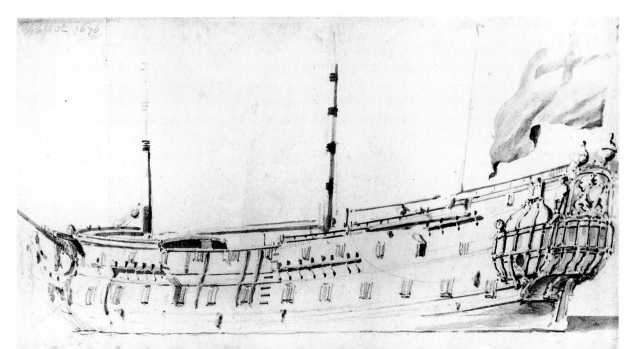
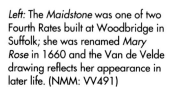

Mediterranean. The war concluded with a compromise peace on 5 April 1654.

Apart from the *Phoenix*, the only other wartime loss among the new frigates was the 46-gun *Sussex*, accidentally blown up on 9 December 1653 at Plymouth. Following the war, the 38-gun *Pelican* was accidentally burnt on 13 February 1656 at Portsmouth, and the 48-gun *Laurel* was wrecked on 30 May 1657 off Great Yarmouth. The 36-gun *Elias* foundered off New England on 19 October 1664, and the 34-gun *Nonsuch* and 38-gun *Phoenix* were both wrecked in a storm in the Straits of Gibraltar on 3 December 1664.

The 1652 Orders – the narrow-beam 40s

Parliament approved the ordering of another thirty frigates on 28 September 1652; ten of these were Third Rates, virtual repeats of the *Speaker*, and carrying around 50 guns and some 200 to 220 men. The majority of the others were Fourth Rates along the lines of the *Foresight*, but from the start designed with 40 guns on two full gundecks and a large quarterdeck (surmounted by a small roundhouse), and each with between 130 and 150 men. The balance of the new frigates were even smaller vessels of just under 300 tons, classed as Fifth Rates and carrying 22 guns.

Of the Fourth Rates, the smaller *Hampshire* was rated as 38 guns and 130 men. Although her Establishment was to rise during Charles II's reign, she was to remain with a lesser armament than the other Fourth Rates for the rest of her career. On the other hand, the *Sussex* – like the *Laurel* – was at some stage reclassed as a Third Rate with 46 guns, and was lost while so rated.

The broad-beam 44s

While the majority of the Fourth Rate frigates had hitherto been completed with 40 guns or less (the 44-gun *Bristol* and 46-gun *Sussex* were exceptions), three frigates were launched in 1653–54 with an establishment of 44 guns and 160 men. The *Newcastle* was built by Phineas Pett II at Deptford, while the *Yarmouth* and *Winsby* were constructed by Edgar at Great Yarmouth (the *Winsby* was renamed the *Happy Return* in 1660). These vessels were to constitute a distinct group among the Fourth Rates, to which all but one of the eight Fourth Rates to be new-built during the following thirty years would adhere. Notably, all were built with a greater breadth, being in excess of 33ft, than the remaining Fourth Rates; more notably, by 1677 they were distinct in retaining a battery of 24pdrs on the lower deck when the narrower Fourth Rates were reduced to culverins or lighter weapons on that deck.

Two more of the broad-beamed vessels were built to the same establishment of men and guns just before the end of the Protectorate, which had replaced the Commonwealth in 1653; the second of these, the *Princess*, as evidenced by the name, was launched after the Restoration.

Table 8: Commonwealth Fourth Rates, 1652 batch – construction history

	Builder	Begun	Launched	Fate
38 or 40-gun type:				
*Kentish**	Henry Johnson, Deptford		1652	Wrecked 15.10.1672
Sussex	John Tippetts, Portsmouth Dyd		1652	Blown up 9.12.1653
Hampshire	Phineas Pett, Deptford Dyd		1653	Rebuilt 1686
Portland	John Taylor, Wapping		1652	Burnt to prevent capture 12.4.1692
Bristol	John Tippetts, Portsmouth Dyd		1653	Rebuilt 1693
*Gainsborough**	Thomas Taylor, Wapping		1653	Wrecked 9.2.1692
*Preston**	Carey, Woodbridge		1653	Sold 11.6.1693
Jersey	Starling, Maldon		1654	Taken by the French 18.12.1691
*Maidstone**	Munday, Woodbridge		1654	Taken by the French 12.7.1691
Dover	William Castle, Shoreham		1654	Rebuilt 1695
*Taunton**	William Castle, Rotherhithe		1654	Rebuilt 1689
*Nantwich**	Francis Bayley, Bristol		13.3.1655	Wrecked 15.8.1666
Broad-beamed (44-gun) type:				
Newcastle	Phineas Pett, Ratcliffe		1653	Rebuilt 1692
Yarmouth	Edgar, Great Yarmouth		1653	BU 1680
*Winsby**	Edgar, Great Yarmouth		1654	Taken by the French 4.11.1691
Later Orders				
Leopard	Jonas Shish, Deptford Dyd	29.9.1657	2.1659	Sunk as breakwater 7.6.1699
Princess	Daniel Furzer, Lydney	1658	8.1660	BU 1680

* these ships were renamed *Kent*, *Swallow*, *Antelope*, *Mary Rose*, *Crown*, *Bredah* and *Happy Return* respectively at the Restoration in 1660.

Table 9: Commonwealth Fourth Rates, 1652 batch – dimensions in feet and inches

Vessel	Gundeck	Keel	Beam	Depth	Tons	Keel/Beam Ratio
38 or 40-gun type:						
Kentish		107 0	32 6	13 6	601 15/94	3.29 : 1
Sussex					600?	
Hampshire	118 0	101 9	29 9	12 8	479 2/94	3.42 : 1
Portland		105 0	32 11	12 10	605 14/94	3.19 : 1
Bristol		104 0	31 1	13 0	534 45/94	3.35 : 1
Gainsborough		100 10	31 10	12 9	543 48/94	3.17 : 1
Preston		101 0	31 0	13 0	516 27/94	3.26 : 1
Jersey		101 10	32 2	13 1	560 43/94	3.17 : 1
Maidstone		102 0	32 0	13 0	555 54/94	3.19 : 1
Dover		104 0	31 8	13 0	554 68/94	3.28 : 1
Taunton		100 6	31 8	13 0	536 6/94	3.17 : 1
Nantwich		100 0	31 0	12 8	511 16/94	3.23 : 1
Broad-beamed (44-gun) type:						
Newcastle	131 0	108 0	33 1	13 2	628 71/94	3.26 : 1
Yarmouth		105 0	33 0	13 3	608 21/94	3.18 : 1
Winsby		104 0	33 2	13 0	608 49/94	3.14 : 1
Later Orders:						
Leopard		109 0	33 9	15 0	645*	3.23 : 1
Princess		104 0	33 0	14 3	602 40/94	3.15 : 1

* this is the tonnage quoted in all records but it does not correspond to figure produced from KB²/188 calculation; the breadth recorded may be in error.

Right: This 1:36 model cannot be identified with certainty, as it is a complete restoration, but would appear to be of a William Castle designed ship of 1654, either the *Dover* or the *Taunton* (the latter was renamed *Crown* in 1660). The decoration, which includes the Stuart Arms and Prince of Wales feathers on the stern, is clearly post-Restoration, and so reflects the ship in later life. (United States Naval Academy Museum, Annapolis model No 50)

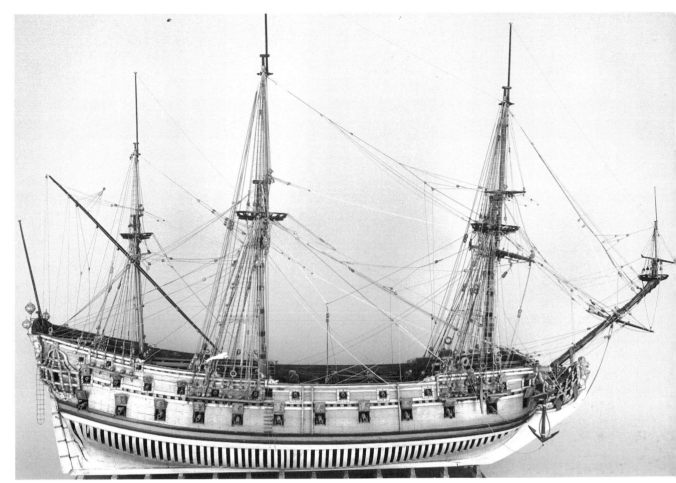

Below: The Commonwealth Fourth Rate in this Van de Velde drawing is not identified, but may be the broad-beamed *Leopard* of 1659. There are 13 gunports per side on the lower deck, while the upper deck ports in the waist have the square wreaths which fell into disuse around 1660. The figures on the quarterdeck give a good impression of the small size of these ships. (NMM: VV1093)

3. The Fourth Rate in the Restoration Navy

Following the restoration of the monarchy in May 1660, a number of frigates whose names derived from the Commonwealth were swiftly renamed by the new regime. Among the Fourth Rates, the *President* became the *Bonaventure*, while the Roundhead victories commemorated in the names of the *Gainsborough*, *Preston*, *Maidstone*, *Nantwich*, *Taunton* and *Winsby* were similarly replaced by names more politically acceptable to the Stuarts.

While few new Fourth Rates were to be built during the quarter-century of Charles II's reign, and none at all were begun in his brother's brief occupation of the throne, several vessels were rebuilt (usually enlarged in the process), especially in James's era, and it appears that this rebuilding programme would have been continued if the regime had not been superseded by the Glorious Revolution of 1688. The fleet was also reinforced by enemy prizes, particularly from the Dutch during the wars of 1665–67 and 1672–74 but also by ships taken from Algerine (*ie* Algerian) corsairs. More importantly, although few structural changes were made to the majority of English Fourth Rates, all vessels underwent a significant increase in their gun armament.

Only two Fourth Rates were recorded as rebuilt during the decade following the Restoration, the *Bonaventure* in 1663 and the *Constant Warwick* in 1666. At Chatham Dockyard, Phineas Pett widened the *Bonaventure* by 14in, other dimensions being unaffected; while not so described, it seems that the ship was girdled to add more structural strength. Sir John Tippets rebuilt the *Constant Warwick* more comprehensively at Portsmouth; she similarly gained 14in in breadth, signifying girdling, but was also lengthened by 2ft along the keel.

While records of other rebuilding are lacking, even from the papers of the scrupulous Pepys, comparison of the known details of the earliest frigates at the time of their original construction with the details quoted immediately prior to their first recorded rebuilding shows a consistent pattern of alterations. Not only did each surviving Fourth Rate acquire a second complete battery on its upper deck (even those built with two complete structural gun decks apparently mounted a relatively limited battery on the upper deck at first) and thus a more extensive armament. But the breadth of most vessels were increased by a foot or more, probably indicating girdling but possibly a more substantial though unrecorded reconstruction, while in

most the depth in the hold was significantly reduced.

Information as to where and when these modifications took place is lacking; the best assumption is that most of these changes were made before 1680, from which date the majority of rebuilding is documented. For example, a model believed to be of the *Bristol* in the National Maritime Museum bears both that name and the date '1666' carved on the stern, but no rebuilding of the *Bristol* is recorded for that date. Table 11 sets out the principal dimensions of all of the surviving Commonwealth frigates as recorded in the 1680s, and should be compared with the earlier tables giving their dimensions at the time of building.

Prior to the outbreak of the Second Dutch War in 1665, new Fourth Rates were ordered. One – the *Greenwich* – was to carry 58 guns and 260 men (like the existing Third Rates), while the others were designed for 50 guns and 220 men. The first two were included in the 1664 Programme on 11 November, the larger *Greenwich* to be built by Christopher Pett at Woolwich Dockyard and the smaller *Saint David* awarded to Daniel Furzer at Bristol, although the latter then decided to set up construction at Conpill, near Lydney in Gloucestershire.

Table 10: Fourth Rates rebuilt 1660–66 – construction history

Vessel	Builder	Ordered	Launched	Fate
Bonaventure	Phineas Pett, Chatham Dyd		1663	BU 1683 to rebuild.
Constant Warwick	Sir John Tippetts, Portsmouth Dyd		1666	Taken by the French 12.7.1691

Table 11: Fourth Rates rebuilt or modified 1660–80 (?) – new dimensions in feet and inches

Vessel	Gundeck	Keel	Beam	Depth	Tons	Keel/Beam Ratio
Constant Warwick		90 0	28 2	12 0	379 $^{75}/_{94}$	3.20 : 1
Assurance	106 7	89 0	29 1½	11 3	401 $^{54}/_{94}$	3.06 : 1
Adventure		94 0	28 0	12 0	392	3.36 : 1
Dragon	119 10	96 0	30 1	12 6	462	3.19 : 1
Portsmouth		100 0	29 6	12 8	463	3.39 : 1
Bonaventure		102 9	30 8	12 4	514	3.35 : 1
later (2nd girdling?)	124 10	102 0	31 10	12 6	550	3.20 : 1
Reserve	118 4	100 0	32 10	12 8	573	3.05 : 1
Advice	118 6	100 0	32 0	12 4	544	3.13 : 1
Foresight	121 2	102 2	32 0	13 0	556	3.19 : 1
Assistance	121 5½	102 0	32 4	13 0	567	3.15 : 1
Bristol	130 0	109 0	34 0	13 6	670	3.21 : 1
Dover	118 6	100 0	32 6	12 11	562	3.08 : 1

The *Adventure* seems to have been slightly enlarged during the 1660s or just after. This 1675 drawing by Van de Velde shows she remained a comparatively small Fourth Rate. On rebuilding in 1688–92 she was re-classed as a Fifth Rate of 42 guns. (NMM: VV442)

The *Saint David* was built near Lydney in the Forest of Dean during the Second Dutch War. Too late to participate in that conflict, she was in action against the Dutch in December 1672, convoying English troops for the successful expedition to capture Tobago. This Van de Velde sketch is dated 1675. (NMM: VV501)

Below: The *Assurance* of 1646 had a long career spanning over fifty years. This Van de Velde drawing dates from about 1671. Note the lower deck sweep ports, and the lids to the waist gunports, the one above the main chains being side-hinged like window shutters so that it does not foul the shrouds. (NMM: VV737)

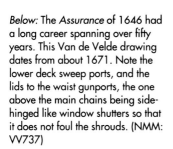

With the outbreak of war in February 1665 it was decided to add a Third Rate (*Warspite*) and three extra Fourth Rates, with the latter ordered from Peter Pett (at Chatham), Edmund and Henry Edgar (at Yarmouth) and Francis Bayley (at Bristol). The orders for Chatham and Yarmouth were subsequently cancelled, while Bayley's vessel at Bristol was named *Saint Patrick*. While the *Saint Patrick* lasted barely a year before being taken by the Dutch off North Foreland, the earlier pair both emerged as 54-gun ships by 1677, when the Establishment allotted them twenty-four 24pdrs on the lower deck, twenty-two 6pdrs on the upper deck, and eight minions on the quarterdeck.

Among several Dutch vessels taken during the first year of the Second Dutch War and incorporated into the Royal Navy were seven established as Fourth Rates of between 48 and 54 guns. The *Charles the Fifth* had a complement of 200, the *Seven Oaks* of 190, and the others of 180. There were eight other smaller Fourth Rate prizes (all 40-gun or 42-gun ships with a wartime complement of 160 or 170 men); the wartime weaponry of most of these prizes appears in Table 109.

The Battle of Lowestoft on 3 June 1665 was catastrophic for the Dutch fleet. The Dutch Admiral, Jacob Wassenaer van Obdam, and most of his crew died when the flagship *Eendracht* blew up, and altogether at least seventeen ships were lost, of which several were added to the English navy as Fourth Rates. The English under James, Duke of York, lost only the 46-gun *Great Charity* and two fireships expended.

The Dutch defeat left them reluctant to contest another fleet action, although small skirmishes and convoy attacks took place during which the several more Dutch ships were taken. During the first four days of June 1666 took place in the southern North Sea a protracted engagement known as the Four Days Battle, in which the Duke of Albemarle's fleet engaged de Ruyter but was finally forced to retreat into the Thames, losing seven Fourth Rates as well as two three-deckers (*Royal Prince* and *Swiftsure*) and other ships.

The Third Dutch War, which broke out on 17 March 1672, was unlike its predecessors in that it unquestionably constituted a war of aggression by the Stuarts against the Dutch. Determined not only to humble the Dutch but also his 'own' English Parliament, Charles entered into a secret pact with Louis XIV, his former enemy. The French, constituting the land element of the alliance, initially scored outstanding successes in their invasion of the Netherlands, while the English navy – which provided the principal maritime element of the attack – gave only a mediocre performance throughout the war.

This war again produced a trio of Third Rates. The *Oxford* and *Woolwich* were 54-gun ships, to carry the same armament as the *Greenwich*. The *Kingfisher* (this name was often spelled *Kings-Fisher*) was established

Table 12: Second Dutch War new building programme – construction history

Vessel	Builder	Ordered	Launched	Fate
Greenwich	Christopher Pett, Woolwich Dyd	26.10.1664	7. 6.1666	BU 1699 to rebuild
Saint David	Daniel Furzer, Conpill	26.10.1664	30. 3.1667	Hulked 1691*; sold 1713
Saint Patrick	Francis Bayley, Bristol	4.1665	9. 5.1666	Taken by the Dutch 5.2.1667

* sunk in Portsmouth harbour 11 November 1690, raised and then hulked.

Table 13: Second Dutch War new building programme – dimensions in feet and inches.

Vessel	Gundeck	Keel	Beam	Depth	Tons	Keel/Beam Ratio
Greenwich	136 0	108 0	33 9	14 6	654 $^{33}/_{94}$	3.20 : 1
Saint David		107 0	34 9	14 8	687 $^{27}/_{94}$	3.08 : 1
Saint Patrick		102	33 0	14 6	621 $^{5}/_{94}$	3.01 : 1

with just 46 guns – twenty-two culverins on the lower deck, twenty 6pdrs on the upper deck and four minions on the quarterdeck; this unusual vessel may have been a fore-runner of the First World War 'Q-ship', being provided with means to mask her identity (screens to hide gunports, removable figurehead, etc), apparently in an effort to act as a lure to Mediterranean privateers.[7]

Most of the Fourth Rates took part in the major actions of the war. On 28 May 1672 the combined Anglo-French fleet were attacked by De Ruyter while at anchor off Southwold; in the resultant battle of Solebay, the Dutch had the best of the contest, although the 50-gun *Stavoreen* was taken by the English and added to the navy. The *Adventure, Advice, Antelope, Bonaventure, Bristol, Crown, Diamond, Dover, Leopard, Mary Rose, Phoenix, Princess, Ruby, Tiger* and *Yarmouth* were participants.

Two battles took place in the early summer of 1673 in the Schooneveld, a channel among the Frisian

The Navy captured a number of Algerian – or as they were termed at the time, Algerine – privateers around 1680, and five were added to the fleet as Fourth Rates. This Van de Velde drawing is unidentified but thought to represent one of these ships. (NMM: VV492)

Table 14: Captured Fourth Rates of the Second Dutch War, 1665–67

Vessel	Former Dutch name	Captured	Guns	Fate
Golden Lion	Gouden Leeuw	29.3.1664	42/34	Given away to Guinea Company 11.1.1668
Unity	Eendracht	2.1665	42/34	Retaken by the Dutch 12.6.1667
Charles the Fifth	Carolus Quintus	3.6.1665	52/44	Burnt by the Dutch 12.6.1667
Mars	Mars	3.6.1665	52/44	Sold 3.1667
Black Bull	Edam	3.6.1665	40/34	Retaken by the Dutch 4.6.1666
Delfe	Delft	3.6.1665	40/34	Sold 22.5.1668
Zealand	Zeelandia	3.6.1665	40/34	Sold 27.11.1667
Young Prince	Jonge Prins	3.6.1665	38/30	Fireship 5.1666; expended 2.6.1666
Clove Tree*	Nagelboom	3.9.1665	62/48	Retaken by the Dutch 4.6.1666
Seven Oaks	Zevenwolden	3.9.1665	52/44	Retaken by the Dutch 1.6.1666
West Friesland	Westfriesland	3.9.1665	54/44	Sold 27.11.1667
Black Spread Eagle	Groningen	3.9.1665	48/40	Foundered after action 2.6.1666
Hope	Hoop	3.9.1665	40/34	Wrecked 16.8.1666
Guilder de Ruyter	Geldersche Ruiter	9.9.1665	48/42	Sold 7.2.1667
Saint Paul	Sint Paulus	9.9.1665	40/34	Foundered in action 2.6.1666
Maria Sancta	Sint Marie	29.12.1665	50/42	Burnt by the Dutch 12.6.1667
Stathouse van Harlem	Raadhuis van Haarlem	7.1667	46/40	Hulked 1669; sunk as foundation at Sheerness 28.10.1690

Vessel	Keel	Beam	Depth	Tons	Keel/Beam Ratio
Golden Lion	101 4	28 6	13 0	438	3.56 : 1
Unity	95 0	24 6	9 2	303	3.88 : 1
Charles the Fifth	102 0	32 0	14 0	555 $^{54}/_{94}$	3.19 : 1
Mars	106 0	26 6	12 2	396	4.00 : 1
Black Bull	103 0	30 0	13 6	493	3.43 : 1
Delfe	94 0	24 0	9 2	288	3.92 : 1
Zealand	93 0	28 6	9 0	402	3.26 : 1
Young Prince	90 0	28 0	10 2	375	3.21 : 1
Clove Tree	103 0	33 0	12 8	596 $^{5}/_{94}$	3.12 : 1
Seven Oaks	105 0	35 0	15 0	684	3.00 : 1
West Friesland	102 0	32 0	12 0	555 $^{54}/_{94}$	3.19 : 1
Black Spread Eagle	86 0	28 4	12 0	367	3.04 : 1
Hope	103 0	30 0	13 6	493	3.43 : 1
Guilder de Ruiter	105 0	35 0	15 0	684	3.00 : 1
Saint Paul	84 0	25 6	9 8	291	3.29 : 1
Maria Sancta	106 0	26 6	12 2	396	4.00 : 1
Stathouse van Harlem	90 0	30 4	11 6	440 $^{45}/_{94}$	2.97 : 1

* this vessel, in spite of her size, was established in the RN with 24 demi-cannon, 26 demi-culverins and 12 sakers (plus 250 men); she is best considered with the 60-gun ships and indeed appeared in some records as a Third Rate.

Table 15: Third Dutch War new building programme – construction history

Vessel	Builder	Ordered	Launched	Fate
Oxford	Francis Bayley, Bristol	11.9.1672	6.1674	BU 1702 to rebuild
Woolwich	Phineas Pett III, Woolwich Dyd	11.9.1672	26.8.1675	BU 1702 to rebuild
Kingfisher	Phineas Pett III, Woodbridge	1674	1.1676	BU 1699 to rebuild

sandbanks off Walcheren Island. Among the Fourth Rates, the *Constant Warwick*, *Advice*, *Assurance*, *Bonaventure*, *Crown*, *Diamond*, *Foresight*, *Hampshire*, *Happy Return*, *Mary Rose*, *Newcastle*, *Princess*, *Ruby* and *Yarmouth* won battle honours here.

De Ruyter again emerged the victor in the final naval action of this war, fought in the shallow waters off the Texel on 11 August 1673. The Fourth Rates *Advice*, *Assurance*, *Bonaventure*, *Bristol*, *Crown*, *Diamond*, *Foresight*, *Hampshire*, *Happy Return*, *Leopard*, *Mary Rose*, *Newcastle*, *Nonsuch*, *Portland*, *Portsmouth*, *Princess*, *Ruby*, *Swallow* and *Yarmouth* took part in this battle.

Two further Fourth Rates were constructed at the close of the war – the galley-frigates named after the king and his brother – but with barely thirty guns apiece these were later reclassed as Fifth Rates and their development does not fall within our present study.

By the time peace arrived on 11 February 1674, only one Fourth Rate had been lost – the 46-gun *Kent* – and that by grounding, although the old *Welcome* had been expended as a fireship during the second battle of Schooneveld.

From about 1662 until 1684, the English navy was engaged in various operations against Salee (Moroccan) and Algerine (Algerian) privateers off the Atlantic and Mediterranean coasts of North Africa. During these years Tangier was English territory, with a garrison maintained at York Castle whose remains still stand in the city. In the course of these operations a number of corsairs were taken by the Royal Navy, and five were added to the fleet as Fourth Rates. The *Tiger Prize* and *Golden Horse* were rated at 46/40 guns and had a complement of 230/200/150 men, while the *Marygold*, *Two Lyons* and *Half Moon* were rated at 44/38 guns and had a complement of 190/160/120 men. The last two ships were allotted only 40 guns in the 1685 proposed Ordnance Establishment, and if they had survived would doubtless have been reduced to Fifth Rates in the early 1690s.

Rebuilding the Commonwealth Frigates

By the start of the 1680s, the Fourth Rates surviving from the Commonwealth orders of 1649 and 1652 were reaching their thirtieth year, and a period of rebuilding began which continued until the close of King William's War. The *Tiger* was the first to undergo rebuilding, and she emerged in 1681 with a (war) armament establishment of 46 guns, comprising twenty demi-culverins (drakes), eighteen sakers and eight saker cutts. In a survey of 1688,[8] she was noted as actually carrying eighteen, seventeen and eight respectively of these weapons, while in the 1696 Survey (*qv*) she actually mounted eighteen demi-culverins and twenty-four sakers (including six cutts).

The *Bonaventure* (originally the *President*) was likewise rebuilt two years later, and was established with a

This Van de Velde drawing of the *Tiger* after her rebuilding at Deptford in 1681 can be compared with the earlier illustration. She is now 5ft longer in the keel and over 3ft broader than when originally built in 1647. The awning framework over the quarterdeck is an interesting feature. (NMM: VV1219)

The *Black Bull* (usually just called *Bull*) of 40 guns was one of some fourteen Dutch ships taken (at least three more were sunk) by the English Navy off Lowestoft in June 1665; she was re-taken by the Dutch a year later in the Four Days Fight off the coast of Flanders. By comparison with her English equivalents, the Dutch ship has loftier afterworks and a rather bluff bow, but no gunports amidships like the original English frigates. (NMM: VV844)

Table 16: Third Dutch War new building programme – dimensions in feet and inches

Vessel	Gundeck	Keel	Beam	Depth	Tons	Keel/Beam Ratio
Oxford		109 0	34 2	15 6	676 ^{77}/94	3.19 : 1
Woolwich	138 3	110 0	35 7	15 0	740 ^{80}/94	3.09 : 1
Kingfisher	136 0	110 0	33 8	13 0	663 ^{17}/94	3.27 : 1

Table 17: Captured vessels of the Third Dutch War, 1672–74

Vessel	Former Dutch name	Captured	Guns	Fate
Stavoreen	Stavoren	28.5.1672	48/42	Sold 2.1682
Arms of Terver	Kampveere (ex Ter Veere)	1673	52/44	Given away 6.1674
Arms of Horn*	Eenhoorn	1673	–	Hulked 1673; sunk as foundation at Sheerness 1694

Vessel	Gundeck	Keel	Beam	Depth	Tons	Keel/Beam Ratio
Stavoreen		100 0	32 0	12 9	544 ^{64}/94	3.13 : 1
Arms of Terver		96 0	32 0	11 9	522 ^{84}/94	3.00 : 1
Arms of Horn*		106 0	30 3	12 0	515 ^{88}/94	3.50 : 1

* used as a hulk in the English Navy; included here as her dimensions indicate she was compatible with English 50s, but had been a 70-gun Dutch ship

Table 18: Fourth Rates captured from Algerine corsairs 1677–82

Vessel	Builder	Built	Captured	Purchased	Fate
Marygold	Algerine		28.10.1677	16.6.1678	Wrecked 31.1.1679
Tiger Prize	Algerine		1.4.1678	16.6.1678	Sunk as a foundation at Sheerness 14.2.1696
Golden Horse	Algerine		9.4.1681		Sunk as a foundation at Chatham 8.1688
Half Moon	Algerine		9.9.1681		Burnt by accident 28.9.1686
Two Lions	Algerine		16.9.1681		Sold 1.1688

Vessel	Gundeck	Keel	Beam	Depth	Tons	Keel/Beam Ratio
Marygold		100 0	30 6	12 6	495	3.28 : 1
Tiger Prize*	112 0	90 0	31 6	12 8	475	2.86 : 1
Golden Horse	125 8	102 0	36 8	14 10	729 ^{41}/94	2.78 : 1
Half Moon	113 1	90 0	34 1	13 4	556	2.64 : 1
Two Lions	115 6	92 6	33 6	13 6	552 ^{16}/94	2.76 : 1

* her dimensions are open to question, as no less than three sets of figures appear in official records; those given above are ones most often quoted.

new (wartime) armament of 52 guns – twenty-two 12pdrs, twenty-two 8pdrs, two sakers (drakes) and six 3pdrs. It is worth noting that by the 1696 Survey her actual armament would be reduced to 40 guns (see Part II).

During 1682 the Navy Board agreed to purchase a two-year-old privateer from a syndicate headed by Lord Mordaunt. A model was made of this vessel either before or just after her purchase, from which her differences from standard navy design can be seen. The main capstan and the riding bitts for the anchor cables are exposed on the upper deck, unlike Navy practice. The beak bulkhead, instead of being positioned some distance behind the knightheads, is actually built far forward, on the knightheads themselves.

The *Mordaunt* (she retained her name in navy service) had twenty-eight gunports on each broadside with, like the earlier ships that William Castle had built for the navy, one more pair of upper deck gunports than on her lower deck, and with five pairs of ports on her quarterdeck; the upper deck ports, at only 21in square (if the model is presumed accurate) were much smaller than those on the lower deck, which measured 33in long and 30in deep; in addition, the ship had four stern gunports in her lower counter, double the usual number. However, she was established in the navy with only 46/40 guns (twenty 12pdrs, eighteen 8pdrs and eight sakers at the higher rating, with two fewer in each calibre at the lower rating) and 230/200/150 men. She was wrecked off Cuba in 1693 while escorting a homeward-bound convoy from Jamaica.

The situation by the Revolution of 1688 is possibly best summed up in the list of vessels published by Thomas in his book *Gloria Britannica*, published in 1689 but probably compiled about 1685, which shows the following Establishments of guns and men for the Fourth Rates in war and peace. The list includes the new *Saint Albans* and *Deptford*, which were completed in '1688' (actually both were launched in 1687, which

This model of the *Mordaunt* bears the Stuart Arms on the stern, so was undoubtedly made after the Navy purchased this privateer from Lord Mordaunt's syndicate in 1683. One unusual feature is the four stern ports in the lower counter, compared with the usual two, while the forecastle reaches far forward so that the beakhead bulkhead is actually built into the bollard timber (the 'knightheads'). The very sharp bow lines can be seen in the concave shape of the forward frames. (NMM: 6145)

might indicate that these entries were *anticipated* details but it gives them no allocation of men or guns. In Pepys's manner, columns 2 to 4 below represent the number of men allotted (2) in war at home, (3) in war abroad and (4) in peacetime everywhere, while columns 5 and 6 represent the number of guns (5) in war at home and (6) in war abroad and at peace everywhere.

Type/group	(2)	(3)	(4)	(5)	(6)
(a) 54-gun group	280	240	185	54	46
(b) 48-gun group	230	200	150	48	42
(c) 46-gun group	220	185	140	46	40
(d) 44-gun group	190	160	120	44	38
(e) 42-gun group	180	150	115	42	36

The 54-gun group comprised the *Newcastle, Yarmouth, Happy Return, Leopard, Princess, Greenwich, Saint David, Oxford* and *Woolwich*; as the *Yarmouth* and *Princess* had been scrapped in 1680 and the *Leopard* recently hulked, this left six vessels of this distinct group. The 48-gun group comprised all of the remaining Fourth Rates which did not fall under any of the other groups, allowing for certain anomalies which may well be clerical errors.

The 46-gun group was composed only of the *Dragon, Hampshire, Kingfisher* and *Portsmouth*. The other smaller Fourth Rates which were later rated with these four in 1703 as a distinct class were at this time all firmly included with the bulk of the Rate in the 48-gun group. It was only when the bulk of the Fourth Rates were raised from 48 guns to 54 guns in 1703 that these smaller vessels were left as 48s to con22222222stitute a separate class.

The *Adventure* was shown as having 48 guns on her higher Establishment, but the other figures all indicate that this was probably a clerical error, and so this has been corrected to 44 guns in the above list, where she joins the rebuilt *Tiger* to fill this intermediate '44-gun group' role. The 42-gun group consisted of the *Constant Warwick* and *Assurance*, plus the former Fifth Rates *Falcon, Sweepstakes, Nonsuch* and *Phoenix*. The *Adventure* was rebuilt as a Fifth Rate in 1691, and all of the surviving 42-gun ships were moved to the Fifth Rate in the same year, except for the elderly *Assurance* which struggled on until sold in 1698.

Table 19: Commonwealth Fourth Rates rebuilt 1681–88 – construction history

Vessel*	Builder	Ordered	Launched	Fate
Tiger (1647)	John Shish, Deptford Dyd		1681	BU 1702 to rebuild
Bonaventure (1650)	Isaac Betts, Portsmouth Dyd		1683	BU 1699 to rebuild
Hampshire (1653)	Fisher Harding, Deptford Dyd		1686	Sunk in action 26.8.1697
Assistance (1650)	R & J Castle, Deptford		1687	BU 1699 to rebuild
Ruby (1651)	Sir Henry Johnson, Blackwall		1687	BU 1705 to rebuild

* with original launch date in parenthesis.

Table 20: Commonwealth Fourth Rates rebuilt 1681–88 – dimensions in feet and inches

Vessel	Gundeck	Keel	Beam	Depth	Tons	Keel/Beam Ratio
Tiger	123 8	104 0	32 8	13 8	590 ³⁰⁄₉₄	3.18 : 1
Bonaventure	124 10	102 6	32 2	12 6	567	3.19 : 1
Hampshire	118 0	101 0	30 2	11 8	489	3.35 : 1
Assistance	121 5½	102 0	32 4	13 0	567	3.15 : 1
Ruby	125 7	105 6	31 6	13 0	556	3.35 : 1

Table 21: Fourth Rate purchased 1682

Vessel	Builder	Built	Purchased	Fate
Mordaunt	William Castle, Deptford	1681	7.10.1682	Wrecked 22.11.1693

Vessel	Gundeck	Keel	Beam	Depth	Tons	Keel/Beam Ratio
Mordaunt	122 6*	101 9	32 4½	13 0	567 ²⁶⁄₉₄	3.14 : 1

* not recorded; taken off scale model in National Maritime Museum.

Table 22: Mid 1680s new building programme – construction history

Vessel	Builder	Ordered	Launched	Fate
Saint Albans	Fisher Harding, Deptford Dyd	29.4.1682	6.1687	Wrecked 8.12.1693
Deptford	Joseph Lawrence, Woolwich Dyd	15.9.1682	6.1687	BU 1700 to rebuild
Sedgemoor	Robert Lee, Chatham Dyd	6.1.1683	5.1687	Wrecked 2.1.1689

Table 23: Mid 1680s new building programme – dimensions in feet and inches

Vessel	Gundeck	Keel	Beam	Depth	Tons	Keel/Beam Ratio
Saint Albans	128 4	107 0	32 10	13 3	614	3.26 : 1
Deptford	125 0	103 0	33 6	13 11	615	3.07 : 1
Sedgemoor	123 0	109 4	34 6	13 7	692	3.17 : 1

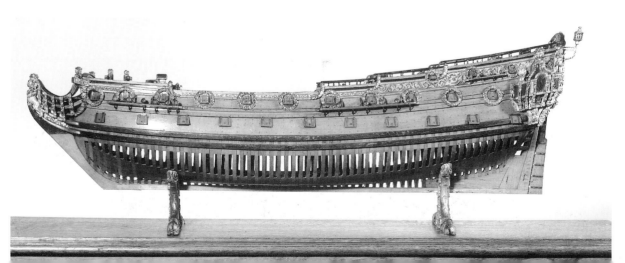

The *Bonaventure* after rebuilding at Portsmouth in 1683 was only slightly enlarged from her earlier dimensions. However, as the records are inconclusive, it is possible that the 'second girdling' referred to in Table 11 reflects this 1683 work rather than any intermediate reconstruction between 1663 and 1683. (NMM: C420)

4. The 12pdr Fifties

In May 1689 England began a century and a quarter of intermittent warfare with France (usually with allies on one or both sides), interrupted by periods of uneasy truce. The initial struggle, sometimes called King William's War but more frequently referred to as the War of the English Succession, came to a close on 20 September 1697 but, two months after William III was succeeded by Queen Anne, England declared war on France and Spain; this renewed conflict, the War of the Spanish Succession, was to last until 13 March 1713.

During King William's War, the Royal Navy lost twenty-one Fourth Rates; of these, nine (plus a hired vessel, the 56-gun *Lumley Castle* in 1694) succumbed to natural causes, although the *Mordaunt* was escorting a convoy when she was wrecked in 1693; two were 60-gun and six were 48-gun ships, plus the 56-gun *Saint David*. The other twelve ships were taken by the French (except the *Hampshire*, which was sunk in action), five of them while acting as convoy escorts and most of the rest while on cruising duties; these war losses are listed below; among them the *Happy Return* and the *Dartmouth* were to be recaptured during the next war.

1689 *Portsmouth* 48
1691 *Constant Warwick* 40, *Mary Rose* (ex-*Maidstone*) 48, *Happy Return* (ex-*Winsby*) 48 and *Jersey* 48
1692 *Portland* 50 and *Phoenix* 40 (both burnt)
1693 *Diamond* 48
1694 *Falcon* 40
1695 *Nonsuch* 40 and *Dartmouth* 48
1697 *Hampshire* 46

The first fleet action of the long French Wars took place in Bantry Bay on May Day in 1689, and in fact was the trigger that caused the formal declaration of war. Admiral Arthur Herbert intercepted a larger French force landing supplies for King James's army in Ireland, but French superiority and discipline resulted in a tactical if bloodless defeat for the English fleet. Among the smaller Fourth Rates, the *Portsmouth*, *Advice*, *Diamond*, *Ruby*, *Portland*, *Antelope*, *Saint Albans*, *Deptford*, *Greenwich* and *Woolwich* fought in the line, as did the *Dartmouth* (since 1688 re-classed as a 36-gun fireship).

Fourteen months later another indecisive battle took place off Beachy Head, again resulting in a tactical French victory, although the French by failing to

This Van de Velde drawing shows an unidentified 50-gun ship of the 123ft group built around 1690. Note the gunport wreaths have disappeared, as has much of the decoration apart from the stern. The drawing also suggests a flat counter, the so-called 'square tuck stern' seen on some of the contemporary models. (NMM: VV679)

This unidentified model is believed to represent a 50-gun ship from around 1691, one of the first batch of new construction for the *guerre de course*. (NMM: 1979)

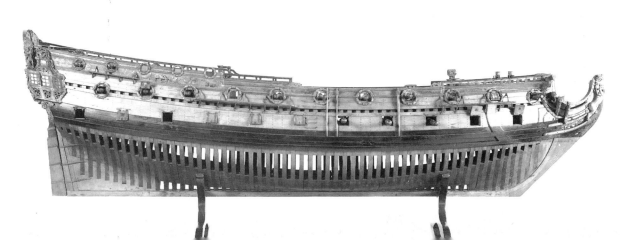

follow up lost the opportunity of inflicting a significant defeat on the Anglo-Dutch forces; Herbert (by now Earl of Torrington) commanded fifty-six allied ships of the line against about seventy French ships. The English squadrons included the *Constant Warwick* (now 36-gun), *Swallow*, *Bonaventure*, *Deptford* and *Woolwich*.

Off Cap Barfleur, the north-eastern promontory of Normandy's Cotentin peninsula, at daybreak on 19 May 1692, a combined Anglo-Dutch fleet under Admiral Edward Russell (later Earl of Orford) intercepted a smaller French fleet under the Comte de Tourville; the English Red squadron in the centre of the line (their Dutch allies formed the van) included two 54s (*Oxford* and *Greenwich*) and five 48s (*Bonaventure*, *Centurion*, *Chester*, *Saint Albans* and *Ruby*) among Russell's twenty-seven ships of the line, while in the rear the Blue squadron under Sir John Ashby numbered a further 54 (*Woolwich*) and four 48s (*Adventure*, *Advice*, *Crown* and *Deptford*) among twenty-nine ships of the line. Neither adversary lost any ships during the day's contest, other than four English fireships unsuccessfully expended in an attempt to burn the French ships at anchor, and a fifth burnt by a lucky shot from a French ship.

Tourville's fleet weighed anchor the next morning; the majority rounded the peninsula and dispersed to Breton ports, but fifteen failed to follow them. Three ships of the line beached themselves at Cherbourg and were destroyed by fireships; the other twelve took refuge at St Vaast La Hougue, seven miles south of Cap Barfleur. On the night of 23/24 May, Sir Cloudisley Shovell, who had shifted his flag to the 70-gun *Kent*, led his inshore squadron into the roads of La Hougue to attack the dozen French ships aground there. Besides eight 70-gun ships and a 64, Shovell had the above-mentioned three 54s from Barfleur and three of the 48s (*Chester*, *Crown* and *Deptford*), as well as a half-dozen smaller vessels and seven fireships.

There were few significant naval actions in the subsequent years of the war, other than the unfortunate expedition to the Mediterranean known as the Smyrna Fleet, in which the *Tiger Prize*, *Woolwich*, *Newcastle* and *Chatham* were among Sir George Rooke's escorting squadron in action against the French in June 1693.

Five of the remaining Commonwealth frigates (including one of the larger 'broad beamed' type) were rebuilt during the war, seemingly a continuation of the programme begun during the 1680s. Of the remainder, the majority were lost in King William's War, while the others – entering their fifth decade of service, were gradually retired.

The 54-gun ships

Few vessels were rated as 54s prior to the 1703 Establishment. At the Glorious Revolution of 1688

Table 24: Commonwealth Fourth Rates rebuilt in Royal Dockyards 1688–95 – construction history

Vessel*	Builder	Ordered	Launched	Fate
Crown (1654)	Joseph Lawrence, Woolwich Dyd		1689	BU 1704 to rebuild
Dragon (1647)	Fisher Harding, Deptford Dyd		1690	BU 1707 to rebuild
Dover (1654)	William Bagwell, Portsmouth Dyd		1695	Became 40-gun Fifth Rate 1716; BU 11.1730

* original launch date in parenthesis.

Table 25: Commonwealth Fourth Rate rebuilt in Royal Dockyards 1688–95 – dimensions in feet and inches

Vessel	Gundeck	Keel	Beam	Depth	Tons	Keel/Beam Ratio
Crown	120 5½	105 11	32 0	13 0	577	3.31 : 1
Dragon	118 11	99 0	31 9	12 2	531	3.12 : 1
Dover	118 0	98 6	34 4	12 7	604	2.87 : 1

Table 26: King William's War new building programme (123ft group) – construction history

Vessel	Builder	Ordered	Launched	Fate
Chatham	Robert Lee, Chatham Dyd	14.3.1690	20.4.1691	BU 1718 to rebuild
Centurion	Fisher Harding, Deptford Dyd	20.3.1690	6.3.1691	BU 1728 to rebuild
Chester	Joseph Lawrence, Woolwich Dyd	20.3.1690	21.3.1691	Taken by the French 10.10.1707
Norwich (i)	William Stigant, Portsmouth Dyd	15.8.1690	16.3.1691	Wrecked 6.10.1692
Falmouth	Edward Snelgrove, Rotherhithe	1.1.1692	25.6.1693	Taken by the French 4.8.1704
Rochester	Robert Lee, Chatham Dyd	28.6.1692	15.3.1693	BU 1714 to rebuild
Portland	Joseph Lawrence, Woolwich Dyd	13.7.1692	28.3.1693	BU 1719 to rebuild
Southampton	John Winter, Southampton	13.7.1692	10.6.1693	BU 1699 to rebuild
Norwich (ii)	R & J Castle, Deptford	5.8.1692	24.8.1693	BU 1712 to rebuild
Dartmouth[1]	John Shish, Rotherhithe	1692	24.7.1693	Wrecked 27.11.1703
Anglesea[2]	Flint, Plymouth	1692?	17.4.1694	BU 1719 to rebuild as 40-gun ship

[1] taken by the French on 4 February 1695, but recovered 12 October 1702 and renamed *Vigo*.
[2] Elias Waffe, the Master Shipwright at the new Plymouth Dockyard, supplied the labour and probably the stores to Flint's private yard.

there were still seven of them, unreconstructed survivors of the 'broad beamed' Commonwealth frigates and the Fourth Rates of Charles II's reign – the *Greenwich* (1666), *Happy Return* (1654), *Leopard* (1659), *Newcastle* (1653), *Oxford* (1674), *Saint David* (1667) and *Woolwich* (1675) – although the *Leopard* had been hulked at Gibraltar since 1686. They were nominally 54/46-gun ships with 280/240/185 men. In fact, the *Greenwich* seems to have carried 60 guns, while the *Happy Return* had only 48. Notably, four of them still carried a gundeck battery of 24pdrs (not carried by any of the smaller Fourth Rates), although only the *Saint David* still had the full Establishment of twenty-four of these guns.

This unidentified model is probably of the *Portland*, launched by Joseph Lawrence in 1693. It shows 12 ports a side on the gundeck and 11 a side on the upper deck, evidence of quite a diverse range of gunport configuration among Fourth Rates of this period. (United States Naval Academy Museum, Annapolis model No 33)

This further model from Annapolis is apparently of another of the 123ft group, and it has been suggested that the ship may be the *Rochester* or *Anglesea*. The details of the stern may be compared with the later draught of the *Lichfield*: although the stern area appears less heavily decorated, the open gallery has been retained. (United States Naval Academy Museum, Annapolis model No 9)

Two swiftly became war losses. The *Saint David* heeled over and sank in Portsmouth Harbour while careening in 1690, and although salved in August the next year, she was only used as a hulk; the *Happy Return* was taken by a force of French privateers off Dunkirk in 1691 – added to the French navy as *L'Heureux-Retour*, she was recovered in April 1708 by the *Burford*, but was not returned to the Royal Navy. The remaining culverin-armed ship, the *Newcastle*, was rebuilt during the early years of the war and either then or later received 8pdrs to replace the demi-culverins on her upper deck. The more recent three ships probably retained their 24pdrs until their post-war rebuilding.

The 1690s vessels – the 48s

Although the Royal Navy inherited by William III include forty-one Fourth Rates, which thus formed the most numerous Rate in the navy, the quantity swiftly proved insufficient for the many functions which the navy found itself called upon to undertake in warfare against the French. The new war, while not on the same global scale as was to be seen during the

following century, still extended over a wider sphere of action than in the three wars against the Dutch. In 1690, an emergency war programme was initiated to expand the number of Fourth Rates. Five ships were ordered from the Dockyards during that year. For the first four the *Sedgemoor*, completed in 1687, seems to have served as a model, and the contracts placed with merchant yards specified dimensions similar to hers (but see footnote to Table 27).

For the fifth new ship ordered in 1690 – the *Weymouth* at Portsmouth – the length was extended by another 7ft. At about the same date, two existing ships – *Newcastle* and *Bristol* – were rebuilt by contract on the Thames to a similar long-hulled design. While no plans enable us to identify the cause of this lengthening (improved speed may be surmised to play a part), one result may have been the addition of a further pair of ports on the lower deck. The *Newcastle* was an existing large ('broad-beamed') ship, so her longer length only improved her proportions.

As the *guerre de course* developed, and the advantages of the 50-gun ship as a heavy cruiser in the convoy escort role became clear, a desperate shortage of such ships emerged; so much so that the capacity of the established British yards and commercial builders became insufficient. Seven new ships of the 123ft type were ordered in 1692, five by contract with commercial builders.[9]

The king, in a speech from the throne in November 1693, blamed the increasing mercantile losses to the deprivations of French privateers on the lack of suitable cruisers, in turn due partly to the lack of a suitable dockyard in the west country.[10] The Navy Board investigated building small two-deckers in Ireland and even awarding contracts to German builders was considered;[11] while neither plan was eventually carried out, the Navy Board placed a series of substantial orders with commercial yards throughout England as well as with the Royal Dockyards between November 1693 and the end of 1695.

The contracts for these ships followed the 1690 order for the *Weymouth* and the rebuilt *Bristol*, and specified a gundeck length of 130ft, a breadth of 34ft (some were 2in more) and a depth of 13½ft although there was no clear distinction in the armament allocated to the 123ft and 130ft versions, most of the latter appear to have been established with 230/200/160 men and 48/42 guns. After 1692, no further orders to build additional ships of the 123ft type were issued, although existing ships continued to be rebuilt to the smaller dimensions, indicating that at this time the process of rebuilding rarely involved taking an existing ship to pieces, which process would have made it fairly easy to extend the length and breadth of a ship.

However, the 1703 Establishment of Guns raised all of the surviving 130ft vessels to 280/240/185 men and to 54/46 guns, comprising in wartime twenty-two 12pdrs (9ft length) on the gundeck, twenty-two 6pdrs (8½ft length) on the upper deck, eight 6pdrs (7ft length) on the quarterdeck, and two 6pdrs (9½ft length) on the forecastle – with the peacetime establishment being respectively twenty, eighteen, six and two guns of these calibres.

Few attempts were made until the middle of the eighteenth century to build naval vessels in Britain's North American colonies, and only a few small craft were constructed for the navy. An exception occurred in 1694, when John Taylor, a mast and timber merchant, had allegedly at his own expense and 'with great difficulty accomplished the building of one ship at Piscataqua fit for a 4th rate frigate'.[12] This vessel may have been built on speculation (at Portsmouth at the mouth of the Piscataqua river), but the order to survey her for possible purchase described her as the 'Falkland mast ship', which implies she might have been used by Taylor to ship his timber from New England between 1690 and 1696.[13]

Her purchase was approved on 4 December 1695, but it was not until early 1696 that the navy actually took her over, and this may have been as she was still completing a merchant voyage. The 1696 Survey revealed the Falkland to be supplied with eighteen culverins, twenty 8pdrs and eight minions, for a total of 46 guns.

The French navy lost one 44-gun ship to the English during King William's War: Le Trident, in company with the larger (68-gun) Le Content, was captured by James Killigrew's six-strong squadron off Pantellaria in early 1695. She was registered ten months later as a 58/50-gun ship with the name of Trident Prize and a maximum establishment of twenty-two culverin, twenty-four sakers, ten 'light sakers' and two 3pdrs (in peacetime, or in war abroad, she had a pair of guns fewer on the gundeck and upper deck, and four fewer 'light sakers'), and with 274/236/182 men.

The Royal Navy also captured a number of French privateers, among them the 50-gun Pontchartrain taken by the Medway in early 1697, and commissioned into the English navy as the Medway Prize, with 48 guns.

The Treaty of Rijswijk on 11 September 1697 brought an end to the war. By its close, the only surviving Fourth Rates from the Commonwealth era which had not been rebuilt were the Foresight (soon to be lost), and the Advice and Reserve, Peter Pett's Woodbridge-built pair of 1650, and these were to undergo rebuilding during the next few years. The newer Fourth Rates built or rebuilt under Charles II and his brother were similarly showing signs of age by the late 1690s, particularly those worn out by punishing employment during the war, and their rebuilding commenced at the same time. In all, the navy finished

Table 27: King William's War new building programme (123ft group) – dimensions in feet and inches

Vessel	Gundeck	Keel	Beam	Depth	Tons	Keel/Beam Ratio
Specification[1]	123 0	100 0	33 6	13 6	597	3.13 : 1
Chatham	126 0	109 6	34 4	13 4	686 54/94	3.19 : 1
Centurion	125 8½	105 0	33 2	13 5	614 35/94	3.17 : 1
Chester	125 1	105 10	34 4	13 10¼	663 55/94	3.08 : 1
Norwich (i)	125 7	102 2	33 8	13 4	616	3.03 : 1
Falmouth	124 0	101 6½	33 7½	13 8	610 64/94	3.02 : 1
Rochester	125 5	107 0	32 8	13 6	607 32/94	3.28 : 1
Portland	125 6	103 6	34 0	14 0	636 39/94	3.04 : 1
Southampton	121 9	100 0	33 10	13 9	608 83/94	2.96 : 1
Norwich (ii)	123 8	101 6	33 10	13 6½	618	3.00 : 1
Dartmouth	122 0	100 0	33 8	13 7	602 84/94	2.97 : 1
after recapture 1702[2]	121 8	101 6	33 6	13 5	605 84/94	3.03 : 1
Anglesea	125 0	106 0	33 2	14 0	620 21/94	3.20 : 1

[1] not all these vessels were contracted to be built to these dimensions; in some the gundeck length was specified at 125ft; in others the breadth is specified at 34¼ft and the depth specified varied from 13ft 4in to 13ft 9in. Nevertheless, the whole group ordered from 1690 to 1692 followed within close parameters which appear to have been based on the completed Sedgemoor of 1687.
[2] as surveyed on 5 January 1703, prior to being re-registered under the name Vigo (Prize) – see PRO – ADM 1/3595.

Table 28: Commonwealth Fourth Rates rebuilt by contract 1690–93 – construction history

Vessel	Builder	Ordered	Launched	Fate
Newcastle (1653)	Pett, Rotherhithe		1692	Wrecked 27.11.1703
Bristol (1653)	R & J Castle, Deptford		1693	Taken by the French 24.4.1709*

* Bristol was recaptured the next day but was holed during the action and then foundered.

Table 29: Commonwealth Fourth Rates rebuilt by contract 1690–93 – dimensions in feet and inches

Vessel	Gundeck	Keel	Beam	Depth	Tons	Keel/Beam Ratio
Newcastle	131 0	108 2	33 4½	13 6	641	3.24 : 1
Bristol	130 2	109 0	35 2	13 0	710	3.10 : 1

the war with fifty-six Fourth Rates, of which eleven were of 60 guns or above.

During the short-lived period of peace, the navy was to lose three more 50s. The old Foresight was wrecked off Cuba in 1698, the Carlisle was destroyed in a massive explosion (attributed to carelessly spilled powder) with the loss of all but eight of her crew while anchored in the Downs in September 1700, and the Harwich broached while careening at Amoy, on the coast of China, a couple of weeks later.

During the peace rebuilding also took place of the three remaining 54-gun ships of the Restoration period, as had already been done for the earlier Newcastle. Their size advantage over the 48-gun ships remained, but no record survives as to what calibre of guns they took on board after the work. All three vessels were widened, the Greenwich (already broadened since her original construction in 1666) by

Right: The draught of the *Lichfield* (here spelt *Litchfield*) reflects the ship prior to her rebuilding in 1727–30. Stylistically the draught is similar to examples firmly dated to the first decades of the eighteenth century, so it should not be assumed to show her exact appearance when first launched at Portsmouth in 1695 as one of the first of the numerous 130ft type built during the Wars of the English and Spanish Succession. All ships underwent a regular series of modernisation and maintenance work described as 'Repairs', so this draught may show the *Lichfield* at the time (1720) when her rebuilding to the 1719 Establishment was approved. (NMM: DR1457)

Table 30: King William's War new building programme (130ft group – wartime orders) – construction history

Vessel	Builder	Ordered	Launched	Fate
Weymouth	William Stigant, Portsmouth Dyd	15.8.1690	8.8.1693	BU 1717 to rebuild
Colchester	Henry Johnson, Blackwall	16.11.1693	23.10.1694	Wrecked 16.1.1704
Romney	Henry Johnson, Blackwall	16.11.1693	23.10.1694	Wrecked 22.10.1707
Lichfield	William Stigant, Portsmouth Dyd	16.11.1693	4.2.1695	BU 1720 to rebuild
Lincoln	Joseph Lawrence, Woolwich Dyd	16.11.1693	19.2.1695	Foundered 29.1.1703
Coventry	Fisher Harding, Deptford Dyd	16.11.1693	20.4.1695	Taken by the French 24.7.1704[1]
Harwich	R & J Castle, Deptford	18.11.1694	14.9.1695	Wrecked 5.10.1700
Severn	Henry Johnson, Blackwall	16.11.1693	16.9.1695	BU 1734 to rebuild
Burlington	Henry Johnson, Blackwall	16.11.1693	16.9.1695	BU 8.1733
Pendennis	R & J Castle, Deptford	18.11.1694	15.10.1695	Taken by the French 20.10.1705
Blackwall	Henry Johnson, Blackwall	12.9.1695	6.7.1696	Taken by the French 20.10.1705
Guernsey	Henry Johnson, Blackwall	12.9.1695	6.7.1696	BU 1716 to rebuild
Nonsuch	R & J Castle, Deptford	25.9.1695	20.8.1696	BU 1716 to rebuild
Warwick	R & J Castle, Deptford	25.9.1695	20.8.1696	BU 1709 to rebuild
Dartmouth	James Parker, Southampton	24.12.1695	3.3.1698	BU 1714 to rebuild
Hampshire	John Taylor, Rotherhithe	24.12.1695	3.3.1698	BU 1739
Winchester	J & R Wells, Rotherhithe	24.12.1695	17.3.1698	BU 1716 to rebuild
Salisbury[2]	Richard Herring, Bailey's Hard	24.12.1695	18.4.1698	BU 1739 to rebuild
Carlisle	Elias Waffe, Plymouth Dyd	24.12.1695	16.5.1698	Blew up by accident 19.9.1700
Worcester	Robert Winter, Northam	24.12.1695	31.5.1698	BU 1713 to rebuild
Jersey	Joseph Nye, East Cowes	24.12.1695	24.11.1698	Hulked 8.1731, sunk 27.5.1763
Tilbury	Daniel Furzer, Chatham Dyd	24.12.1695	22.9.1699	BU 1726 to rebuild

[1] retaken 17 March 1709 but not re-added. [2] the building site was on the Beaulieu River, halfway between Beaulieu town itself and Buckler's Hard; the *Salisbury* was captured by the French on 10 April 1703, retaken by *Leopard* on 15 March 1708 and renamed *Salisbury Prize*, but renamed *Preston* on 2 January 1716.

almost another 2ft, and the other two by lesser amounts. But nevertheless when the majority of the 48s were re-rated as 54-gun ships in 1703, no alterations were made to the establishments of the four existing 54s, and in due course any distinctions between the two groups were to disappear.

During the War of the Spanish Succession, the English ('British' from 1707) navy lost a further twenty-four Fourth Rates, including five 60s; but of these, thirteen ships (including three of the 60s) succumbed to natural causes. Of the eleven ships taken by the French, four were later to be recovered by the Royal Navy – although the *Bristol* in 1709 and the 60-gun *Pembroke* in 1711 were to founder upon their recaptures.

Significantly, seven were lost while on convoy escort: the *Salisbury* (in 1703), *Coventry* (1704), *Blackwall* and *Pendennis* (1705), *Chester* and *Ruby* (1707) and the 60-gun *Gloucester* (1709) were all lost while defending convoys against attack by enemy squadrons – all (except the *Coventry*) after gallant defences against unequal odds. Of the other four, the *Falmouth* was taken by two French 50-gun ships (curiously both former English ships, the *Salisbury* and *Jersey*) while cruising off the Scillies in 1704; like the *Bristol* and 60-gun *Pembroke* in 1709 and the *Advice* in 1711, which were also cruising when they encountered French squadrons, the *Falmouth* only surrendered after horrific casualties and in a disabled condition.

The 1703 Establishment of Guns

This Establishment, at least in theory, altered almost every 48-gun ship, raising them to a total of 54 guns.

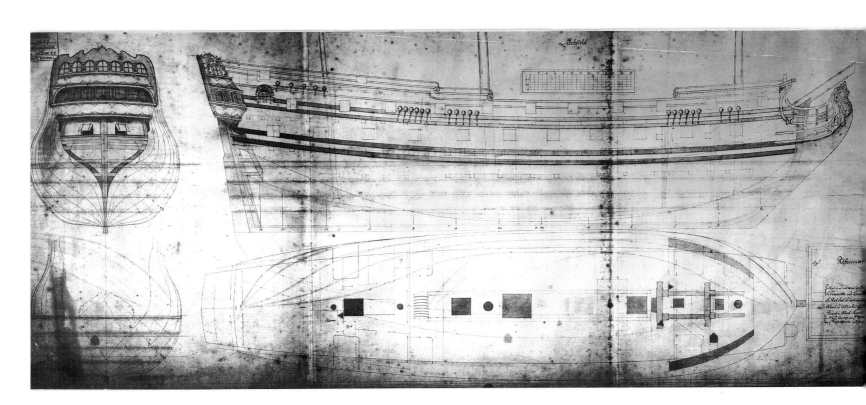

But while the four existing 54s had formerly 24pdrs on the gundeck and 8pdrs on the upper deck, the new Establishment prescribed, for all but the smallest of the existing 48-gun ships, a new allocation of 12pdrs (of 9ft length) for the gundeck and 6pdrs (8½ft length) on the upper deck; the sakers on the quarterdeck and forecastle were likewise to become 6pdrs – although of 7ft length on the former and of 9½ft length (bow chasers) on the latter. The four existing 54-gun ships were also scheduled to exchange their heavy weapons for the new calibres.

While the Establishment of almost all of the smaller 48-gun ships was raised to that of the 54-gun ships, seven vessels were deemed to be too small or weak to bear the increased armament, and these remained as 48-gun ships (the *Advice*), or raised to just 50 guns (the *Assistance, Bonaventure, Crown, Dover, Ruby* and *Reserve*). The three remaining 46-gun ships, the *Dragon, Kingfisher* and *Tiger* were raised to 48 guns (in the case of the *Dragon* to 50 guns) to join them, and they were joined by the newly-captured *Triton Prize*. Significantly, all of the ships (except the prize) were vessels which had been rebuilt.

There were few differences between the gun establishment for the 50-gun and 48-gun classes. Both were to carry twenty 12pdrs on the lower deck,

Table 31: King William's War new building programme (130ft group – wartime orders) – dimensions in feet and inches

Vessel	Gundeck	Keel	Beam	Depth	Tons	Keel/Beam Ratio
Specification	130 0	107 0	34 2	13 6	664 $^{38}/_{94}$	3.13 : 1
Weymouth	132 4	107 10	34 3	13 10	672 $^{80}/_{94}$	3.15 : 1
Colchester	131 4	111 8	34 3	13 7	696 $^{72}/_{94}$	3.26 : 1
Romney	131 0½	109 0	34 4	13 7	683 $^{41}/_{94}$	3.17 : 1
Lichfield	130 3	107 7	34 7½	13 6	682	3.11 : 1
Lincoln	130 7	108 4	34 3½	13 6½	675 $^{91}/_{94}$	3.16 : 1
Coventry		106 0	34 5	13 6	670	3.08 : 1
Harwich	130 2	109 0	34 4	13 8	683 $^{41}/_{94}$	3.17 : 1
Severn	131 3	109 0	34 4	13 6	683 $^{41}/_{94}$	3.17 : 1
Burlington	131 3	109 0	34 3	13 7	680 $^{12}/_{94}$	3.18 : 1
Pendennis	130 2½	109 0	34 3½	13 6½	681 $^{74}/_{94}$	3.18 : 1
Blackwall	131 1½	109 0	34 2½	13 7½	678 $^{44}/_{94}$	3.19 : 1
Guernsey	131 9	109 0	34 3	13 6	680 $^{12}/_{94}$	3.18 : 1
Nonsuch	130 5	109 0	34 2	13 9	676 $^{77}/_{94}$	3.19 : 1
Warwick	130 5	109 0	34 5	13 9	686 $^{71}/_{94}$	3.17 : 1
Dartmouth	131 3¾	108 10½	34 3½	13 6½	681 $^{47}/_{94}$	3.17 : 1
Hampshire	132 0	110 7	34 3	13 8	690 $^{1}/_{94}$	3.23 : 1
Winchester	130 0	107 5	34 4	13 7	673 $^{48}/_{94}$	3.13 : 1
Salisbury	134 4½	109 9½	34 2	13 6	681 $^{67}/_{94}$	3.21 : 1
Carlisle		112 0	34 6	13 2	709 $^{8}/_{94}$	3.25 : 1
Worcester	131 8¾	109 7	34 4¾	13 6¼	689 $^{50}/_{94}$	3.19 : 1
Jersey	132 1	109 0	34 2	13 8	676 $^{77}/_{94}$	3.19 : 1
Tilbury	130 1½	110 3	34 4	13 7½	691 $^{26}/_{94}$	3.21 : 1

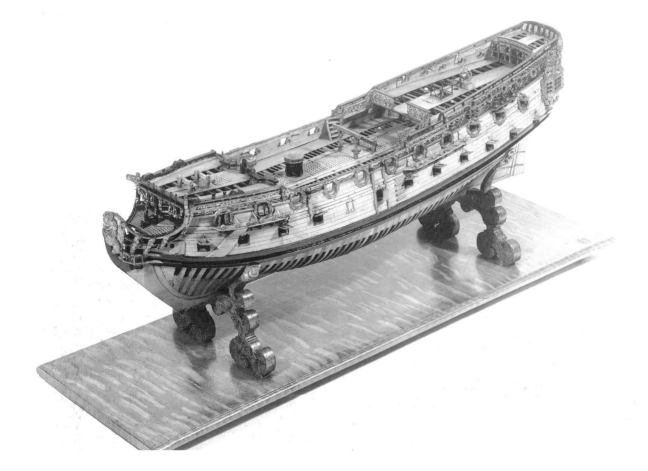

This classic 'Navy Board' framed model of a 50-gun ship is dated to the end of the seventeenth century. It bears the date 1701 in a small cartouche and Queen Anne's monogram carved on the stern, honouring the queen's accession on 8 March 1701/2 (modern dating records this as 1702, but by contemporary dating, the year 1701 ended on 25 March); this may be when the model was made, for the ship itself would appear to be one built during King William's War, and the shipwright's initials 'JL' carved on the model may indicate it was the work of Joseph Lawrence, who built three 50-gun ships at Woolwich in this period. If so, the most likely of these three vessels would appear to be the *Lincoln*, launched in 1695. Gunport wreaths certainly disappeared very quickly after 1703. The presence of a steering wheel on the quarterdeck and the absence of gunport lids in the waist might also indicate a somewhat later ship, but they may equally be subsequent alterations. (NMM: DR 6672)

Table 32: Fourth Rate purchased 1696

Vessel	Builder			Built	Purchased	Fate
Falkland	Thomas Holland, Portsmouth*, New Hampshire			1690	2.3.1696	Rebuilt 1702

Vessel	Gundeck	Keel	Beam	Depth	Tons	Keel/Beam Ratio
Falkland	128 6	109 0	33 2	13 9	637 ^{71}/94	3.29 : 1

* building site may have been at New Castle, nearer the coast, rather than near the site of the later Portsmouth Navy Yard.

Table 33: Prizes taken (both from French) during King William's War, 1689–97

Vessel	Builder	Built	Captured	Purchased	Fate
Trident Prize	F Coulomb, Toulon	1688	19.1.1695	23.11.1695	Sunk as a breakwater 3.7.1702
Medway Prize	H Hendrick, Dunkirk		30.4.1697	20.8.1697	Hulked 1699; sunk as foundation 1712

Vessel	Gundeck	Keel	Beam	Depth	Tons	Keel/Beam Ratio
Trident Prize	129 6	107 1½	36 7	13 4	762 ^{57}/94	2.93 : 1
Medway Prize	116 7		34 1	13 1	600?	2.83 : 1?

Note that the *Medway Prize* is listed in Dimensions Book 'B' as only 500 tons; however, this is inconsistent with the recorded dimensions which would imply a vessel of about 96ft or 97ft on the keel (no keel length is listed) which would in turn indicate a burthen of some 600 tons.

Table 34: Commonwealth Fourth Rates rebuilt 1698–1701 – construction history

Vessel	Builder	Ordered	Launched	Fate
Advice	Fisher Harding, Woolwich Dyd	24.5.1698	1698	Taken by the French 27.6.1711
Assistance	Samuel Miller, Deptford Dyd	29.4.1699?	1699	Rebuilt 6.1710
Southampton	Samuel Miller, Deptford Dyd	29.4.1699?	1699	Hulked 5.1728; BU 1734 (or 1771?)
Bonaventure	Fisher Harding, Woolwich Dyd		1699	Rebuilt 1711
Kingfisher	Fisher Harding, Woolwich Dyd		1699	Hulked 17.8.1706, BU 1728
Deptford	Fisher Harding, Woolwich Dyd	7.7.1699	1700	Rebuilt 2.1717
Reserve	Fisher Harding?, Deptford Dyd		1701	Foundered 27.11.1703

Like many contemporary models, this one – which originated in the collection of Charles Sergison, Pepys' successor at the Navy Board – cannot positively be identified with a particular vessel, and may be one of several from the 130ft class built around the turn of the century. (United States Naval Academy Museum, Annapolis model No 11)

although in the case of the 48-gun ship these were to be of 8½ft length rather than the 9ft variety allocated to the 50-gun ship (and to the 54). The main difference occurred on the upper deck, where the 50-gun ship carried twenty-two 6pdrs compared with twenty for the 48-gun ship; in both classes these were 8ft guns compared with the 8½ft weapons of the 54-gun ship. Both classes carried six 6pdrs of 7ft length on the quarterdeck, and two 6pdrs of 8½ft length as chase guns on the forecastle. These were of course wartime establishments at home; in peacetime or on overseas service, each class was reduced by one pair of guns from each deck (except the chase guns). The complement for the 48-gun ship remained at 230/200/150 (including the widows' men) although the peacetime figure was in some records recorded as 160, while the equivalent figures for the 50-gun ship was fixed at 250/220/165.

This rating of eleven of the smallest Fourth Rates as 50/44 or 48/42 gun ships was not to stand for long. In August 1704 (by Admiralty Order of 9 August 1704) the two classes were abolished and all the ships were re-rated as 54/46 guns. In any case, it is doubtful if any of these vessels ever carried the weaponry set out in the 1703 Establishment. In most cases the seventeenth-century guns were to remain in place until the ship was rebuilt, and those that were partially re-armed usually received antiquated guns, since the new models were issued predominantly to newly built vessels.

In September 1701, England and the Netherlands concluded a secret treaty with Austria, fearing that Louis XIV's plans to secure a favourable inheritance of the Spanish dominions overseas would result in French domination of the Mediterranean. The two maritime powers declared war on Spain and France in May 1702, with the aim of seizing portions of Spain's American territories. Sir George Rooke led a fifty-strong fleet in an abortive attack against Cadiz, but subsequently attacked the Spanish treasure fleet, with its French escorts, in Vigo Bay on 12 October 1702.

The small French 40-gun, *Le Triton*, was among the

ships taken there (the other prizes being Third Rates or 64s/60s), while the *Dartmouth* was retaken, re-named *Vigo Prize* in honour of the battle and returned to the Royal Navy on 29 January 1703 at her former rating. The *Triton* was added to the navy under the same name, and in 1703 was rated as a 48/42-gun ship with the same establishment of men and guns as the *Advice*, *Dragon* and *Tiger*.

At the close of 1703, the French 50-gun *Le Hasar-deux* was captured by an English squadron including the 70-gun *Warspite* and *Orford*, and added under the name *Hazardous*; on 25 March 1704 she was rated as a 54-gun ship in the Royal Navy, but with twenty-two 18pdrs on the gundeck and the same number of 12pdrs on the upper deck, and her complement was fixed at 320/240. She grounded off Selsey in 1706 and was wrecked there. A third naval prize was the 36-gun storeship (*flûte*) *La Seine*, which was taken by the *Falk-land* after a stiff resistance, and sailed as a prize into the Downs on 8 August 1704. She was surveyed at Woolwich on 28 August, and against the Dockyard's advice[15] she was added to the navy as the *Falkland's Prize*; she was rated, manned and armed as a standard 54-gun ship under the 1703 Establishment, but was run ashore in Sandwich Bay in late 1705 after her cables parted in a storm; her remains were salved, but were ordered to be sold on 11 March 1706.

The major battles of this war were between the Anglo-Dutch fleet and French fleets off Malaga on 13 August 1704 (in which the 50-gun ships *Tilbury*, *Swal-low*, *Centurion*, *Panther* and *Triton Prize* participated), and at Marbella on 10 March 1705 (in which the *Ti-ger*, *Swallow*, *Newcastle*, *Leopard*, *Antelope* and *Green-wich* took part). The *Leopard* was also to take part in the action in Gaspé Bay in August 1711.

Several other French Fourth Rates were taken by the Royal Navy during the later stages of the war. In the spring of 1708 the *Happy Return* and *Salisbury* were retaken (by the *Burford* and *Leopard* respectively), and while the former was broken up the latter was re-instated in the navy as the *Salisbury Prize* (a new *Salis-bury* having been built while she was in French hands). In November 1708 the 44-gun *Le Thétis* (built at Rochefort in 1697) was captured in the West Indies, but not purchased for the navy. The *Coventry* was also retaken on 17 March 1709 by the *Portland*, but not returned to the navy. In 1710 the 52-gun *Le Maure* (a near-sister to *Le Trident* captured in 1695) was taken, and she was added to the navy as the *Moor*, rated a 54-gun under the 1703 Establishment.

Various French Third Rates of between 50 and 54 guns were also captured in this war – *Le Modéré* at Vigo in 1702, *L'Arrogant* and *L'Auguste* in 1705 – but all three were rated as Fourth Rate 60s or 64s in the Royal Navy and armed with twenty-four 24pdrs on the gundeck, and so fall outside this study.

Table 35: Commonwealth Fourth Rates rebuilt 1698–1701 – dimensions in feet and inches

Vessel	Gundeck	Keel	Beam	Depth	Tons	Keel/Beam Ratio
Advice	118 0	99 3	32 4	12 1	551	3.07 : 1
Assistance	119 7	103 4	33 3	12 0	607	3.07 : 1
Southampton	122 3	102 2	34 2½	13 2	635 88/94	2.99 : 1
Bonaventure	125 5	102 5	33 1½	12 5	597	3.10 : 1
Kingfisher	125 8	110 0	34 4½	12 9	691 36/94	3.20 : 1
Deptford	128 4	106 9	34 4	13 5	669 31/94	3.11 : 1
Reserve	117 6	96 5	33 7½	13 0	579 80/94	2.87 : 1

Table 36: 54-gun ships of Restoration Era rebuilt 1699–1702 – construction history

Vessel	Builder	Ordered	Launched	Fate
Greenwich (1666)	Elias Waffe, Portsmouth Dyd	25.2.1699	1699	Rebuilt 7.1724
Oxford (1674)	Fisher Harding, Deptford Dyd		1702	Rebuilt 7.1723
Woolwich (1675)	William Lee, Woolwich Dyd		1.1702	Rebuilt 8.1736

Note that technically the work on these ships was classed as repair rather than the rebuilding which it amounted to in actuality. The 1699 order for work on the *Greenwich* (ADM 2/179) was an instruction to 'repair' her, while the work on *Oxford* and *Woolwich* was categorised as 'Great Repair'.

Table 37: 54-gun ships of Restoration era rebuilt 1699–1702 – dimensions in feet and inches

Vessel	Gundeck	Keel	Beam	Depth	Tons	Keel/Beam Ratio
Greenwich	135 10	110 0	36 0	13 6½	785	3.06 : 1
Oxford	126 8½	103 5	35 0½	14 9½	675 44/94	2.95 : 1
Woolwich	139 0	110 0	36 1	14 11	761 76/94	3.05 : 1

Table 38: War of the Spanish Succession new building programme (130ft group) – construction history

Vessel	Builder	Ordered	Launched	Fate
Antelope	John Taylor, Rotherhithe	[1]	13.3.1703	Rebuilt 2.1738
Leopard	Edward Swallow, Rotherhithe	[1]	15.3.1703	Rebuilt 12.1718
Swallow	Fisher Harding, Deptford Dyd	6.3.1702	22.2.1703	Rebuilt 12.1717
Newcastle	Joseph Allin, Sheerness Dyd	6.3.1702	24.3.1704	Rebuilt 5.1728
Panther	Edward Popely, Deptford	8.7.1702?	15.3.1703	Rebuilt 1713
Reserve[2]	Fisher Harding, Deptford Dyd	19.3.1703	18.3.1704	Hospital ship 6.1741; BU 1754
Saint Albans	Richard Burchett, Rotherhithe	16.11.1705	10.12.1706[3]	Rebuilt 3.1716
Colchester	Joseph Allin, Deptford Dyd	16.11.1705	13.2.1707	Rebuilt 12.1718

[1] one of these contracts was placed on 4.6.1702, but it is unclear which, and no date is known for the other ship. [2] renamed *Sutherland* 2.1.1716. [3] also recorded as 27.8.1706.

Table 39: War of the Spanish Succession new building programme (130ft group) – dimensions in feet and inches

Vessel	Gundeck	Keel	Beam	Depth	Tons	Keel/Beam Ratio
Specification	130 0	107 0	34 2	13 6	664 38/94	3.13 : 1
Antelope	131 5	108 11½	34 4½	13 9	684 78/94	3.17 : 1
Leopard	131 1	108 9	34 4½	13 6½	683 52/94	3.16 : 1
Swallow	130 0	106 3	34 6	13 6	672 64/94	3.08 : 1
Newcastle	130 2	109 0	34 2	13 7	676 77/94	3.19 : 1
Panther	131 3½	108 9½	34 4	13 8¼	683 27/94	3.17 : 1
Reserve	130 0	107 0	34 5½	13 6½	675 74/94	3.11 : 1
Saint Albans	130 8	109 7	34 4	13 7½	687 8/94	3.19 : 1
Colchester	130 6	108 3	34 5	13 6½	682 3/94	3.15 : 1

Table 40: Rebuilds 1701–04 – construction history

Vessel	Builder	Ordered	Launched	Fate
Falkland	Robert Shortis, Chatham Dyd	26.6.1701	1702	Rebuilt 6.1718
Tiger	Richard Wells, Rotherhithe	9.10.1701	4.1703	Rebuilt 2.1717
Crown	Fisher Harding, Deptford Dyd	10.6.1703	24.6.1704	Wrecked 21.1.1719
Ruby	Joseph Allin, Deptford Dyd	29.2.1704	18.2.1706	Taken by the French 10.10.1707

Table 41: Rebuilds 1701–04 – dimensions in feet and inches

Vessel	Gundeck	Keel	Beam	Depth	Tons	Keel/Beam Ratio
Falkland	128 6	109 0	33 2	13 9	637 $^{71}/_{94}$	3.29 : 1
Tiger	124 8½	103 6	33 4½	13 9	613 $^{7}/_{94}$	3.10 : 1
Crown	126 8	103 4	34 5½	13 6	652 $^{59}/_{94}$	3.00 : 1
Ruby	128 4	105 7	34 8	13 7	674 $^{88}/_{94}$	3.05 : 1

Table 42: Prizes taken (all from French) during War of the Spanish Succession 1702–13

Vessel	Builder	Built	Captured	Purchased	Fate
Triton	B Panglot, Brest	1696–97	12.10.1702	29.1.1703	Sold 4.10.1709
Hazardous	Lorient	1698	6.11.1703	8.12.1703	Wrecked 19.11.1706
Falkland's Prize	Rochefort	1688	15.7.1704	29.8.1704	Wrecked 19.12.1705; wreck salved, sold 11.3.1706
Moor	B Panglot, Toulon	1687–89	13.12.1710	1.5.1711	Sunk as a breakwater at Plymouth 7.3.1716

Vessel	Gundeck	Keel	Beam	Depth	Tons	Keel/Beam Ratio
Triton	128 0	105 7	34 4	13 4	661 $^{93}/_{94}$	3.08 : 1
Hazardous	136 5¾	114 11	37 10	15 0	874 $^{88}/_{94}$	3.04 : 1
Falkland Prize	133 6	112 4	35 0	15 1	731 $^{90}/_{94}$	3.21 : 1
Moor	135 4	116 2	36 2¾		811 $^{3}/_{94}$	3.21 : 1

1706 Establishment – nineteen ships completed as 12pdr type

Since 1694, the 50-gun ships had continued to be built to the dimensions specified in contracts issued that year, but in February 1706 the first steps were taken to introduce a more formalised basis for ship design by the creation of an 'Establishment of Dimensions'. This system, which was to become increasingly rigid over the next four decades and was to 'set in stone' most of the Navy Board's requirements for design, was introduced almost as an afterthought by Prince George, the Lord High Admiral (and Queen Anne's consort); while ordering the Navy Board to 'consult such officers you judge most proper, and then report to me what proportions may be most proper' for the rebuilding of several ageing Second Rates, added a request that similar proportions should be devised for future Third, Fourth and Fifth Rates.[16]

At the Navy Board's request, Daniel Furzer, the Surveyor, produced in May 1705 a list of the required dimensions. To produce the 'most proper' dimensions for the 50-gun ship, he adopted the proportions of the existing ships of the 130ft class, slightly broadening their design to 35ft. The Prince ordered the Navy Board to adopt these dimensions for all future warships of these Rates, and the Navy Board on 13 June passed on the instructions to the dockyards, making it clear that the new dimensions were to apply to the rebuilding of ships as well as to new vessels.

The new Establishment was to suffer some reconsideration before it came into practice. Admiral George Churchill, acting for Prince George's

The *Antelope* was built at Rotherhithe in 1702–3, and armed with 20 × 12pdrs and 30 × 6pdrs – see Table 115. The annotation on the draught includes the details taken off at Plymouth in March 1712/13, which provides the latest possible date for the drawing, but it may be the actual building draught. (NMM: DR1580)

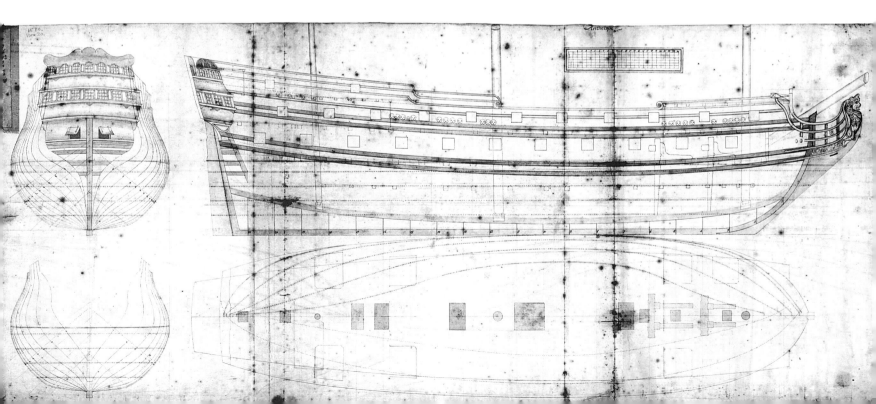

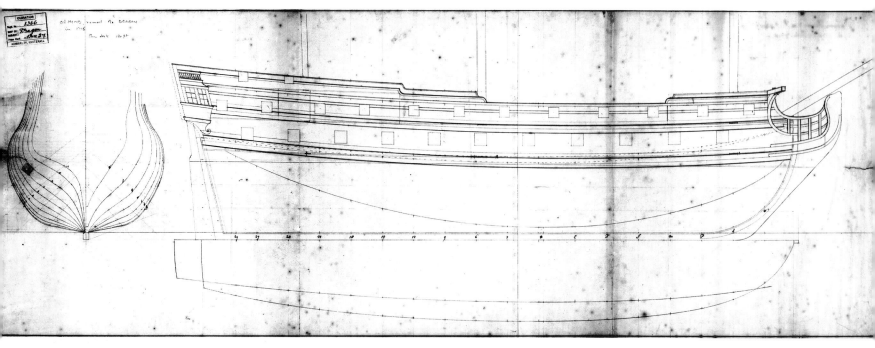

Above: Until Anson's reforms in the late 1740s, the design of dockyard-built vessels was the responsibility not of the Surveyor's office but of the master shipwrights in the individual ports. Thus, notwithstanding the issuance of Establishments setting common standards for ships' principal dimensions and (after 1719) for the thickness of the scantlings, common designs only evolved slowly. This vessel, constructed at Woolwich in 1710–11, was the sole 50-gun ship to be built by Jacob Acworth, subsequently Surveyor from 1715 until his death in 1746. Unlike the pre-Establishment ships, a twelfth pair of gunports was introduced on the upper deck, right aft in the great cabin; and the Acworth design dispensed with any roundhouse on the quarterdeck. Initially named *Ormonde* to honour James Butler, 2nd Duke of Ormonde and Marlborough's successor as C-in-C of British forces at the end of the French war, she was hastily renamed *Dragon* following the Duke's impeachment for treason in June 1715. (NMM: DR1366)

Below: The *Strafford* (incorrectly spelt *Stratford* on the draught) was the first of four 50-gun ships built by John Phillips at Plymouth Dockyard between 1712 and 1719. She was named after Thomas Wentworth, 3rd Earl of Strafford and First Lord of the Admiralty during the years she was building; this proved as politically unsound as with the *Ormonde* when the Earl was similarly impeached in 1715 following the Hanoverian bloodless coup in 1714, but the *Strafford* was at least able to retain her name. It is well to note that a number of contemporary naval vessels were named not after towns and counties – as modern readers might assume – but after peers whose titles included those places. (Science Museum photo B004823)

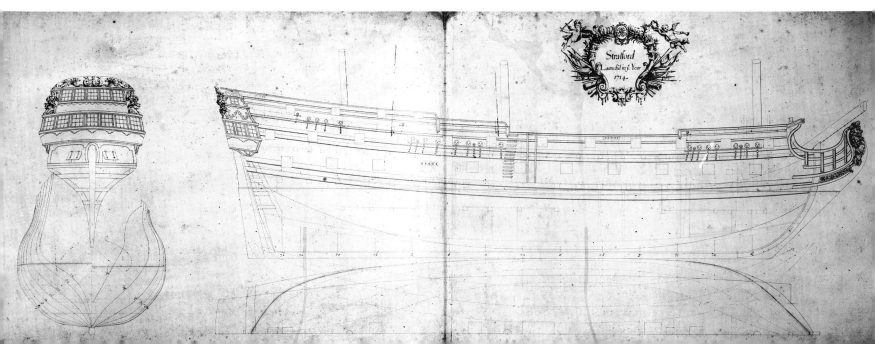

Table 43: Fourth Rates of 1706 Establishment (12pdr group) – construction history

Vessel	Builder	Ordered	Begun	Launched	Fate
Salisbury	Benjamin Rosewell, Chatham Dyd	27.4.1706		3.7.1707	Rebuilt 3.1716
Dragon (RB)	James Taylor, Rotherhithe	7.11.1706		?10.1707	Wrecked 26.3.1711
Falmouth	Richard Stacey, Woolwich Dyd	8.2.1707		26.2.1708	Rebuilt 5.1724
Ruby[1]	Joseph Allin, Deptford Dyd	26.3.1707		25.3.1708	44-gun Fifth Rate 1.1744; sold 19.5.1748
Chester	Benjamin Rosewell, Chatham Dyd	29.12.1707		18.10.1708	Hospital ship 8.1743, BU 2.1750
Romney	Joseph Allin, Deptford Dyd	29.12.1707		2.12.1708	Rebuilt 6.1723
Bonaventure[2] (RB)	Benjamin Rosewell, Chatham Dyd	(1711)		19.9.1711	Rebuilt 1.1720
Warwick (RB)	Richard Burchett, Rotherhithe	9.5.1709		9.1.1711	Rebuilt 3.1727 (as 60-gun ship)
Pembroke	John Lock (I), Plymouth Dyd	26.2.1707		18.5.1710	Rebuilt 9.1726 (as 60-gun ship)
Advice[1]	Joseph Allin, Deptford Dyd	27.7.1711		8.7.1712	44-gun Fifth rate 5.1745; sold 11.5.1749
Bristol	John Lock (I), Plymouth Dyd	24.4.1709		8.5.1711	BU 11.1742
Gloucester	Joseph Allin, Deptford Dyd	29.7.1710		4.10.1711	Rebuilt 11.1724
Ormonde[3]	Jacob Acworth, Woolwich Dyd	9.6.1710		18.10.1711	BU 1733 to build new 60-gun ship
Assistance (RB)	William Johnson, Blackwall	15.6.1710	23.6.1710	16.2.1713	Rebuilt 1.1720
Strafford	John Phillips, Plymouth Dyd	11.7.1712		16.7.1714	BU 7.1726 (to build new 60-gun ship)
Worcester (RB)	Joseph Allin, Deptford Dyd	(1713)		31.8.1714	BU 1733 to build new 60-gun ship
Panther (RB)	John Hayward, Woolwich Dyd	26.1.1714	11.12.1713	26.4.1716	Hulked 1743, sold 26.4.1768
Dartmouth (RB)	John Hayward, Woolwich Dyd	3.3.1714	7.5.1714	7.8.1716	Rebuilt 10.1736
Rochester (RB)	Richard Stacey, Deptford Dyd	(1714)	30.7.1714	19.3.1716	BU 10.1748[4]

Note that eleven of the above were new-built and eight (indicated by 'RB' after name) were rebuilds. The years in brackets given in the 'Ordered' column are estimated dates, as no official date of ordering can be found in the records for the ships concerned.
[1] renamed *Mermaid* and *Milford* respectively on 23 May 1744. [2] renamed *Argyll* 2 January 1716. [3] renamed *Dragon* 30 September 1715.
[4] became hospital hulk at Port Mahon and renamed *Maidstone* on 27 September 1744.

Advisory Council, overturned the new rules on 31 July and asked the Navy Board to reconsider the dimensions, consulting the Master Shipwrights at the principal dockyards and commercial builders, as well as the Surveyor. Following a meeting of all these parties, fresh dimensions were sent to the Admiralty, who promulgated them on 18 April 1706; while the dimensions of the Second and Third Rates were further enlarged from the previous year's figures, those of the Fourth Rates remained the same. They governed the construction of all ships for the next thirteen years.

Between the promulgation of this Establishment and Queen Anne's death, eleven 'new' vessels were ordered from the dockyards, and instructions for the rebuilding of eight existing vessels issued (six from the dockyards, plus two from private builders on the Thames). The eleven new ships were not additional units but replacements for Fourth Rates lost to the French (or, in one case, wrecked) during the war years from 1703 onwards – indeed, nine of them received the names of the lost vessels, and a tenth (*Ormonde*) was soon re-named after another of the 1711 losses. Only *Strafford* and (while she bore the name) *Ormonde* were new names, drawn from contemporary political leaders.

These, and the fact that other of these vessels were laid down before the loss of the ships whose names they took (*eg* the *Ruby*), seems to show that the Navy Board anticipated an attrition rate and placed orders for replacements beforehand in order to maintain the number of Fourth Rates at a constant sixty-two. Two of the last losses – *Gloucester* and *Pembroke* in 1709 – had been 60-gun ships, their replacement by new 50s indicating that the Navy Board's preference at this time was for the smaller of the Fourth Rates (no new 64s/60s were ordered until 1721).

The dimensions established for the 50-gun ship were a modification of the standard 130ft type. The gundeck remained at 130ft, while the keel was lengthened by a foot to 108ft; the breadth (outside the plank) was raised 10in to 35ft (20ft 8in at the main transom) and the depth in hold by 6in to 14ft. The new design was therefore slightly squarer and slower, but with increased stability.

The Establishment also set firm heights for each deck and for the sizes of the gunports; from the

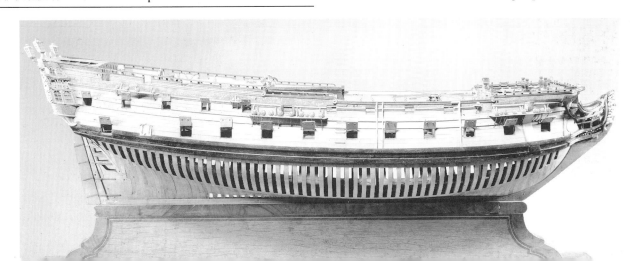

A broadside view of the model of a 1706 Establishment ship. The twelfth upper deck gunport added in the captain's accommodation generally distinguishes these vessels from pre-Establishment ships, but this example has a twelfth lower deck port as well. (NMM: A9951)

gundeck to the upper edge of the upper deck beams at the side ranged from 6ft 4in amidships to 6ft 6½in aft; the headroom on the upper deck below the quarter-deck beams ranged from 6ft amidships to 6ft 5in aft, while below the forecastle it ranged from 5ft 6in at its rear end to 5ft 8in below the bulkhead. The freeboard (the height of the lower gunport sills midships above the waterline) was to be 4½ft, and the draught ranged from 14½ft forward to 16ft aft.

By April 1714 it is clear that the 1703 Establishment had been adapted, at least in the application to individual vessels, for all the smaller (ie excluding 64-gun ships) Fourth Rates with the exception of the *Assistance* and the *Dover*, both still listed as 50-gun ships, and the *Tiger*, listed as 48-gun. The *Assistance* had just (1713) been rebuilt, while the *Dover* was shortly to be re-rated as a 40-gun Fifth Rate due to her small size. The *State of the Navy* List also refers to a ship under construction at Plymouth which 'may be finished in two or three months' (presumably the new *Strafford*) specifically as of 50 guns; however it is probable that both she and the *Worcester* described as 'now rebuilding at Deptford' were completed later that year as 54-gun ships, and the three ships listed as needing to be rebuilt were also rebuilt as 54-gun ships and fitted according to the 1703 Establishment of Guns.

The condition of all the 54s/48s was reported to be as follows in April 1714:

1A. In sea pay; in good condition: *Advice, Anglesea, Antelope, Bristol, Centurion, Colchester, Crown, Dover* (50), *Greenwich, Guernsey, Moor, Newcastle, Ormonde, Pembroke, Romney, Ruby, Salisbury, Southampton, Swallow, Tiger* (48), *Warwick, Weymouth, Winchester, Woolwich*.

1B. Lying in ordinary; in good condition: *Assistance* (50), *Falkland, Jersey, Leopard, Saint Albans, Severn, Tilbury*.

2B. Lying in ordinary; wants but small repairs: *Bonaventure, Chatham, Chester, Gloucester, Hampshire, Oxford*.

3A. In sea pay; wants great repair: *Lichfield, Reserve, Salisbury Prize* (renamed *Preston* 2 January 1716).

3B. Lying in ordinary; wants great repair: *Deptford, Falmouth, Norwich, Nonsuch, Portland*.

4A. In sea pay; wants rebuilding: *Panther* (was rebuilt 1713–16).

4B. Lying in ordinary; wants rebuilding: *Dartmouth* and *Rochester* (were both rebuilt 1714–16).

– Now under repair at Chatham: *Burlington*.

– Now rebuilding at Deptford: *Worcester* (was rebuilt 1713–1714).

In 1711 Robert Harley, Chancellor of the Exchequer (and *de-facto* Premier) organised the creation of the South Seas Company to participate in trade with Spanish America following the anticipated conclusion

Table 44: Fourth Rates of 1706 Establishment (12pdr group) – dimensions in feet and inches

Vessel	Gundeck	Keel	Beam	Depth	Tons	Keel/Beam Ratio
Establishment	130 0	108 0	35 0	14 0	703 68/94	3.09 : 1
Salisbury	130 0	108 0	35 0	14 0	703 68/94	
Dragon	131 8	108 5¼	35 3¾*	14 0	719 33/94	
Falmouth	130 0	107 0	35 1	14 0	700 49/94	
Ruby	130 4¾	108 0	35 1	14 0	707 7/94	
Chester	130 0	108 0	35 0	14 0	703 68/94	
Romney	130 6	108 0	35 2	14 0	710 41/94	
Bonaventure	130 0	108 0	35 0	14 0	703 68/94	
Warwick	130 0	107 2½	35 7	14 0	722 4/94	
Pembroke	130 0	108 0	35 0	14 0	703 68/94	
Advice	130 8	108 1	35 3	14 0	714 34/94	
Bristol	130 0	108 0	35 0	14 0	703 68/94	
Gloucester	130 8	108 1	35 3	14 0	714 34/94	
Ormonde	130 0	108 0	35 0	14 1½	703 68/94	
Assistance	132 1½	108 11	35 0	14 0½	709 65/94	
Strafford	130 10	108 0	35 0	14 0	703 68/94	
Worcester	131 5	108 7	35 3½	14 0	719 34/94	
Panther	131 1½	108 3½	35 3	14 4	715 70/94	
Dartmouth	130 3	108 9	35 1	14 4	711 87/94	
Rochester	131 3	108 7	35 3½	14 0	719 34/94	

* Dimensions Book 'B' list the *Dragon*'s breadth as 33ft 3¾in, but this would appear to be a clerical error.

of the War of the Spanish Succession. During the autumn of 1712 the *Anglesea* and *Warwick* were lent to the Company to act as transports. Reduced to 30 guns and 130 men, they were re-rigged as Fifth Rates; the great cabins were shortened by 6ft and the quarter-decks extended forward to the mainmast, while the lower decks were boarded in using feather-edged deals to act as a storage area, leaving only four guns on the lower deck (the usual armament of twenty 6pdrs remained on the upper deck, with two guns on the fore-castle and four on the quarterdeck). The bottoms were ordered to be 'fully drove with nails' as protection against worm, since they were being sent into tropical waters.

In 1714 this arrangement was renewed for the *Anglesea*, except that her armament was increased to 40 guns, with fourteen 12pdrs on the lower deck, sixteen 6pdrs on the upper deck, and ten 3pdrs on the half-deck (resulting from the extended quarterdeck). The *Anglesea* was broken up in 1719 for rebuilding, and as she was rebuilt as a 40-gun ship it seems likely that she remained at that rating from 1714 onwards.

Other 54-gun ships were by this time showing signs of age. At the start of 1715 the captains of the *Centurion* and *Weymouth* complained that their elderly vessels were unable to safely carry the 54 guns assigned to them. To reduce the strain, the two ships were each ordered to carry only 50 guns in future. In 1716 both the *Dover* and *Southampton* were reduced to 40-gun Fifth Rates; the latter underwent a Large Repair at Chatham between 1722 and 1724 (remaining at 40 guns), but was hulked at Jamaica in 1728.

5. The 18pdr Fifties

Queen Anne died on 1 August 1714, leaving her successor a fleet of 247 vessels that included fifty 54-gun ships; notwithstanding the end of the war, few Fourth Rates were disposed of. The new Hanoverian administration rapidly replaced the membership of the Admiralty and Navy Boards. But its placemen, although younger, were no less conservative than their predecessors, and the regime of the Establishment continued to impose its restraining effect upon British naval design. In the following quarter-century, the size of the warships built by Britain's rivals was to leap-frog over the equivalent ships of the Royal Navy.

Nevertheless, one great weakness – the relative lack of firepower – was identified and on 6 July 1716 a new Establishment of Guns was promulgated. The smaller Fourth Rates were substantively restored to their pre–1703 armament, with 18pdrs (the old name 'demi-culverin' was dropped – all guns now being identified by their weight of shot) on the lower deck and 9pdrs on the upper deck. To compensate for the greater weight of these batteries, the 6pdrs on the quarterdeck were cut from eight to four in number, so the total (rated) number of guns became 50.

The Gun Establishment of 1716 not only provided a significant increase in the firepower allotted to each ship, it also aimed to ensure that all vessels of the same number of guns, irrespective of their age, carried the same armament and were within the same Rate. It was, however, recognised that it would require a number of years before all existing vessels could be re-armed to the new Establishment.

Proportionately, the 54-gun ships were those most affected by the new standard. Their 12pdr guns were to be superseded by 18pdrs. While these were 9ft weapons like the 12pdrs, the new 18pdrs weighed 39cwt apiece, an increase of 8cwt on the 12pdrs. Moreover the 6pdrs on the upper deck were similarly to be replaced by 9pdrs of the same 8ft 6 inch length, and at 26cwt apiece these were 4cwt heavier than the existing 6pdrs. To compensate in part for the extra weight, half of the eight 6pdrs on the quarterdeck were to be struck from the complement of guns, so that the vessels became 50-gun instead of 54-gun. The new 6pdrs were 8ft, 20cwt weapons, while the pair of chase guns on the forecastle were to become 9ft, 24cwt weapons.

Accordingly, not only was the firepower of the 'new' 50-gun ships more than 38 per cent higher than that of the 54s (they were, of course, actually the same vessels), in spite of the nominal decrease by four guns, the broadside rose from 228 pounds to 315 pounds. But the actual weight of ordnance also rose by about 15 per cent to 77.9 tons, placing a tremendous strain on the vessels.

The Navy Board expressed its concern that stand-ardisation was being taken too far. It pointed out that several ships, including the *Dover*, *Tiger* and *Chatham* were smaller than the other 54s and would find it a strain to carry the 10 tons of extra weight. The reference to the *Chatham* is obscure as she was certainly not among the smaller of the 54s – although she was certainly ageing and in line for a rebuild. However, it was clearly the vessels formerly contained in the short-lived 48-gun class of 1703–04 which most worried the Navy Board.

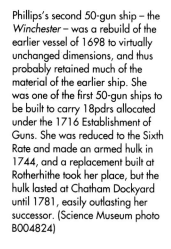

Phillips's second 50-gun ship – the *Winchester* – was a rebuild of the earlier vessel of 1698 to virtually unchanged dimensions, and thus probably retained much of the material of the earlier ship. She was one of the first 50-gun ships to be built to carry 18pdrs allocated under the 1716 Establishment of Guns. She was reduced to the Sixth Rate and made an armed hulk in 1744, and a replacement built at Rotherhithe took her place, but the hulk lasted at Chatham Dockyard until 1781, easily outlasting her successor. (Science Museum photo B004824)

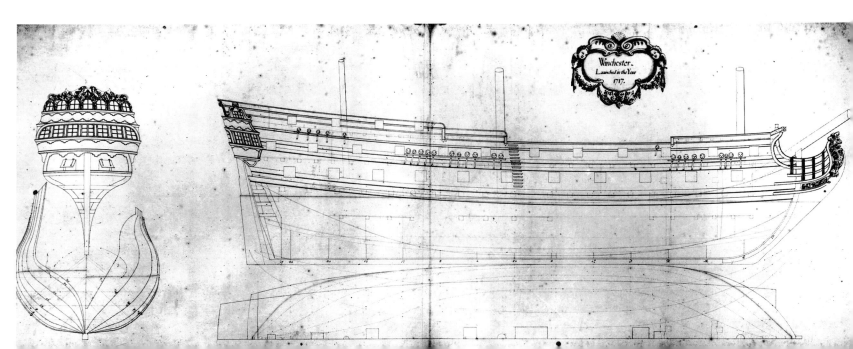

The early Hanoverian orders of 1716 to 1719 – the last ships to the 1706 Establishment

The replacement of many senior officials at the time of the Hanoverian accession, and a resulting discontinuity and confusion in the records, makes it difficult to be certain, but it would appear likely that the first orders for Fourth Rates placed by the Earl of Orford's final administration were in early 1716 and, even if they were not initially intended to comply with the new Establishment of Guns, certainly by the time that work on these vessels was well advanced, they were clearly to be armed according to the new pattern, although their hulls still conformed to the dimensions laid down in the 1706 Establishment. Orford's policies were at first to be maintained by his successor, the Earl of Berkeley (the former Admiral James Berkeley). Ten vessels – all rebuilds of existing 54s – were to be completed before reconsideration of the specifications for the weapon platforms resulted in more appropriate designs being introduced.

In June 1744 the *Norwich* was to be reduced to a 44-gun Fifth Rate.[17] Renamed *Enterprise*, she retained twenty of her 18pdrs on the lower deck, but was re-armed with twenty 6pdrs on the upper deck and four more 6pdrs on the quarterdeck; her complement was reduced to 250 men.

At the Battle of Cape Passaro on 11 August 1718, Sir George Byng's fleet took or burnt a number of Spanish ships, including one 50-gun – the *San Isidro*,

The *Deptford*, another ship rebuilt by John Phillips at Plymouth in 1718–19, had a short and uneventful career lasting only four years (mostly on convoy and cruising duties) before she was paid off in 1723 and the hulk sold three years later. She differed from the *Winchester* by having an extra quarter light instead of her sistership's twelfth pair of upper deck gunports aft. The short life of most Plymouth-built ships is attributed not so much to the quality of workmanship but more usually to the bad quality of materials sent down from Deptford. (Science Museum photo B004825)

Table 45: Fourth Rates of 1706 Establishment (18pdr group) – construction history

Vessel	Builder (& Dockyard)	Ordered	Begun	Launched	Fate
Nonsuch	John Naish, Portsmouth	(1716)	8.1716	29.4.1717	Hulked 1740, BU 1745
Salisbury	Richard Stacey, Deptford	8.3.1716	25.5.1716	10.10.1717	BU 1724 to RB (by 1726)
Winchester	John Phillips, Plymouth	8.3.1716	10.7.1716	10.10.1717	Hulked 1744, BU 1781
Guernsey	John Hayward, Woolwich	16.5.1716	7.9.1716	24.10.1717	BU 1737 for RB (by 1740)
Saint Albans	John Phillips, Plymouth	8.3.1716	3.4.1717	6.3.1718	BU 9.1734 to RB (by 1737)
Norwich*	Ben Rosewell, Chatham	(1716)		20.5.1718	BU 1771
Weymouth	John Hayward, Woolwich	6.9.1717	13.6.1717	26.2.1719	BU 6.1.1732
Swallow	Ben Rosewell, Chatham	4.12.1717	11.9.1717	25.3.1719	BU 1728
Deptford	John Phillips, Plymouth	1.2.1717	21.3.1718	19.6.1719	Sold by AO 3.5.1726 (?BU 1729)
Tiger	John Ward, Sheerness	1.2.1717	1.5.1718	13.11.1722	Wrecked 12.1.1743

Note all the above ten ships were rebuilds. * renamed *Enterprise* 23 May 1744, and re-armed and re-classed as a 44-gun ship in June 1744.

Table 46: Fourth Rates of 1706 Establishment (18pdr group) – dimensions in feet and inches

Vessel	Gundeck	Keel	Beam	Depth	Tons	Keel/Beam Ratio
Establishment	130 0	108 0	35 0	14 0	703 $^{68}/_{94}$	3.09 : 1
Nonsuch	131 2	107 9	34 7½	13 7	687 $^{12}/_{94}$	
Salisbury	130 7½	107 9	35 2½	14 0	710 $^{44}/_{94}$	
Winchester	131 4	108 7	35 1	14 0	710 $^{84}/_{94}$	
Guernsey	130 0	107 4	35 2	14 1	706 $^{5}/_{94}$	
Saint Albans*	130 8	109 7	34 4	13 7½	687 $^{8}/_{94}$	
Norwich	130 0	108 0	35 0	14 4	703 $^{68}/_{94}$	
Weymouth	130 0	107 8	35 4	14 0	714 $^{92}/_{94}$	
Swallow	130 4	107 0	35 4	14 4	710 $^{54}/_{94}$	
Deptford	131 9	109 0	35 0	14 0	710 $^{22}/_{94}$	
Tiger	130 0	106 6	35 5½	14 0	712 $^{22}/_{94}$	

* no trace of *Saint Albans*'s rebuilding appears in the Dimensions Book, and it is assumed here that her dimensions were unaltered.

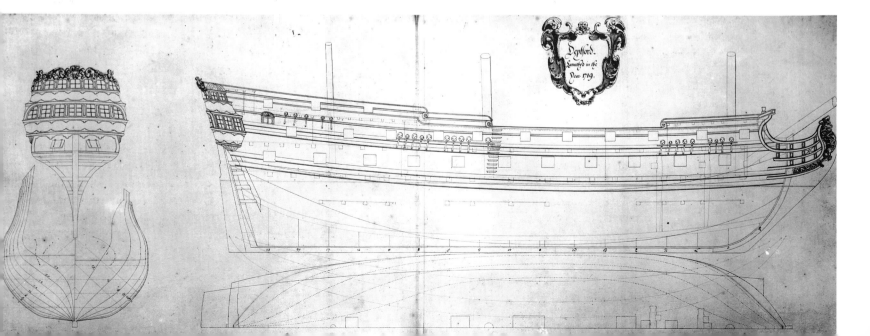

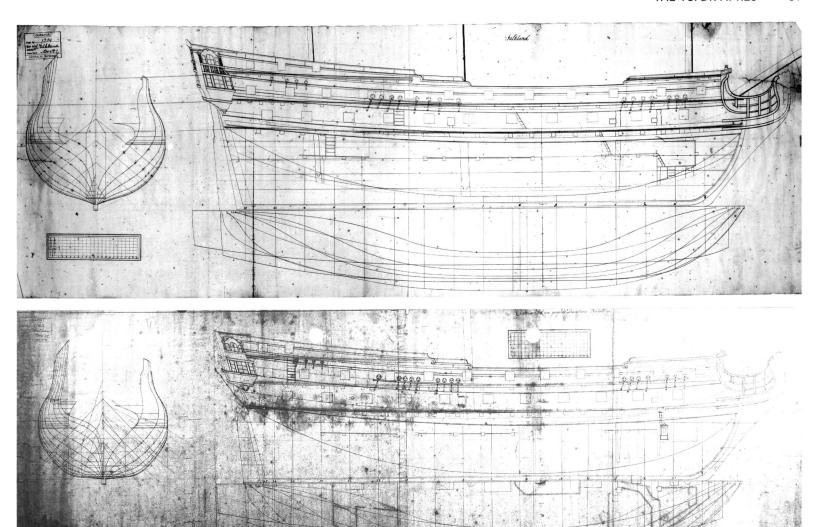

In early 1719 a new Establishment was issued, enlarging the dimensions of the 50-gun ship and setting standards for the scantlings (the thickness of timbers used in construction). Two 50s had begun rebuilding at Deptford Dockyard in the previous year, and both were completed to the new standards – the *Falkland* of 1720 (top) and the *Chatham* launched a year later (above). Other than the 4ft increase in length, the main visual change was that the rigidly straight cutwater was replaced by a gently concave curve. Note the radically different hull forms exhibited by the two ships, *Falkland* being very fine indeed, clearly demonstrating that the early Establishments were *not* standard designs, although often described as though they were. (NMM: DR1359 *Falkland* and DR1362 *Chatham*)

built in 1716 at Pasajes; like the other prizes, she was not added to the Royal Navy, but was laid up until 1731, when she was found to be rotten and was broken up. The *Bonaventure* – newly renamed the *Argyll* – and the *Rochester* were among Byng's fleet at Passaro. With the cream of the Spanish navy lost, the War of the Quadruple Alliance was a brief affair, and few British warships were to see any action for another two decades.

The 1719 Establishment

A year later the established dimensions were revised to take account of the new weight of weapons. In June 1719 the Admiralty requested the Navy Board to report on building and rebuilding of its ships, and Jacob Acworth, the new Surveyor, called a conference of the Master Shipwrights from which emerged in December a new and more detailed Establishment. Whereas the 1706 Establishment had sought only to fix the principal dimensions of each class of warship (except the largest and smallest), the new rules laid down the dimensions of each scantling and practically every

other part of a ship's structure for all six Rates. While the master shipwright in the dockyard concerned retained the task of drawing the actual lines of each new (or rebuilt) ship, the rigid requirements of the new Establishment precluded any significant experimentation or development.

The new Establishment lengthened the gundeck by 4ft to 134ft, while the keel was only stretched by 20in to 109ft 8in. The breadth was increased by a foot to 36ft, and the depth in the hold by 14in to 15ft 2in. The tonnage thereby was increased by 51 to almost 756 tons. The established complement of men remained at 280 (185 in peacetime).

No additional ships were built to these new specifications, but they were applied to each new rebuilding of a 50-gun ship as the more aged vessels approached the end of their useful lives. Altogether fourteen 50-gun ships were authorised to be rebuilt – all in the Royal Dockyards – between June 1718 and the summer of 1725, and thirteen were completed to this Establishment; work on the *Gloucester* – ordered from Sheerness – was deferred for nearly a decade and she was finally built to the revised Establishment of 1733, but another vessel – the *Newcastle* from Woolwich – although not ordered until 1728, was instead built to the 1719 Establishment.

In December 1718 orders were passed to rebuild the *Portland* and *Lichfield*. On the same day Plymouth Dockyard was ordered to 'take down' the *Leopard* and *Colchester*, and to send their remains (*ie* serviceable timbers) to Woolwich and Chatham.[18] With approval for the new Establishment being given in 1719, all four ships, together with the *Falkland* and *Chatham* on which work had begun at Deptford in the previous year, were to be built to the new dimensions and strict code of scantlings now in force. Work on rebuilding the *Lichfield*, however, was delayed and she was not re-launched until 1730.

In early 1720 Woolwich Dockyard was ordered to rebuild the *Argyll* (the former *Bonaventure*, renamed in 1716) and *Assistance* to the new dimensions.[19] No further rebuilding of 50s was approved until June 1723, when Deptford was ordered to rebuild the *Romney* from her serviceable remains, and Portsmouth was instructed to take to pieces the *Oxford* and rebuild her.[20] During the next two years four more 50s were ordered to be rebuilt, including the seven-year-old *Salisbury* whose 'Great Repair' in 1716 had apparently proved deficient. The work on the *Falmouth* and *Gloucester* was clearly major, as both ships were ordered to be taken to pieces before being rebuilt. However, work on the new *Gloucester* was not proceeded with, and it was not until after the adoption of the next Establishment in 1733 that Sheerness Dockyard began work on their new Fourth Rate.

Further 50-gun ships became in need of rebuilding from early 1726, with instructions being issued to rebuild to the 1719 Establishment the *Deptford* (although only seven years old), *Strafford*, *Pembroke*, *Tilbury* and *Warwick* during the next twelve months. But no work had begun on these five ships before they were overtaken by a change in policy.

Modified 1719 Establishment – 50s replaced by 60s

It is a general axiom among naval historians that the period of the Establishments – in particular the years from 1719 to 1733 – is one extreme fossilisation in ship design, at the end of which the qualities of British warships had been overtaken by advances in design made by the Continental navies, particularly those of France. This viewpoint is substantiated by much evidence. But all conservatism is relative, and notwithstanding the restrictions imposed by the Establishment, considerable thought was given to improving the designs, and in many cases implemented. From 1727, in particular, the incoming Torrington administration authorised the construction of a considerable number of 'exceptions'

Table 47: Fourth Rates of 1719 Establishment – construction history

Vessel	Builder (& Dockyard)	Ordered	Begun	Launched	Fate
Falkland	Richard Stacey, Deptford	11.6.1718	8.4.1718	28.8.1720	BU 3.1742 to RB
Chatham	Richard Stacey, Deptford	19.6.1718	4.7.1718	15.8.1721	Breakwater 5.1749[1]
Colchester	Benjamin Rosewell, Chatham	5.12.1718	1.4.1719	26.10.1721	BU 9.1742
Leopard	John Hayward, Woolwich	5.12.1718	1.8.1719	18.4.1721	BU 1739
Portland	John Naish, Portsmouth	5.12.1718	6.2.1720	25.2.1723	BU 6.1743
Lichfield	Peirson Lock, Plymouth	5.12.1718	11.1727	25.3.1730	BU 7.1744
Argyll	John Hayward, Woolwich	27.1.1720	20.10.1719	5.7.1722	Breakwater 23.11.1748[2]
Assistance	John Hayward, Woolwich	27.1.1720	1.1721	25.11.1725	Breakwater 14.12.1745
Romney	Richard Stacey, Deptford	11.6.1723	21.8.1723	17.10.1726	44 guns in 1.1746; sold 21.7.1757
Oxford	Joseph Allin, Portsmouth	29.6.1723	13.3.1724	10.7.1727	BU 10.1758
Greenwich	Benjamin Rosewell, Chatham	16.4.1724	1.7.1724	15.2.1730	Wrecked 20.10.1744
Falmouth	John Hayward, Woolwich	14.5.1724	24.6.1724	30.4.1729	BU 8.1747
Gloucester	Jeremiah Rosewell, Sheerness	6.11.1724	–	–	Altered to 1733 Estab
Salisbury	John Naish, Portsmouth	9.4.1725	23.12.1725	30.10.1726	Hulked 8.1744, sold 1.5.1749
Deptford	Richard Stacey, Deptford	3.5.1726	–	–	Re-ordered 6.1729 as 60-gun ship
Strafford	Benjamin Rosewell, Chatham	14.7.1726	–	–	Re-ordered 3.1733 as 60-gun ship
Pembroke	John Hayward, Woolwich	8.9.1726	–	–	Re-ordered 6.1729 as 60-gun ship
Tilbury	Benjamin Rosewell, Chatham	15.12.1726	–	–	Re-ordered 6.1729 as 60-gun ship
Warwick	Peirson Lock, Plymouth	14.3.1727	–	–	Re-ordered 6.1729 as 60-gun ship
Newcastle	John Hayward, Woolwich	31.5.1728	3.1729	6.1.1732	BU 4.1746
Swallow	Peirson Lock, Plymouth	7.1.1729	–	–	Re-ordered 6.1729 as 60-gun ship
Centurion	Joseph Allin, Portsmouth	17.2.1729	–	–	Re-ordered 6.1729 as 60-gun ship

[1] sunk as breakwater at Sheerness; raised and BU 1762. [2] sunk as breakwater at Harwich; BU 1762.

which provided incremental development of British naval designs away from the restricted dimensions of the 1719 Establishment.

By the middle of the 1720s, the role of the lightly armed 50-gun ship was being questioned. Too small to be effective in the line of battle, it was considered that there should be a move towards the 60-gun ship as a replacement. Following the accession of George II and the replacement of Berkeley's ten-year-old administration by a new Board in July 1727 under Viscount Torrington (the former Sir George Byng), this policy began to be implemented. In March 1728 the

Table 48: Fourth Rates of 1719 Establishment – dimensions in feet and inches

Vessel	Gundeck	Keel	Beam	Depth	Tons	Keel/Beam Ratio
Design (Establishment)	134 0	109 8	36 0	15 2	755 $^{89}/_{94}$	3.05 : 1
Falkland	134 5	110 0	36 5	15 2	775 $^{89}/_{94}$	
Chatham	134 0	109 8	36 0	15 2	755 $^{89}/_{94}$	
Colchester	134 0	109 8	36 0	15 4	755 $^{89}/_{94}$	
Leopard	134 3	109 10¾	36 2	15 2	762 $^{25}/_{94}$	
Portland	134 5	110 0	36 4	15 3	772 $^{38}/_{94}$	
Lichfield	134 2	109 8	36 0	15 2	755 $^{89}/_{94}$	
Argyll	134 2	110 4	36 1	15 2	764 $^{11}/_{94}$	
Assistance	134 0	109 9	36 1	15 2	750 $^{17}/_{94}$	
Romney	134 0	109 8	36 0	15 2	755 $^{89}/_{94}$	
Oxford	134 6	109 10	36 3	15 2	767 $^{66}/_{94}$	
Greenwich	134 2	110 1	36 0	15 0	758 $^{82}/_{94}$	
Falmouth	134 2	109 0	36 1	15 2	760 $^{61}/_{94}$	
Salisbury	133 5	109 8	36 0	15 2	755 $^{89}/_{94}$	
Newcastle	134 0	109 8	36 1	15 2	759 $^{47}/_{94}$	

This Navy Board model of a 50-gun ship of the 1719 Establishment should be compared with the rigging draught for the *Oxford* in Chapter 10. The protruding external gallery on the quarterdeck level is just visible below the stern lanterns. This broadside view gives a good idea of the sheer still remaining at this time, although much reduced from seventeenth century vessels. (NMM: 6042)

Navy Board was instructed to send Josiah Burchett, the Admiralty Secretary, a list of ships of 50 guns and above that were to be rebuilt. In the meantime, Hayward at Woolwich Dockyard was ordered to rebuild another 50 – the *Newcastle* – to the 1719 Establishment. During early 1729, it was also instructed that the *Swallow* and *Centurion* should be taken to pieces and rebuilt.[21]

The new Board ordered that eight 50s which were to undergo rebuilding should be replaced, not by new 50s, but by six 60s.[22] Clearly the new ships – at 951

tons in the 1719 Establishment – could not be considered to be rebuilds, so the fiction was dropped, although the allocation of the names of earlier 50s to the new ships showed clearly that they were replacements for the older vessels. The *Lichfield* and *Newcastle* had both been laid down and were to proceed as 50-gun ships, but the other eight Fourth Rates which had been ordered rebuilt had not been commenced and six of these were now to be laid down as 60s; the rebuilding of the remaining two, the *Gloucester* and *Strafford*, was not proceeded with at this time, but in 1733 they were re-ordered to the Establishment of that year, the former as a 50-gun and the latter as a 60-gun ship.

Two of these ships were to become 50-gun vessels later in their lives. In September 1746 the *Centurion* was reduced to 350 men and 52 guns – twenty-two 24pdrs, twenty-four 9pdrs and six 6pdrs (four on quarterdeck and two on forecastle), by Admiralty Order of 1 December 1744. In 1752 the *Deptford* was reduced to 350 men and 50 guns – the same breakdown except one fewer pair of 9pdrs on the upper deck – by Admiralty Order of 29 November 1750.

While the first five of the 60-gun ships were built to the 1719 Establishment, these dimensions – like those of the 50s – were being reconsidered by the Torrington Board. The *Centurion*'s design was proposed by Allin to be widened by a foot to provide extra stability, and on 17 October 1729 this alteration was ordered to be made. In December 1737 this ship came under the command of 40-year-old Captain George Anson, and in September 1740 was his flagship when he led a small squadron – including the 50-gun ships *Gloucester* and *Severn* and five smaller vessels – out from Portsmouth at the start of a historic 41-month voyage of circumnavigation.

Six months after the return of the survivors in 1744, Anson was appointed to the Board of Admiralty of which he was to be First Lord from 1751 to 1762 (apart from one gap of seven months); but prior to that the worn-out *Centurion* had already been reduced to a 50-gun ship and renamed *Eagle* (she regained her original name a year later by exchanging names with a new 58-gun ship building at Harwich). Significantly, by this time the latest 50-gun ships built to the 1741 Establishment equalled her dimensions. The ship outlasted her most illustrious commander by seven years – being broken up in December 1769, with a new 50 ordered to bear her name a year later.

The 1733 Establishment

In early 1732 the Admiralty began to give consideration to creating a new Establishment of dimensions. Being aware that the Navy Board, and especially Acworth, were opposed to a radical enlargement of dimensions, the Admiralty decided to obtain a wider range of opinion from the Master Shipwrights at the principal dockyards. In April it instructed the Navy Board to request each of the senior Master Shipwrights to recommend to what principal dimensions they would propose new ships of each Rate should be built, and after some delays received the following proposals in respect of 50-gun ships:

Existing (1719)	134 0	109 8	36 0	15 2	755 89/94
Richard Stacey	134 0	109 2	36 10	15 5	787 74/94
John Ward	134 9	111 0	37 1	14 9	818 3/94
Peirson Lock	135 9		37 4	15 2	*c.*830 estimated
Joseph Allin	135 0		38 4¾	15 4½	*c.*870 estimated
John Hayward	136 0		38 6	15 4	*c.*883 estimated
Adopted (1733)	134 0	108 3	38 6	15 9	853 45/94

Allin was the only one to offer an estimate of the draught of water his design would require, offering 14ft 11¾ ins forward and exactly 2ft more aft. It is significant that none of the shipwrights felt much need for increased length, but all wanted more beam, suggesting – as borne out by surviving Sailing Quality Reports – that the 1719 ships were rather tender, lacking a good reserve of stability. After further consultation it was Acworth in May 1733 who finally came forward with compromise proposals which the Admiralty could endorse. The 50-gun was not increased in length – indeed, the keel length was shortened by 17in to 108¼ft; but the breadth was increased by 2½ft (to 38½ft) and the depth in hold by 7in to 15¾ft. As a consequence the tonnage jumped to just under 853½ tons.

While the dimensions were adopted in practice, with all orders for new or rebuilt ships from 1733 onwards being to Acworth's compromise dimensions, this Establishment was never formally confirmed by the King in Council, and thus the 1719 Establishment was technically kept in being. Notwithstanding the enlarged dimensions, the measurements of all the scantlings set out in 1719 were retained. The increased breadth was also designed to allow the 50s to carry 24pdrs on their lower decks instead of 18pdrs, and a new Establishment of Guns which incorporated this proposal was approved by the Council in January 1733, but there was swift opposition by the Ordnance Board, and the approval was suspended (see below). For the next decade the 1719 armaments were to remain in force.

Orders were thus issued to authorise work on the *Gloucester* at Sheerness, on which the start of work had been deferred since 1729, and now to be built to the proposed new Establishment for 50-gun ships. In 1733 it was also decided to replace more ageing 50-gun ships by new 60s, and four of the surviving ships of the 1706 Establishment, plus the even older *Burlington* and *Jersey*, were broken up and six more 60s to

Table 49: 60-gun replacements for 50-gun ships – construction history

Vessel	*BU (as 50)*	*Builder & Dyd as 60)*	*Ordered*	*Keel Laid*	*Launched*	*Fate*
Deptford	1726	Richard Stacey, Deptford	3.5.1726	12.12.1729	26.9.1732	Sold 23.6.1767
Pembroke	8.1726	John Hayward, Woolwich	8.9.1726	9.1729	27.11.1733	Wrecked 13.4.1749
Tilbury	1726	John Ward[1], Chatham	15.12.1726	25.3.1731	2.6.1733	Burnt 21.9.1742
Warwick	1726	Peirson Lock, Plymouth	14.3.1727	4.1730	25.10.1733	Taken 11.3.1756[2]
Swallow[3]	1728	Peirson Lock, Plymouth	7.1.1729	1.12.1729	6.10.1732	BU 3.1742
Centurion	1729	Joseph Allin, Portsmouth	17.2.1729	9.9.1729	6.1.1733	BU 12.1769
Strafford	1726	John Ward, Chatham	14.7.1726	15.9.1733	24.7.1735	Breakwater 8.1756
Weymouth	1731	Peirson Lock, Plymouth	6.1.1733	9.1733	31.3.1736	Wrecked 16.2.1745
Jersey	1731[4]	Peirson Lock, Plymouth	19.4.1733	11.1733	14.6.1736	Hospital ship 3.1771 abandoned 11.1783
Augusta	8.1733[5]	Richard Stacey, Deptford	22.5.1733	7.11.1733	1.7.1736	BU 6.7.1765
Worcester	1733	Joseph Allin, Portsmouth	4.9.1733	13.11.1733	20.12.1735	BU 9.1765
Dragon	1733	John Hayward, Woolwich	19.10.1733	12.11.1733	11.9.1736	Breakwater 7.1757
Saint Albans	1744[6]	Thomas West (Deptford)	6.8.1745	9.1745	23.12.1747	Sold 14.3.1765

Note that the 'ordered' dates for the first seven are when their rebuilding as 50-gun ships was ordered; the first six were ordered to be rebuilt as 60s instead of as 50s by Admiralty Order on 7 June 1729, and the *Strafford* by Admiralty Order on 22 March 1733.

[1] completed by Ward but early building done by Benjamin Rosewell (Ward moved from Sheerness to take over as Master Shipwright at Chatham in 1732). [2] by the French; retaken 24 January 1761 but then broken up. [3] renamed *Princess Louisa* on 16 January 1737. [4] hulked August 1731 (hull not disposed of until 1763). [5] date predecessor *Burlington* broken up. [6] predecessor wrecked 20 October 1744 (this was 1737-launched ship); West was a merchant builder.

Table 50: 60-gun replacements for 50-gun ships – dimensions in feet and inches

Vessel	*Gundeck*	*Keel*	*Beam*	*Depth*	*Tons*	*Keel/Beam Ratio*
Design (1719 Establishment)	144 0	117 7	39 0	16 5	951 27/94	3.01 : 1
(Modified type – *Centurion*)	144 0	117 7	40 0	16 5	1000 67/94	2.94 : 1
Deptford	144 0	117 7	39 0	16 5	951 27/94	
Pembroke	144 2	117 8	39 1	16 5	956 34/94	
Tilbury	144 2	118 0	39 2	16 5	962 58/94	
Warwick	144 0	117 0	39 0	16 5	951 27/94	
Swallow	144 0	117 0	39 0	16 7	951 27/94	
Centurion	144 1	117 5	40 1½	16 5	1005 50/94	
Design (1733 Establishment)	144 0	117 0	41 5	16 11	1067 49/94	2.82 : 1
Strafford	144 0	116 4	41 5	16 11	1061 41/94	
Weymouth	144 0	116 10	41 5	16 11	1065 35/94	
Jersey	144 0	116 10	41 5	16 11	1065 35/94	
Augusta	144 0	116 7	41 5	16 11	1067 23/94	
Worcester	144 0	116 4	41 5	16 11	1061 41/94	
Dragon	144 0	116 7	41 6	16 11	1067 23/94	
Design (1745 Establishment)	150 0	123 0½	42 8	18 6	1191 41/94	2.88 : 1
Saint Albans	149 10	121 4⅛	43 3	18 6	1207 33/94	2.81 : 1

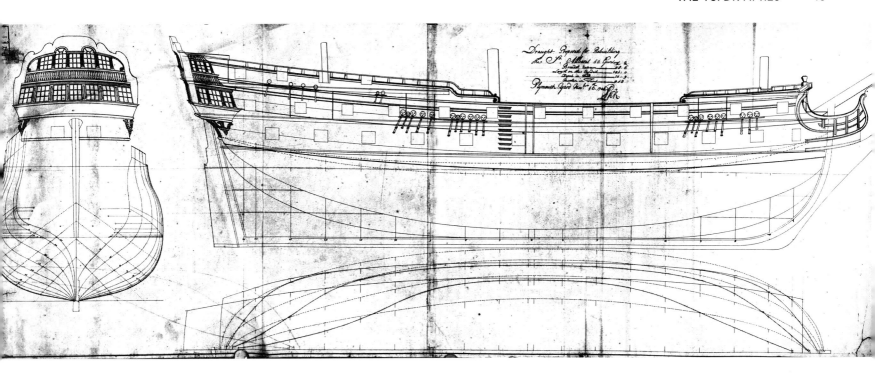

Above: The proposed 1733 Establishment was never formally adopted, and certainly the scantlings fixed in 1719 – and the guns allocated under the 1716 Establishment – were unaltered, but in practice the new dimensions proposed in 1733 came into effect, broadening the 50-gun ships to make them more stable and give their lower deck ports more freeboard. Note the re-introduction of the fourth pair of quarterdeck gunports on this group. The *Saint Albans* was rebuilt by Pierson Lock at Plymouth to the new Establishment in 1736–37 following this proposed draught. (NMM: DR1417)

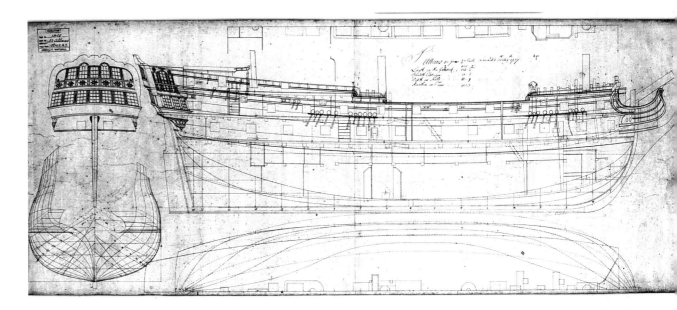

Centre: The draught taken off the *Saint Albans* after completion in 1737 shows a much enlarged roundhouse compared with the original design, and also shows the internal profile and the centreline deck fittings of this group of vessels. (NMM: DR1418)

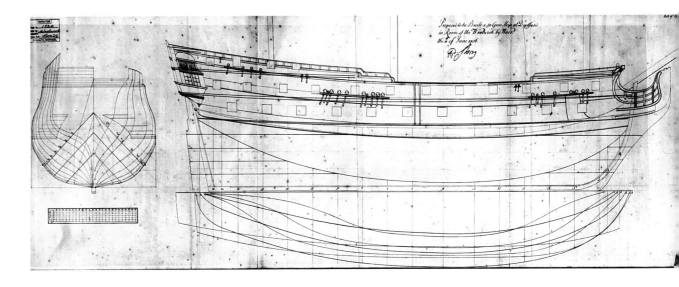

Bottom: The *Woolwich* was 'rebuilt' at Deptford Dockyard by Richard Stacey in 1738–41, but the draught actually describes the process as 'proposed to be built a 50-gun ship at Deptford in room of the *Woolwich*' (*ie* a new-built replacement). The proposed draught indicates no roundhouse or lights on the quarterdeck, and also omits any bridle port on the gundeck. (NMM: DR1520)

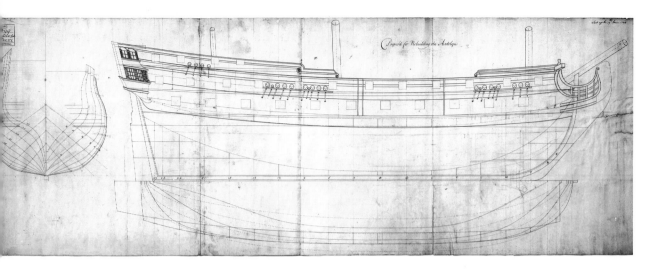

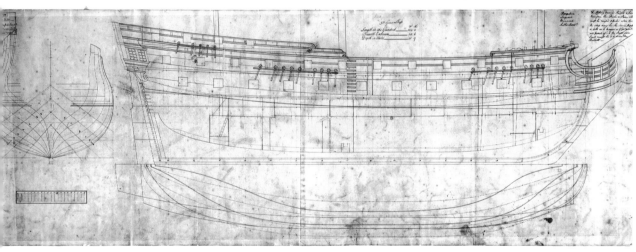

Top: A draught 'proposed for rebuilding the *Antelope*': the ship appears to differ from other Dockyard rebuildings of the period by retaining the straight cutwater. She was the last of eleven 50-gun ships delivered from Woolwich Dockyard by John Hayward, Master Shipwright there from 1715 to 1742, and remained in service for over forty years before being sold in 1783. (NMM: DR1399)

Centre: Following the outbreak of war with Spain in October 1739 (caused more by commercial rivalry than by the particular act of auriclectomy from which the war took its name), four new 50-gun ships were ordered in April 1740 to the 1733 Establishment. Although replacements for unserviceable vessels (whose names they took), the urgent needs of war meant that all pretence of rebuilding was dropped and contracts signed with commercial builders, who began construction the same year and all were in the water by the end of 1741. Copies of a common draught were sent for all four, which copied the straight cutwater of the *Antelope* and *Guernsey*, and – while having a small roundhouse – lacked any quarter lights at this level. (NMM: DR1484)

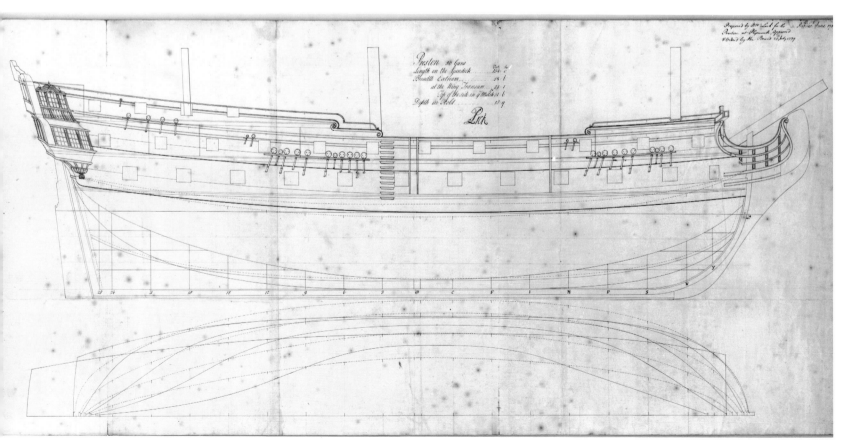

Table 51: Vessels of the 1733 Establishment – construction history

Vessel	*Builder*	*Ordered*	*Begun*	*Launched*	*Fate*
DOCKYARD-BUILT					
Gloucester	Jeremiah Rosewell, Sheerness	22.5.1733	19.8.1734	22.3.1737	Scuttled 16.8.1742
Severn	Peirson Lock, Plymouth	13.5.1734	10.2.1735	28.3.1739	Taken by the French 19.10.1746
Saint Albans	Peirson Lock, Plymouth	10.9.1734	12.1.1736	30.8.1737	Wrecked 20.10.1744
Guernsey	John Ward, Chatham	23.2.1737	3.1738	11.8.1740	Hulked 4.1769; sold 1786
Woolwich	Richard Stacey, Deptford	10.6.1736	8.1738	6.4.1741	BU 6.1747
Dartmouth	John Hayward, Woolwich	8.10.1736	19.10.1736	22.4.1741	Blew up 8.10.1747
Antelope	John Hayward, Woolwich	9.1.1738	28.9.1738	27.1.1742	Sold 30.10.1783
Preston	Thomas Fellowes, Plymouth	8.5.1739	12.1739	18.9.1742	Hulked 23.9.1748, BU 11.1749
CONTRACT-BUILT					
Hampshire	John Barnard, Ipswich*	28.4.1740	11.6.1740	13.11.1741	BU 22.12.1766
Leopard	Philip Perry, Blackwall	28.4.1740	20. 6.1740	30.10.1741	BU 7.1761
Sutherland	James Taylor, Rotherhithe	28.4.1740	1.7.1740	15.10.1741	Sold 5.6.1770
Nonsuch	John Quallett, Rotherhithe	28.4.1740	19.10.1740	29.12.1741	BU 11.1766

* actually at John's Ness, about two miles downstream from Barnard's St Clements Yard; towed to King's Yard at Harwich to be rigged.

Table 52: Vessels of the 1733 Establishment – dimensions in feet and inches

Vessel	*Gundeck*	*Keel*	*Beam*	*Depth*	*Tons*	*Keel/Beam Ratio*
Design (Establishment)	134 0	108 3	38 6	15 9	853 45/94	2.81 : 1
Gloucester	134 0	108 6	38 8	15 9	865 91/94	
Severn	134 0	108 3	38 6	15 9	853 45/94	
Saint Albans	134 0	108 3	38 6	15 9	853 45/94	
Guernsey	134 0	108 6	38 8	15 9	862 81/94	
Woolwich	134 0	109 10⅞	38 6	15 9	866 44/94	
Dartmouth	134 0	108 2	38 7	15 9	856 48/94	
Antelope	134 3	108 8	38 7	15 9	860 44/94	
Preston	134 1	108 7	38 7	15 9	859 60/94	
Hampshire	134 2	108 3	38 6½	15 9	854 61/94	
Leopard	134 0	109 8	38 8	15 9½	872 13/94	
Sutherland	134 2	109 10⅛	38 8	15 9	873 51/94	
Nonsuch	133 3	107 8⅛	38 8¾	15 10	852 7/94	

Left: The *Preston* was the final 50-gun ship to be 'rebuilt', although by now the term was a legal fiction and in practice the ship was virtually, if not entirely, new-built. Although completed in 1742 at Plymouth by Thomas Fellowes, the draught bears the signature of his predecessor Pierson Lock, who as Master Shipwright there was responsible for the *Preston* until his transfer to Portsmouth earlier in 1742. (NMM: DR1472)

the newly proposed 1733 Establishment were ordered (including the postponed *Strafford*); one of these involved a change of name, the 50-gun *Burlington* being replaced by the 60-gun *Augusta*. Altogether, while the number of Fourth Rates was to remain totally unchanged at sixty-four throughout the whole period, the initial breakdown of eighteen 60s and forty-six 50s was to change after 1727 to become thirty 60s and thirty-four 50s by the outbreak of war in 1739.

From 1734 to 1739 another seven 50-gun ships were ordered to be rebuilt on the same basis as the *Gloucester*. The eight ships were nominally 'rebuilds', but the term had become increasingly a technicality. Increasingly it had come to mean the incorporation of timber from a broken-up ship into that ship's replacement, usually a vessel which took the same name. But the exigencies of war meant that the leisurely process of taking an old ship to pieces in the dockyard could not be sustained, and it was simpler to contract to build an entirely new ship, while the old vessel was increasingly likely to endure as a harbour hulk (most often to accommodate seamen awaiting their assignment to a new ship) rather than be immediately taken to pieces.

After 1739, therefore, the concept of 'rebuilding' was quietly dropped. When the last quartet of 50-gun ships to the 1733 Establishment were ordered on 28 April 1740, they were clearly authorised as new vessels even though they were replacements for decaying fifty-gun ships of the same names, broken up or hulked during 1739–41; for the first time since Queen Anne's reign, the additional burdens of war meant that these ships were ordered to be built by contract in commercial yards. The draughts for these four indicate that they (and possibly some of the earlier rebuilds) were constructed without the quarter lights on the roundhouse level.

Body plan of the *Preston* of 1742. (NMM: DR1472)

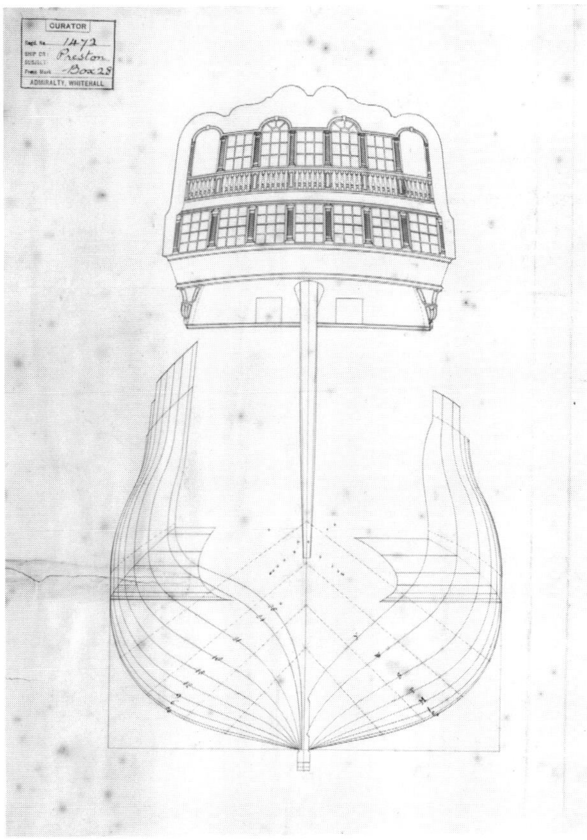

6. The 24pdr Fifties

As early as 1732, when the new Establishment of Dimensions was planned to enlarge the 50-gun Fourth Rate from 755 to 853 tons, it had been recognised that British warships of all Rates, but particularly the smaller ships of the line, remained seriously under-gunned. In April 1733 it was argued that guns of heavier calibre should be carried so that 'they may be in a much better condition, not only of defending themselves, but of annoying (sic) the ships of war of other maritime princes in time of war, who have not only (according to their several rates and classes) increased their weights of ordnance, but also their number of men, compared to what were formerly allowed'.[23]

The 50-gun ships were to be the greatest beneficiaries of this up-gunning. Whereas the 60-gun ship was only to exchange its upper deck 9pdrs for 12pdrs (and in the process, in order to compensate for the extra weight of metal, were to have one pair of ports on this deck left empty, reducing them to 58-gun ships), the 50-gun had both upper and lower decks upgraded, with 24pdrs on the lower deck and 12pdrs on the upper deck; moreover it retained the same number of guns, so that there was now little difference in broadside between the two types.

The proposals were approved by King George in Council in January 1733, but they ran into strong opposition from the Board of Ordnance, who complained that they would have great difficulty in complying with the new scheme in the immediate future.[24] Accordingly, the proposals were shelved indefinitely (in effect for a decade) so that when war arrived in 1739, the Fourth Rates were to meet it still poorly armed to face their opponents of similar nominal rating.

The capture of the Spanish 70-gun *Princessa* in 1740 showed how far behind British vessels lagged. While not carrying a heavier armament than her British equivalents, she measured 1709 tons compared with the 1224 tons of her British equivalent – the 1733 Establishment 70-gun ship. At last the Admiralty recognised the inadequate size of domestic designs, and cast around for proposals to improve British naval building. It was agreed that the dormant 1733 proposals to up-gun each Rate would be needed, and as a preliminary step it was recognised that another increase in dimensions would be necessary. The breadth of the 50-gun ship was enlarged by a further 18in to 40ft, and this time the length was also increased, by 6ft on the gundeck.

Eight vessels were ordered to these new dimensions

Table 53: Fourth Rates of 1741 Establishment – construction history

Vessel	Builder	Ordered	Keel Laid	Launched	Fate
Harwich[1]	John Barnard, Harwich	21.8.1742	11.1742	22.12.1743	Wrecked 4.10.1760
Colchester (i)	John Barnard, Harwich	6.9.1742	14.12.1742	14.8.1744	Wrecked 21.9.1744
Falkland	Philemon Ewer, Bursledon	13.11.1742	20.1.1743	17.3.1744	Victualling hulk 10.8.1768
Chester	Thomas Bronsden, Deptford	24.2.1743	2.1743	18.2.1744	Floating battery 1757–62; sold 28.7.1767
Winchester	Elias Bird, Rotherhithe	28.3.1743	7.5.1743	3.5.1744	Sold 20.6.1769
Portland	Thomas Snelgrove, Limehouse	26.4.1743	29.4.1743	11.10.1744	Sold 15.3.1763
Maidstone[2]	Thomas Bronsden, Deptford	16.5.1743	30.5.1743	12.10.1744	Wrecked 27.6.1747
Panther	Thomas Fellowes, Plymouth Dyd	16.5.1743	27.6.1743	24.6.1746	BU 7.1756
Gloucester	Whetstone, Rotherhithe	15.6.1743	12.7.1743	23.3.1745	Hospital ship for soldiers 1758, receiving ship 1759; BU 13.2.1764
Norwich	Philip Perry, Blackwall	30.9.1743	23.11.1743	4.7.1745	Sold 24.5.1768
Ruby	Philemon Ewer, Bursledon	30.9.1743	18.2.1744	3.8.1745	BU 28.5.1765
Advice	George Rowcliffe, Northam	27.3.1744	6.1744	26.2.1746	BU 10.1756
Salisbury	Philemon Ewer, East Cowes	2.5.1744	23.5.1744	29.1.1746	Condemned 24.4.1761
Lichfield	John Barnard, Harwich	1.6.1744	24.7.1744	26.6.1746	Wrecked 29.11.1758
Colchester (ii)	Robert Carter, Southampton[3]	6.11.1744	1744	20.9.1746	BU 2.1773

[1] ordered as *Tiger*, renamed 29 November 1743. [2] ordered as *Rochester*, renamed 27 September 1744.
[3] built at Chapel shipyard ; probably completed for Carter by Henry Bird.

from commercial builders during the latter half of 1742 and the first half of 1743, with a ninth ship being ordered at Plymouth Dockyard. While the system of 'rebuilding' had effectively ended, all were replacements for other 50-gun ships – two to replace the losses of the *Tiger* and *Gloucester* in 1742 (the former's replacement was renamed *Harwich* a month before her launch at that port), and the others supplanting antiquated ships of the 1706 and 1719 Establishments.

In August 1742 the 34-year-old *Chester* was reclassed as a Fifth Rate and was re-armed as a 44-gun ship with a complement reduced to 250 and mounting twenty 18pdrs and twenty 9pdrs, plus four 6pdrs on

Right. Although built to the same dimensions and scantlings as other ships of the 1741 Establishment, the *Panther* was the sole Dockyard-built vessel of the batch and differs significantly. The quarterdeck gunports and roundhouse (with its quarter lights) retain the layout of the 1733 Establishment. The bow is much altered, with a raked stempost and a curved cutwater compared with the straight edge of the contract-built vessels, while the *Panther*'s midship section shows a sharp turn of bilge unlike the continuous sweep of the merchant-built vessels. (NMM: DR1443)

the quarterdeck. She was not to last for long, and in August 1743 was disarmed and relegated to harbour duties as a hospital ship, being broken up in 1750; but in 1744 three other 50-gun ships of similar age – the *Ruby*, *Norwich* and *Advice* – were similarly converted (all by Admiralty Order of 23 May 1744) in January 1744, June 1744 and May 1745 respectively, being re-named *Mermaid*, *Enterprise* and *Milford* respectively in their new roles; the *Mermaid* and *Milford* were sold after the war (on 19 May 1748 and 11 May 1749 respectively), while the *Enterprise* lasted until 1771. Three new 50-gun ships ordered in the autumn of

1743 (two) and spring of 1744 (one) were given the names *Ruby*, *Norwich* and *Advice* as replacements.

A fifth 50 – the *Romney* – was likewise reduced to a 44-gun ship by Admiralty Order of 22 June 1745, in January 1746. Her new establishment of men was 280. She was sold on 21 July 1757.

Two further vessels to this Establishment were ordered in the early summer of 1744 to take the place of the (1719 Establishment) *Salisbury* and *Lichfield*, and a final ship was contracted for at the end of the year to replace the new *Colchester*, which was stranded on a sandbank and had to be abandoned less than a month

The 1741 Establishment substantially increased the dimensions of the 50-gun ship, by 6ft in length and 1½ft in beam; sadly much of this potential advantage to sailing qualities was lost by increasing the firepower (and the weight) of the guns carried, so that a further increase in dimensions was required within a few years. The new ships were also deeper in the hold, while the gunports on the quarterdeck were moved forward to allow an enlargement of the roundhouse. (NMM: DR1485)

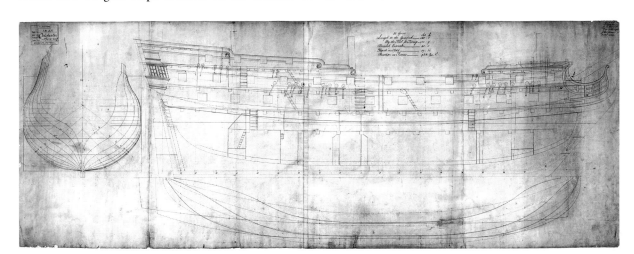

All of the contract-built vessels to the 1741 Establishment were apparently built to an identical draught, although the roundhouse provided here on the *Falkland* is shorter and provides only four cabins for officers rather than the six accommodated in the *Colchester* and other vessels. (NMM: DR1360)

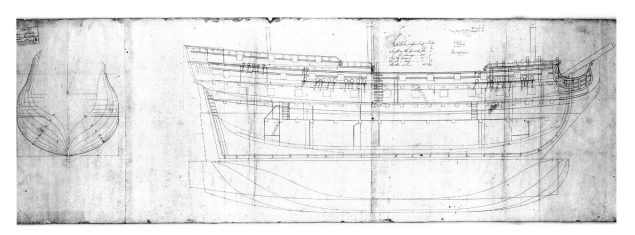

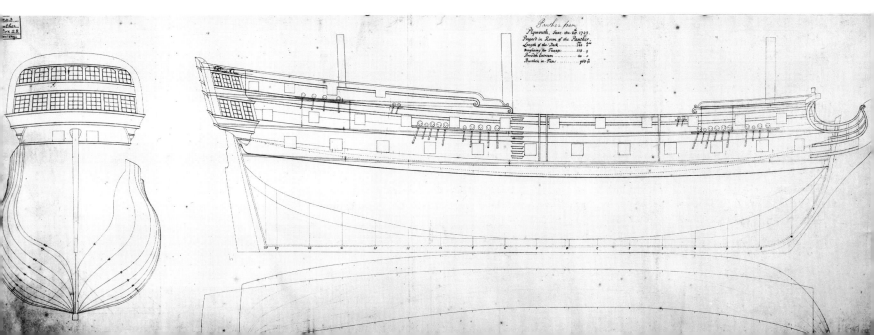

after completion. All the 1741 Establishment 50s built to contract were seemingly to a single design, as the draught bears the names of all fourteen ships for which contracts were placed; the *Panther*, the sole Dockyard-built vessel, was built to slightly altered lines.

In February 1742 Sir Robert Walpole's government was defeated over its tentative prosecution of the war, and out of office with him went Wager's Board. The new Prime Minister, the Earl of Wilmington (Spencer Compton), brought in a civilian – the Earl of Winchelsea – to head the Board for the first time since 1714. While the new Board was scarcely innovatory, it did swiftly sanction, as an experiment, the building of a 50-gun ship to be 6ft longer than the new Establishment (and 2ft longer than the 60-gun ships of the 1733 Establishment). John Holland, the Master Shipwright at Woolwich from 1742 to 1746, was asked to produce a plan for the re-building of the old *Bristol*, whose defects were found so advanced that she had to be taken to pieces.[25] He recommended a length of 146ft, retaining the Establishment breadth, and this plan was accepted; Holland subsequently became Master Shipwright at Deptford (1746–52) where in March 1747 he was instructed to appoint an overseer to built a second ship to the same draught in a merchant yard as near as possible to Deptford; five weeks later the building was transferred to Deptford Dockyard itself.

The Establishment of Guns first proposed in 1733 was finally approved again by the King in Council in 1743. It was not retrospective – vessels built to the pre-1741 Establishment specifications would never be strong enough to carry the new armament, and so they continued to carry 18pdrs and 9pdrs for the rest of their days. But all the new vessels ordered from the start of 1741 onward were completed with the heavier weaponry.

The Winchelsea Board made few other changes. In spite of continuing criticism of the design of British warships of all classes, there was so much inertia built into the system that radical innovations were beyond its means. The chief officers of the Navy had in many cases been in post since George I's reign; Sir Jacob Acworth, the Surveyor, had held office since March 1715 and bore the brunt of the criticisms. Nevertheless, his detractors could not dislodge him. Three final vessels to the 1741 Establishment were ordered later in 1744 to replace remaining ships of the 1720s, but by the end of that year the Board was sacked, and a new one under the nominal leadership of the Duke of Bedford was set up.

Table 54: Fourth Rates of 1741 Establishment – dimensions in feet and inches

Vessel	*Gundeck*	*Keel*	*Beam*	*Depth*	*Tons*	*Keel/Beam Ratio*
Design:	140 0	113 9	40 0	17 2½	968 8/94	2.84 : 1
Harwich	140 2	113 9	40 2	17 2½	976 16/94	
Colchester (i)	140 1	113 9	40 2	17 2½	976 16/94	
Falkland	140 2¾	113 6¼	40 2	17 3¼	974 19/94	
Chester	139 11	113 5⅞	40 2¾	17 2	976 91/94	
Winchester	140 6	114 3¾	40 3½	17 2½	987 11/94	
Portland	140 3	113 4⅛	40 2¼	17 2½	973 65/94	
Maidstone	140 6	113 9¼	40 2¾	17 2½	979 37/94	
Panther	140 0	113 9	40 0	17 2½	968 8/94	
Gloucester	140 8½	114 7½	40 2½	17 2½	985 68/94	
Norwich	140 2½	114 1	40 5½	17 2½	993 28/94	
Ruby	141 5	114 6	40 3½	17 3	988 69/94	
Advice	140 2	113 11	40 3½	17 2½	983 65/94	
Salisbury	140 0	113 10	40 2	17 2½	976 83/94	
Lichfield	140 2	113 9	40 2¾	17 3	979 20/94	
Colchester (ii)	140 4	114 0	40 2	17 2½	978 30/94	

Table 55: The *Bristol* class (Holland design 1742) – construction history

Vessel	*Builder*	*Ordered*	*Begun*	*Launched*	*Fate*
Bristol	John Holland, Woolwich Dyd	22.11.1742	24.6.1743	9.7.1746	BU 10.1768
Rochester	John Holland, Deptford Dyd	4.3.1747	24.9.1747	3.8.1749	Sold 3.4.1770

Table 56: The *Bristol* class (Holland design 1742) – dimensions in feet and inches

Vessel	*Gundeck*	*Keel*	*Beam*	*Depth*	*Tons*	*Keel/Beam Ratio*
Design:	146 0	120 0	40 0	16 10	1021 26/94	3.00 : 0
Bristol	146 0	120 0	40 0	16 10	1021 26/94	
Rochester	146 0	120 6	40 2	16 10	1034 9/94	

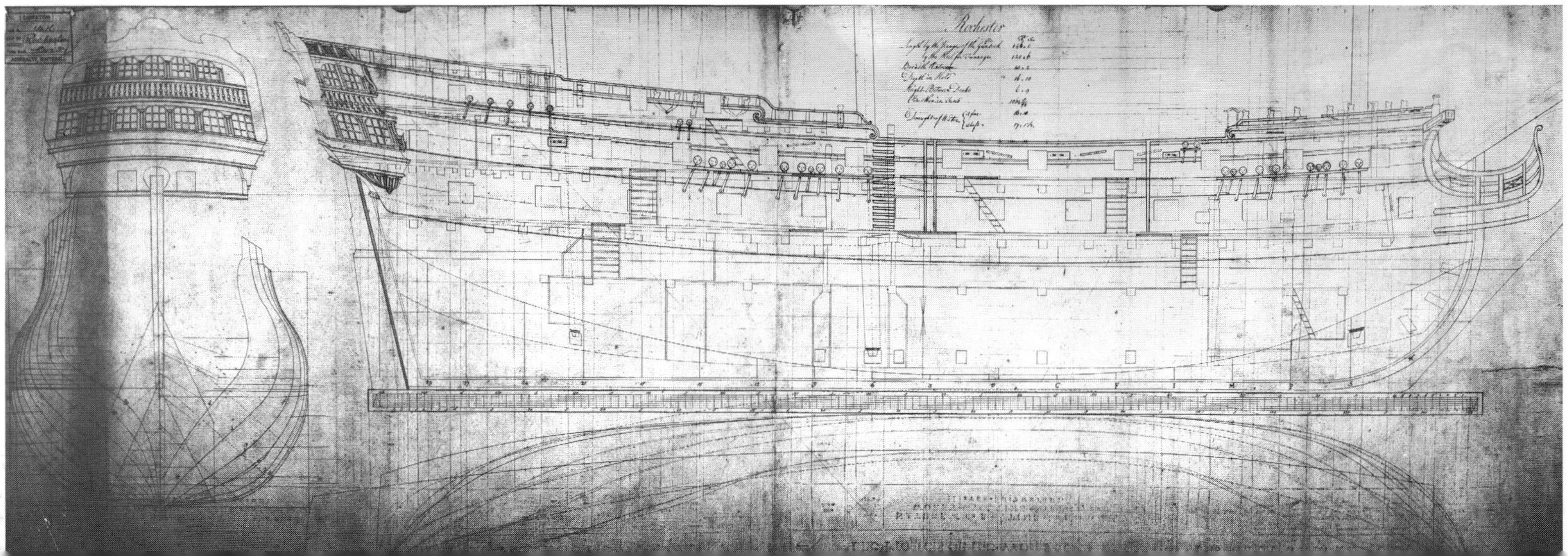

In practice, Bedford left naval administration to his political ally on the Board, the Earl of Sandwich, and to the latter's able assistant, the 47-year-old George Anson, newly promoted to rear-admiral; and it was Anson who became the professional head of the administration. Even then, Sandwich and Anson were unable to engineer Acworth's retirement, and it was not until June 1746 that they were even able to secure the appointment of Joseph Allin, the Master Shipwright at Deptford, to share the surveyorship with Acworth.

The 1745 Establishment

It was Bedford's new Board which in June 1745 at last began to tackle the problems that the earlier Establishments had left. Recognising that the innate conservatism of the Surveyor and the Master Shipwrights was a stumbling block, the Admiralty appointed a new committee, chaired by Sir John Norris, to produce new proposals. The deficiencies in size of even the 1741 Establishment were recognised, and the 50-gun ship was lengthened for a further 4ft and broadened by 1ft, so that it was now virtually the same size as the 60-gun ship of the 1733 Establishment. While this increase still left British warships much smaller than equivalent classes of foreign ships, the worst aspects had been mitigated by the Norris Committee, which had also referred to seagoing officers as well as commercial builders.

A more important result was that the new Establishment provided not just a standard set of principal dimensions, but actually centralised design. No longer were builders in each yard to prepare their own plans in conformity with the Establishment, but in future a single plan for each class of vessel was to be drawn up by the Surveyor and the Master Shipwrights in concert and approved by the Privy Council so that no subsequent alterations could be made without that body's consent. The aim was to standardise in order that every vessel would match the approved designs, but the corollary was that the new Establishment, finally produced in December 1745, was to be even more rigid than its predecessors. This proved swiftly unworkable, and after a few years a growing list of alterations finally resulted in the abandonment of the Establishment system altogether.

The *Falmouth* and *Lichfield* were in Vice-Admiral Edward Vernon's fleet for the unsuccessful attempt to capture Cartagena in 1741. The *Norwich* and *Assistance* were in Charles Knowles's squadron for the attack on Porto Cavallo in 1743, and were joined by the *Advice* for the attack on La Guayra in the same year.

The entry of France into the war on Spain's side in March 1744 had seen a widening of the conflict. Throughout the war period most 50s saw continuous service on convoy and cruising duties. On 25 January 1745 the *Preston* and *Deptford* took three French East Indiamen; the *Preston*, *Winchester* and *Harwich* were in Edward Peyton's squadron in the East Indies on 25 June 1746 for the action with La Bourdonnais's fleet.

Eight 50-gun ships were lost during the nine years of war – the *Tiger* and *Gloucester* (both 1742), *Colchester*, *Greenwich* and *Saint Albans* (all 1744), *Severn* (1746), *Maidstone* and *Dartmouth* (both 1747) – although only the *Severn* and *Dartmouth* were through enemy action, and the first of these was later recovered. The *Gloucester*, worn out during Anson's exploration in the Pacific, was scuttled, and the other five ships were wrecked.

A final replacement of a 50-gun by a 60-gun ship was to occur in 1745, when the 50-gun *Saint Albans*, lost in 1744, was replaced by a new 60; but by this time the rigid system of direct replacements, by which the number of ships of the line was maintained constant by only building replacements for or rebuilding worn-out vessels on a one-for-one basis, was being abandoned. The extra demands of war meant that the Admiralty was no longer constrained to keep the fleet at the same nominal strength, although this was to mean only small increases in numbers of Fourth Rates.

On 19 October 1746 the *Woolwich* and the *Severn* were escorting a homeward-bound convoy of fifty ships from the Caribbean when it was intercepted off the Scilly Isles by a French squadron of three ships of the line. Ordering the convoy to scatter, the two 50-gun ships positioned themselves between the French

Lower left: The 'as-built' draught of the *Rochester* shows a slight enlargement from her sister *Bristol* built four years earlier. The two ships were built by John Holland with a considerable increase in length over the original 1741 Establishment. The *Rochester* has a full gallery at quarterdeck level (unlike *Bristol*), indicating she was built with a view to accommodating a flag officer on an overseas station, although early in her career the captain's quarters were to be relocated to this deck on newer 50-gun ships. (NMM: DR1416)

Below: This model is usually believed to represent a 50-gun ship of the 1745 Establishment, but the position of the channels below the upper deck ports may indicate that it is of an early stage of the design. (NMM: C600)

and the merchantmen. A running fight developed, but the *Severn* found herself pinned between two French 70s (*Le Terrible* and *Le Neptune*). After a gallant three-hour defence, with his ship disabled and with a dozen casualties, Captain William Lyle surrendered – later to be exonerated and given a larger command for his bravery which had allowed the whole convoy and the *Woolwich* to escape. The *Severn* was recaptured a year later in Edward Hawke's victory off Cape Finisterre on 14 October 1747, but was condemned as unfit to be reinstated in the Royal Navy and was broken up.

The *Dartmouth* likewise succumbed to a much larger opponent. Captain James Hamilton valiantly attacked the Spanish 74-gun *Glorioso* off the Atlantic coast of Spain on 8 October 1747, and held her to action for some two hours until joined by her consort, the 80-gun *Russell*. At this point the *Dartmouth* was destroyed by a tremendous explosion which took the lives of all but a dozen of her crew; the *Russell* continued the action and captured the *Glorioso* after another day's exhaustive combat, the Spanish ship subsequently being added to the British navy.

During this war, the French lost (besides the recaptured *Severn*) six of their 50-gun ships to British action. Three were captured in 1746 (*L'Auguste*, *Le Mercure* and *Le Ferme*) but of these only *L'Auguste*, taken by the *Portland* while cruising in the Soundings on 9 February, was added to the Royal Navy, being renamed *Portland's Prize*.

In 1747 the tide of war at sea moved decisively in Britain's favour. On 3 May George Anson, now Vice-Admiral of the Blue, won a decisive victory over a French squadron off Cape Finisterre. Although Anson now flew his flag in a Second Rate, his fleet included his old *Centurion*, as well as two other 50-gun ships (the *Bristol* and *Falkland*) and five 60-gun ships; five months later, Rear-Admiral Edward Hawke gained a second victory in the same location; these were to be the last fleet actions in which the majority of the British line comprised Fourth Rates.

Three (apart from the *Severn*) of the French participants – all of which were taken by the British in these two contests – were ships of 50 or 56 guns from de la Jonquiere's squadron captured by Anson in the first battle off Cape Finisterre, but of these the small *Le Jason* was sensibly re-rated and re-armed by the British as a Fifth Rate of 44 guns (and by 1757 had been reduced to 30 guns), like her near-sister *La Gloire*; and the similar *Le Rubis*, serving as a storeship with only 26 guns, was incorporated into the British navy as a transport, subsequently classed as Sixth Rate and quickly broken up.

Only the larger *Le Diamant* joined the ranks of the British 50s, where she served under the new name of *Isis* throughout the Seven Years War. A longer vessel than the British ships, the *Isis* was established with 350 men and carried twenty-four 24pdrs on the gundeck (replacing her old French 18pdrs), with the same number of 9pdrs on the upper deck, and a single pair of 6pdrs on the quarterdeck – the forecastle being unarmed.

The ships of the 1745 Establishment

When the new Establishment was approved in December 1745, the replacement 50s which had begun to be ordered in the preceding months were all specified to conform to the new dimensions. Seven vessels were ordered in the space of as many months, four to be built by contract and three in the Royal Dockyards. A fourth order was issued to a dockyard (Chatham) in 1747, but by the end of that year only the four vessels being built by contract were complete, while only two of the vessels allocated to the dockyards had been laid

Table 57: Captured vessels of the War of the Austrian Succession, 1744–49

Vessel	Builder	Built	Captured	Purchased	Fate
Portland's Prize	Brest	1738–40	9.2.1746	2.1746	Sold 17.5.1749
Isis	Toulon	1730–33	3.5.1747	10.1747	Sold 1.7.1766

Vessel	Gundeck	Keel	Beam	Depth	Tons	Keel/Beam Ratio
Portland's Prize	134 2	109 5¼	38 7	15 3½	866 ^{50}/94	2.84 : 1
Isis	142 3	117 3	40 2¼	17 2	1013 ^{4}/94	2.92 : 1

The draught used for the three contract-built ships of the 1745 Establishment (the Dockyard vessels were built to a copy of the same draught) shows vessels of greater depth than their predecessors, drawing 3in more forwards and 5in more aft than the 1741 Establishment. This increased headroom internally, as well as making the vessels more stable to carry the heavier 24pdrs for which they were the first 50-gun ships designed. Note the channels have now been moved above the upper deck gunports. (NMM: DR1394)

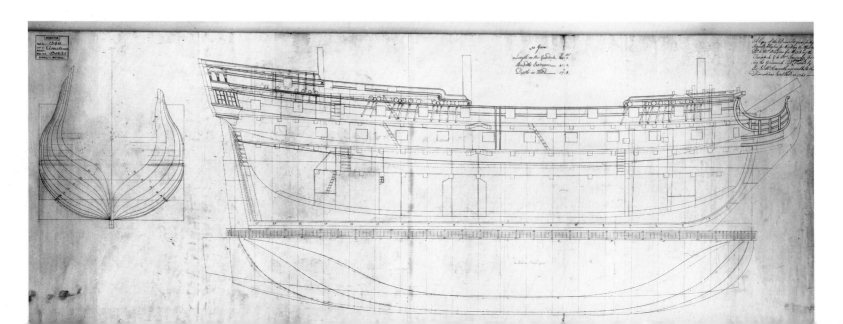

Table 58: Fourth Rates of 1745 Establishment – construction history

Vessel	Builder	Ordered	Begun	Launched	Fate
Assistance	Sedger & Hogben, Chatham	6.8.1745	8.1745	22.12.1747	Hulked 1770, sold 11.8.1773
Greenwich	Moody Janverin, Lepe	3.10.1745	11.1745	19.3.1747	Taken by the French 18.3.1757
Tavistock	Hugh Blaydes, Hull	18.10.1745	11.1746	26.8.1747	Hulked 1760, sold 24.12.1768
Falmouth	Adam Hayes, Woolwich Dyd	15.11.1745	22.8.1746	7.12.1752	Beached and abandoned 16.1.1765
Newcastle	Peirson Lock, Portsmouth Dyd	11.12.1745	17.6.1746	4.12.1750	Wrecked 1.1.1761
Dartmouth	Benj. Slade, Plymouth Dyd	16.1.1746	–	–	Cancelled 20.3.1748
Severn	John Barnard, Harwich	18.3.1746	4.1746	10.7.1747	Sold 2.1.1759
Woolwich	John Ward, Chatham Dyd	6.5.1747	–	–	Cancelled 8.5.1748

Table 59: Fourth Rates of 1745 Establishment – dimensions in feet and inches

Vessel	Gundeck	Keel	Beam	Depth	Tons	Keel/Beam Ratio
Establishment:	144 0	117 8½	41 0	17 8	1052 $^{47}/_{94}$	2.87 : 1
Assistance	144 0	117 8½	41 2½	17 8	1063 $^{20}/_{94}$	
Greenwich	144 6½	116 1½	41 3½	17 7	1053 $^{15}/_{94}$	
Tavistock	144 0	117 8½	41 2	17 ½	1061 $^{6}/_{94}$	
Falmouth	144 0	116 1¼	41 2	17 8	1046 $^{57}/_{94}$	
Newcastle	144 0	117 8½	41 0	17 8	1052 $^{46}/_{94}$	
Severn	144 0	117 8½	41 2	17 8½	1061 $^{6}/_{94}$	

down. As war drew to a close early in 1748 and peace negotiations were conducted at Aix-la-Chapelle, the two unstarted vessels were cancelled, while work on the pair on the stocks at Portsmouth and Woolwich was given a lower priority.

Under the new Establishment, these 50-gun ships reached the dimensions that the 60-gun ship had enjoyed before the war. The vessels were to sit much deeper in the water, draught being 17ft 2in forward and 18ft 4in abaft. The freeboard improved to provide a height of 5ft 11in amidships from the waterline to the upper edge of the lower gunport sills. Internally the headroom also improved, with the height on the orlop deck and on the upper deck each becoming 6ft 8½in.

The collapse of the Establishments

The war came formally to an end in October 1749. The Earl of Sandwich had taken over the leadership of the Admiralty Board from the Duke of Bedford in 1748, and after the war the now ennobled Anson swiftly became the First (indeed, the only) Naval Lord. He was soon to stamp his mark on the Navy; indeed, what is widely regarded as the 'Anson revolution' was to blow through the whole of naval administration, sweeping away the outmoded and restrictive system of Establishments and creating a fleet of vessels more capable of dealing with the strategic needs of the expanding empire.

While the 1745 Establishment had again raised the dimensions of the 50-gun ship, within a few years the new vessels built to it were already proving a disappointment, particularly in their sailing and handling. As any further change in the strict regulations was only possible with the approval of the Privy Council, the Admiralty were unable to introduce any further improvements of any significance. Application to the Privy Council in 1750 for the right to make further changes in design was met only with the response that the Admiralty should draw up proposals and submit them to the Privy Council, who were clearly unwilling to lose their veto over the Navy's designs.

The situation clearly could not continue. With several new orders being placed in 1751, including one for a new 50-gun ship to replace the *Preston*, which had been broken up at Trincomalee in November 1749, the Navy Board proposed increases in the scantlings, but had the request turned down by the Admiralty on the grounds that they were not authorised to alter the dimensions contained in the Establishment.

With the death of Jacob Acworth in 1749, Allin had become the sole Surveyor. He lacked his predecessor's overbearing nature and his work as a shipwright had shown fair competence, but he was clearly not inclined to affect or even to disagree with the conservative mould in which the Surveyor's Department worked. Accepting that he could make no major alterations to the 1745 Establishment, he produced a slightly amended draught which stuck rigidly to the same dimensions and scantlings, and the new *Preston* was built to this design. She was to enjoy a long service life; but she underwent a great repair at Portsmouth from January 1772 to July 1773 at a cost of £20,124 – virtually the cost of a new ship – and, while hulked in 1785, survived until the close of the Napoleonic War.

Eighteen months later another 50-gun ship was ordered to replace the *Chatham*, sunk as a breakwater at Sheerness in May 1749. Again the Navy Board requested changes in the Establishment, and finally the Admiralty took the proposals to the Privy Council, which authorised a 3ft extension to the length of the class, and for the breadth to be cut by a foot to produce finer lines. Allin drew up a variant of his earlier plan for this second new ship, with its narrower hull form.[26]

Britain was not the only power to continue to build 50-gun ships, in spite of their increasingly obvious limitations in a battlefleet role. Across the Channel, Rouillé, the French Navy Minister, acknowledged the lack of firepower of France's 18pdr-armed ships, although orders were placed in order to utilise the large amount of appropriate timbers on hand in the dock-yards. It should be noted that French 50s (but not their other two-deckers) of the 1740s carried no carriage guns on their upperworks ('*gaillards*'); thus their twenty-four 18pdrs and twenty-six 12pdrs equated numerically with the 24pdr and 12pdr weapons carried by the British 60-gun ship on the same gundecks, missing only the ten 6pdrs of the 60-gun ship. Hence their total broadside of 372 *livres* (407 English pounds) was closer to the 474-pound broadside of the English 60 rather than the English 50's broadside of 315 pounds. But following Britain's adoption of the 1743 Establishment of Guns with its 24pdrs for 50-gun ships, France also moved to augment their firepower, with *L'Amphion* being laid down at Brest in 1749 to carry twenty-four 24pdrs on her lower deck. She was followed by another 50 with this increased weaponry, *Le Sagittaire*, built at Toulon, and by the end of the Seven Years War all remaining French 50s would be based in this Mediterranean port.

In early August 1755 Allin suddenly became ill, and Anson moved swiftly to replace him with more talented and creative designers. Thomas Slade, hitherto Master Shipwright at Deptford (and previously at other dockyards), and William Bately, until then Assistant Surveyor under Allin, were to share the Surveyorship, seemingly hand-picked by Anson to implement the restructuring of naval design that he had been seeking. Allin was pensioned off, and on 25 November a new Navy Board was appointed by the Crown, confirming the new Surveyors in office.

The Seven Years War

When war broke out again in 1756, the French navy possessed eleven small two-deckers of 50 guns, but they quickly suffered the loss of the *Arc-en-Ciel*, taken

Table 60: The Modified 1745 Establishment (Allin design 1751) – construction history

Vessel	Builder	Ordered	Begun	Launched	Fate
Preston	Adam Hayes, Deptford Dyd	28.3.1751	13.6.1751	7.2.1757	Sheer hulk 11.1785; BU 1.1815

Table 61: The Modified 1745 Establishment (Allin design 1751) – dimensions in feet and inches

Vessel	Gundeck	Keel	Beam	Depth	Tons	Keel/Beam Ratio
Design:	144 0	117 8½	41 0	17 8	1052 $^{47}/_{94}$	2.87 : 1
Preston	143 3	115 4	41 3	17 3	1043 $^{81}/_{94}$	

Table 62: The Modified 1745 Establishment (Allin design 1752) – construction history

Vessel	Builder	Ordered	Begun	Launched	Fate
Chatham	Edward Allin, Portsmouth Dyd	20.10.1752*	14.12.1752	25.4.1758	Convalescent ship 3.1793; powder hulk 12.1805; renamed *Tilbury* 29.6.1810; BU 5.1814

* design approved 8 November 1752.

Table 63: The Modified 1745 Establishment (Allin design 1752) – dimensions in feet and inches

Vessel	Gundeck	Keel	Beam	Depth	Tons	Keel/Beam Ratio
Design:	147 0	124 0	40 0	17 8	1055 $^{30}/_{94}$	3.10 : 1
Chatham	147 0	123 0¼*	40 3	17 8	1067 $^{37}/_{94}$	

* later re-measured at 122ft 2in (equating to 1052 $^{71}/_{94}$ tons).

Following the death of Sir Jacob Acworth, the Navy Board – with encouragement from Anson – moved slowly to loosen the restrictions of the Establishment system and finally to abandon it. Allin, succeeding Acworth as Surveyor, introduced few changes in the *Preston*, his first attempt to vary Acworth's 1745 design. As in the *Panther*, the *Preston* has a noticeably curved cutwater. (NMM: DR1474)

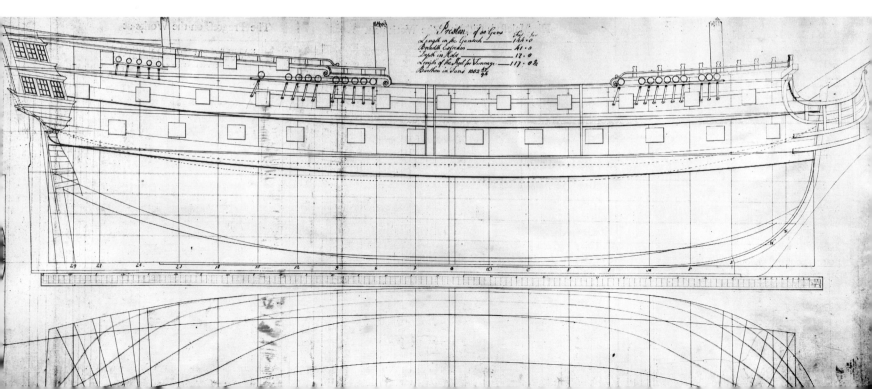

Table 64: Captured vessel of the Seven Years War, 1756–63

Vessel	Builder	Built	Captured	Purchased	Fate
Arc-en-Ciel	Bayonne	1745	12.6.1756	3.1758	Sold 6.9.1759

Vessel	Gundeck	Keel	Beam	Depth	Tons	Keel/Beam Ratio
Arc-en-Ciel	146 0	119 3	41 2½	18 4	1077 ^{12}/94	2.89 : 1

Table 65: The *Warwick* class (Bately design 1758) – construction history

Vessel	Builder	Ordered	Begun	Launched	Fate
Warwick	Thomas Bucknall, Portsmouth Dyd	13.12.1758	27.8.1762	28.2.1767	Receiving ship 8.1783; sold 24.3.1802 (for £1205)

Table 66: The *Warwick* class (Bately design 1758) – dimensions in feet and inches

Vessel	Gundeck	Keel	Beam	Depth	Tons	Keel/Beam Ratio
Design:	151 0	122 9	40 2	18 3	1053 ^{36}/94	3.06 : 0
Warwick	151 0	124 7¼	40 3	18 3	1073 ^{71}/94	

Centre: After his first attempt with the Preston, Allin's draught for the Chatham saw a much greater departure from the 1745 Establishment, displaying a longer and narrower hull. She has a wide gallery on the quarterdeck, where a fifth pair of gunports is introduced. Note that the mizzen channels on are unusually raised above the quarterdeck ports, indicating that this vessel has a full-scale poop deck rather than just a roof to the cabin. The position of the foremost of the twelve lower deck ports suggests a useable gunport rather than just a bridle port. (NMM: DR1361)

Bottom: The only draught for a 50-gun ship by William Bateley, the Warwick was the largest design to date, and was not to be exceeded in size until the 1780s. Note the aft magazine was raised on this ship almost up to the level of the orlop deck, which must have severely inconvenienced the residents of the cockpit. This was the last 50-gun ship to have a twelfth pair of ports on the gundeck, which could rarely if ever have been used except as a bridal port, but the 'spare' was typical Bateley practice – his contemporary frigates of the Richmond class also had an extra pair. In contrast, the quarterdeck gunports were reduced to three pairs. (NMM: DR1571)

by a British squadron in North American waters; she was added to the Royal Navy with her name unchanged, with the 1743 Establishment of guns. On 18 March 1757 a squadron of eight French vessels captured the British *Greenwich* off Cape Cabron, Santo Domingo; but she was wrecked on 14 January 1758.

The Royal Navy also suffered the loss of three 50-gun ships wrecked during the war – the *Lichfield* in 1758 (off the Atlantic coast off Morocco, with 130 casualties), the *Harwich* in 1760 (off Jamaica) and the *Newcastle* on New Year's Day 1761 (in the cyclone off Pondicherry which also claimed the 60-gun *Sunderland* and three other British warships, with over a thousand lives lost); but no others were lost through enemy action. On the other hand, the French navy suffered four more 50-gun ships lost to British action, of which *L'Aquilon* and *L'Alcyon* were sunk in action on 14 May and 23 November 1757, while *L'Apollon* was taken at the capture of Louisbourg on 17 July 1758 and *L'Oriflamme* (a Toulon-built near-sister to *L'Arc-en-Ciel*) was captured while armed *en flute* by the *Isis* on 1 April 1761 – although neither of the latter were taken into service.

Notwithstanding the decision taken to exclude 50-gun ships from the line of battle, they more than occasionally found themselves in fleet actions. When Vice-Admiral Byng brought the French fleet to action off Minorca in May 1756, he originally called for the *Deptford*, the sole 50 in his squadron, to stand in the line; later he decided to remove her (on the curious grounds that his squadron would otherwise outnumber the enemy), but later ordered her in to take the place of the disabled 64-gun *Intrepid*.

The first 50-gun ship to be ordered following the outbreak of war showed that the Establishment dimensions had been well and truly buried. This ship took her name not from any of the old 50s then being

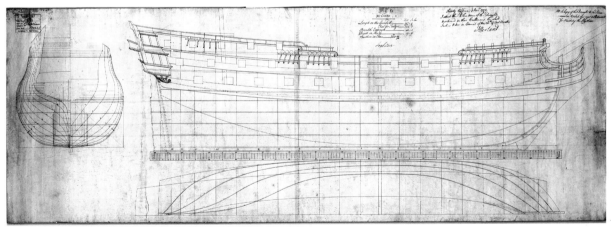

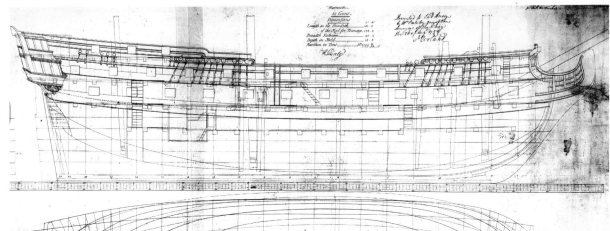

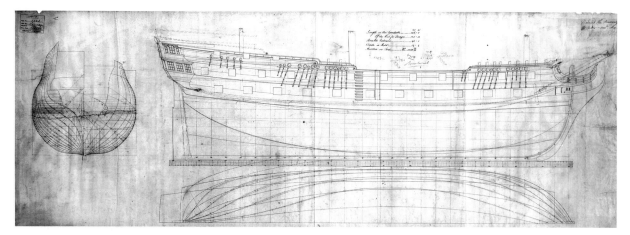

Thomas Slade's first 50-gun ship reverted to smaller dimensions compared with Bateley's contemporary design; she was named *Romney* in November 1760. Although there is space, the bridle ports on the gundeck were dispensed with. Dotted lines indicate the later addition of solid barricades around the poop deck. (NMM: DR1425)

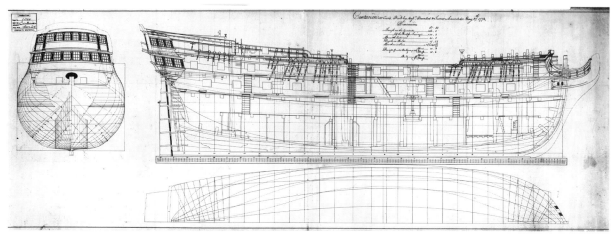

The *Centurion*, Slade's third and final 50-gun ship, was to the same specification as the *Salisbury* but this 'as-built' draught shows the two differed in detail as much as the earlier vessel had from the *Romney*. The quarter lights on the quarterdeck have been enlarged, with all three panels now of similar size. (NMM: DR1368)

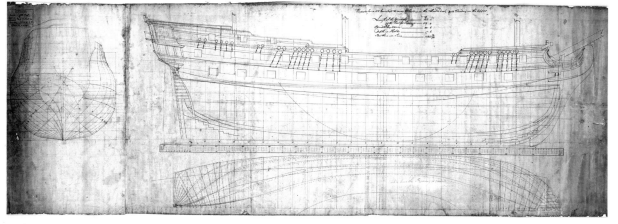

The *Renown*, a typical ship to William's 1767 design, was built by Robert Fabian at the Chapel yard leased by him at the mouth of the Itchen. She saw much service throughout the American Revolutionary War, and was one of five 50-gun ships (the others being *Chatham*, *Preston*, *Centurion* and *Experiment*), comprising – with smaller craft – Sir Peter Parker's squadron which successfully occupied Newport, Rhode Island on 8 December 1776, thereby providing the British Navy with its most useful base in America for the next three years. (NMM: DR1479)

retired from service, but from a 60-gun ship of the 1719 Establishment which had been captured by the French in 1756; the old *Warwick* (see above) had itself been the replacement for an earlier 50-gun ship. Bately's plan extended the new ship by 7ft beyond the Establishment, 4ft more than the *Chatham*, although the breadth was virtually the same. The *Warwick* was built at Portsmouth at a cost of £23,853 of which £17,420 was for her hull, masts and yards and £6433 for rigging and stores.

A second ship was ordered in the following year, to replace the old *Romney* broken up in 1757; for this second ship Slade, who prepared the design, shortened the hull proportions again, although not quite to the dimensions of the Establishment of 1745. It had

previously been the practice for the Navy Board, when two designers shared the surveyor's post, to allow both to prepare competitive draughts and to split orders for ships between both designs to enable them to evaluate the qualities of each; this practice was to continue under the new team and indeed with subsequent Surveyors.

The new *Romney* drew 10ft 9in forward and 15ft 5in abaft when normally stored. She proved an expensive ship, costing £31,142 of which £23,230 was for hull, masts and yards. She underwent a great repair at Woolwich from 1790 to 1792 at the cost of a further £31,375 (£23,776 for hull, masts and yards and £7599 for her rigging and stores).

In 1765 both Slade and his new fellow-Surveyor

Table 67: The *Romney* class (Slade design 1759) – construction history

Vessel	Builder	Ordered	Begun	Launched	Fate
Romney	Israel Pownoll,* Woolwich Dyd	20.7.1759	1.10.1759	8.7.1762	Wrecked 19.11.1804

* the Dimensions Book ascribes this ship to Joseph Harris, but as the latter only moved from Sheerness to Woolwich in 1762 it seems clear that his predecessor should be given the credit for this ship.

Table 68: The *Romney* class (Slade design 1759) – dimensions in feet and inches

Vessel	Gundeck	Keel	Beam	Depth	Tons	Keel/Beam Ratio
Design:	146 0	120 10	40 0	17 2	1028 $^{34}/_{94}$	3.02 : 0
Romney	146 0	120 8½	40 4½	17 2	1046 $^{61}/_{94}$	

John Williams (Bateley retired in June 1765) were asked to produce competitive designs for new 50-gun ships. Both Surveyors retained the 146ft length of the *Romney*, while slightly broadening the vessels to improve stability. Slade prepared what was basically a modification of his *Romney* draught, while Williams brought forward a design that was a fraction larger, and an order for one ship to each design was placed with the Royal Dockyards at the start of 1766, Williams' newer design being approved in April of that year.

Another vessel to Williams's design for the *Portland* was ordered in 1768 from Sheerness Dockyard (although her design was not confirmed until May 1769, and she was named *Bristol* in September[27]) while they still had the first under construction, and when in the latter half of 1770 the rupture with Spain over the Falkland Islands led the Admiralty to demand more deep-water cruisers, the Navy Board turned to commercial yards with orders for two further ships to the *Portland* design, plus a single sister to Slade's *Salisbury*.

Table 69: The *Salisbury* class (Slade design 1766) – construction history

Vessel	Builder	Ordered	Begun	Launched	Fate
Salisbury	Joseph Harris, Chatham Dyd	18.1.1766	19.8.1766	2.10.1769	Wrecked 13.5.1796
Centurion	John Barnard, Harwich	25.12.1770	5.1771	22.5.1774	Hospital ship 1808; sank at her moorings 21.2.1824; raised and BU 1825

Table 70: The *Salisbury* class (Slade design 1766) – dimensions in feet and inches

Vessel	Gundeck	Keel	Beam	Depth	Tons	Keel/Beam Ratio
Design:	146 0	120 7⅝	40 4	17 4	1043 $^{77}/_{94}$	2.99 : 1
Salisbury	146 0	120 5¼	40 6¼	17 4	1051 $^{81}/_{94}$	
Centurion	146 0	120 2	40 5	17 3½	1044 $^{11}/_{94}$	

The last 12pdr 50s

In 1772, shortly after Slade's death left him as the sole Surveyor, an attempt was made by Williams to design a new light, fast two-decked cruiser which would overcome the deficiencies of the existing 50-gun ships. At the onset he believed he could establish this without reducing the firepower of the type. Writing to Philip Stephens, the Admiralty Secretary, he urged:

Being of [the] opinion that a new class of strong frigates [*sic*] to carry 50 guns will be very useful in HM's Navy, to be built of a less[er] scantling and dimensions than the previous ships of 50 guns, to bear fewer men [300] and yet to be of equal force to the old 50-gun ships, and in some respects superior, by carrying the lower ports higher out of the water and a heavier battery on the upper deck; and by having no roundhouse and being of a different body to the old 50 or 44 gun ship, we expect she will also answer better in points of sailing. As such ships will be very useful in time of war for cruisers and convoys, we beg you will please to lay before the Rt Hon the Lords Commissioners of the Admiralty the draughts which accompany this [letter], by which we propose to build a ship of 50 guns to carry 300 men, to be established with the number and nature of guns described in the same draughts; and to prevent any interruption to the buildings and repairs carrying on in HM's Yards, if their Lordships shall approve of it, we would propose to contract for building her in a merchant shipping yard.[28]

To accomplish his stated aims, Williams' design was for a ship of only 140½ft length and 38½ft breadth, a retreat to the dimensions of the 1741 Establishment. To carry 24pdrs without reducing the cramped space between the gunports, he eliminated one pair of guns and ports from the lower deck, at the same time eliminating the unused twelfth pair of ports from the upper deck. The deleted pair of 24pdrs were replaced by an extra pair of 6pdrs on the quarterdeck, made possible by the removal of the roundhouse.

Notwithstanding Williams' belief that the new ships would be capable of carrying 24pdrs sufficiently high enough out of the water to make them an attractive alternative to the single-deck frigate, the Admiralty felt that the new design would suffer from problems of stress as they lacked the structural strength of the *Portland*s. It therefore decided to arm the new design with 12pdrs on both lower and upper decks, and the Navy Board accordingly placed an order with Adams and Barnard's yard at Deptford. Williams was ordered to amend his draught to take into account the reduced armament. The result, early in the new year, showed that the Surveyor still saw the new type as a realistic alternative to the single-deck ship, and both he and the Admiralty still extended the designation of 'frigate' to the small two-deckers: 'Agreeable to your request, I have herewith sent you a copy of the draught approved by the Rt Hon the Lords Commissioners of the Admiralty for building a frigate of 50 guns, called the *Experiment*, in a merchant yard.'[29]

Although lacking any roundhouse or other structure on the quarterdeck, the *Experiment* was built with a trio of false lights along the quarterdeck which gave the illusion of two levels. Nonetheless, an additional fourth pair of ports along the quarterdeck was built far back towards the taffrail seemingly an unnecessary addition as she already had the traditional three pairs of ports to accommodate her six quarterdeck 6pdrs. Launched in 1774, the result seems to have been encouraging, for within a year of the *Experiment* coming into service, a second ship was ordered from Plymouth Dockyard. This ship was modified somewhat from the original Williams design, with the upper lights being omitted to produce an overtly frigate-like stern.

The small 50s were, however, unfortunate in service. The *Experiment* surrendered off the American coast in 1779 to a much larger French 50-gun ship – *Le Sagittaire* (originally built as a 64 at Toulon from 1759 to 1761, although based on the 1748 design of the 50-gun *L'Amphion*); as *L'Expérimente*, she served in the French navy until 1794, when she was razeed into a frigate; the conversion was a failure, since she was broken up the next year. And on her first commission in 1786, the *Medusa* was badly damaged and underwent a Great Repair at Plymouth until 1788 from which she emerged re-armed, with her twenty lower deck and two forecastle guns all being replaced by 32pdr carronades. Notwithstanding Williams' optimism that this class would 'carry their lower ports higher out of the water', her ports were only 4¼ft above the surface of the water when victualled and stored for Channel service.[30] The contemporary 32-gun frigates of the *Amazon* class, in comparison, had more than 2ft greater freeboard.

Table 71: The *Portland* class (Williams design 1767) – construction history

Vessel	Builder	Ordered	Begun	Launched	Fate
First Batch:					
Portland	Edward Hunt, Sheerness Dyd	18.1.1766	1.1767	11.4.1770	Storeship 10.1800; prison hulk 5.1802; sold 19.5.1817 (for £800)
Bristol	George White, Sheerness Dyd	12.10.1768	5.1771	25.10.1775	Prison ship 11.1794; BU 10.1810
Renown*	Robert Fabian, Southampton	25.12.1770	5.1771	4.12.1774	Lazarette 3.5.1794; BU 12.1794
Isis	John Henniker, Chatham	25.12.1770	12.1772	19.11.1774	BU 9.1810
Later Batch:					
Leopard	Edward Hunt, Portsmouth Dyd	16.10.1775	1.1776	–	Frames taken up in 1785 and moved to . . .
	William Rule, Sheerness Dyd		7.5.1785	24.4.1790	Troopship 4.1811; wrecked 28.6.1814
Hannibal	Henry Adams, Buckler's Hard	24.5.1776	7.1776	26.12.1779	Taken by the French 21.1.1782
Jupiter	Randall & Co, Rotherhithe	21.6.1776	7.1776	13.5.1778	Hospital ship 1805; wrecked 10.12.1808
Leander	Nicholas Phillips, Chatham Dyd	21.6.1776	1.3.1777	1.7.1780	Medical depot ship 11.1806; renamed *Hygeia* 1813; sold 14.4.1817 (for £2100)
Adamant	Peter Baker, Liverpool	13.11.1776	6.9.1777	24.1.1780	Receiving ship 4.1809, BU 6.1814
Europa	John Jenner, Woolwich Dyd	12.1.1778	26.9.1778	19.4.1783	Troopship 4.1798; sold 11.8.1814
Assistance	Peter Baker, Liverpool	11.2.1778	4.7.1778	12.3.1781	Wrecked 29.3.1802

* named 19 November 1774, but stuck on the ways and launched 15 days later; built at Chapel shipyard (some sources erroneously give Northam).

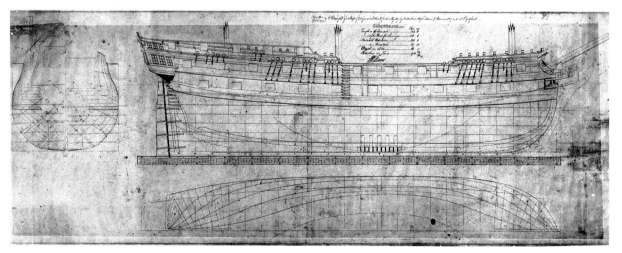

Williams' original draught for the small 50-gun *Experiment*, at this stage intended to carry twenty 24pdrs on the gundeck. More than 5ft shorter than the *Portlands*, the reduced length meant the removal of one pair of gunports from this deck and a similar deletion on the upper deck. There was no roundhouse (the stern and quarter lights at this level were fakes) and the space used to provide a fifth pair of gunports on the quarterdeck. (NMM: DR1372A)

Table 72: The *Portland* class (Williams design 1767) – dimensions in feet and inches

Vessel	Gundeck	Keel	Beam*	Depth	Tons	Keel/Beam Ratio
Design:	146 0	119 9	40 6	17 6	1044 ^{73}/94	2.96 : 1
Portland	146 0	119 9	40 6	17 6	1044 ^{73}/94	
Bristol	146 0	119 9	40 7	17 6	1049 ^{9}/94	
Renown	146 0	119 8	40 7½	17 4½	1050 ^{48}/94	
Isis	146 0	119 8¼	40 7½	17 6	1050 ^{66}/94	
Leopard	146 5	120 0¾	40 8	17 6	1055 ^{75}/94	
Hannibal	146 3½	119 9⅞	40 8	17	1054 ^{4}/94	
Jupiter	146 1½	119 8	40 10	17 6	1061 ^{30}/94	
Leander	146 0	119 7¾	40 8	17 5	1052 ^{46}/94	
Adamant	146 3	120 0	40 9	17 7½	1059 ^{88}/94	
Europa	145 11	119 4⅝	40 7¼	17 5½	1046 ^{91}/94	
Assistance	145 1	119 9	40 8	17 6	1053 ^{37}/94	

* beam outside the planking but inside the wales; extreme breadth was 5in more; moulded breadth 39ft 10in.

Table 73: The *Experiment* class (Williams design 1772)

Vessel	Builder	Ordered	Begun	Launched	Fate
Experiment	Henry Adams and William Bernard, Deptford	9.11.1772	12.1772	23.8.1774	Taken by the French 24.9.1779
Medusa	John Henslow (until 1784), then Thomas Pollard, Plymouth Dyd	1.8.1775	3.1776	23.7.1785	Receiving ship 1793; troopship 1796; hospital ship 1797; wrecked 26.11.1798

Table 74: The *Experiment* class (Williams design 1772) – dimensions in feet and inches

Vessel	Gundeck	Keel	Beam	Depth	Tons	Keel/Beam Ratio
Design:	140 6	115 6	38 6	16 7	910 ^{60}/94	3.00 : 1
Experiment	140 9	115 6	38 9	16 7	922 ^{47}/94	2.98 : 1
Medusa	140 9½	115 11½	38 7½	16 7	920 ^{16}/94	3.00 : 1

While the *Medusa* proved a successful sea-boat, reported as sailing and steering well, no further vessels of this type were begun, and instead construction of small two-deckers was to concentrate during the American War on the 44-gun ships of the *Roebuck* and *Adventure* classes. Hulked as a receiving ship at Plymouth following the outbreak of war in 1793, the *Medusa* was recommissioned as a troopship in 1796 before becoming a seagoing hospital ship in 1797, but was lost in Rosas Bay a year later.

For the next batch of 50-gun ships, Williams reverted to his proven *Portland* design, with her 24pdrs. The Admiralty were clearly disappointed with the lightly-armed *Experiment*, whose 276-pound broadside was less than that of the cheaper *Roebuck* class 44s. In late 1775, only eleven weeks after ordering *Medusa*, an order for another 50 to the *Portland* design was placed at Portsmouth, and during 1776 another four were ordered, with a final pair being ordered in 1778. The first two ships were named *Leopard* and *Hannibal* on 13 November 1775 and 27 August 1776 respectively. In May 1776, Williams and Maurice Suckling, the Controller, wrote jointly to Philip Stephens: 'Pursuant to an order from the Rt Hon the Lords Commissioners of the Admiralty of 24th instant, we send you herewith draughts by which it is proposed to build in merchant yards at the outports in different yards one ship of 50 guns to carry 24pdrs on her lower deck . . . and desire you will lay them before their Lordships for their approval and directions accordingly.'[31]

The *Leander* had an additional pair on 6pdrs mounted on her quarterdeck (Admiralty Order of 15 August 1780), and was uniquely rated as a 52-gun ship. During the French Revolutionary War, the *Jupiter* had two extra 12pdrs and two extra 6pdrs added on her quarterdeck. The *Assistance* had four 6pdrs removed (leaving just one pair on her quarterdeck), and had eight 24pdr carronades added, two pairs on the quarterdeck and two pairs on the forecastle; she also had an extra pair of 12pdrs installed on the gundeck. The complement of each ship was reduced from 350 to 343 in 1794.

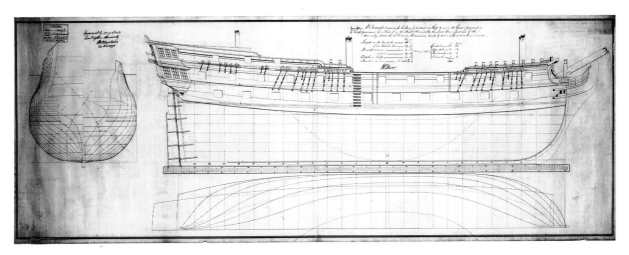

Although long since regarded, in theory, as unsuitable for the line of battle, some 50s nevertheless found themselves in fleet engagements right to the closing years of the 18th century. The Liverpool-built *Adamant*, like the *Isis*, fought at Camperdown in 1797 and continued to serve almost until the conclusion of the Napoleonic Wars. (NMM: DR1478)

Most of the class were complete by the close of the American War. The Portsmouth vessel – named *Leopard* in November 1775 – was, however, only partly built during 1776 and work then stopped on her. She remained there 'quietly rotting in the open, for ten years or more' (Patrick O'Brian's novel *Desolation Island*, containing an accurately detailed and highly graphic description of this ship). During May 1785 the frames were taken down and 'such part as was sound' was transported to Sheerness where work commenced again on 9 May, and she was completed by William Rule over the next five years at a final cost of over £21,000.

By 1774, with the situation in North America deteriorating as the colonists' hostility to British control and taxation flared towards open revolt, the Admiralty grew concerned over the provision of suitable vessels for deployment on that station. It was recognised that ships of the line could play little part in any counter-insurgency operations; there was no hostile battlefleet for them to oppose, and the likely American participants in any seaborne conflict would be the fast brigs and schooners produced in the Thirteen Colonies. Yet frigates lacked both the firepower and the troop-carrying capacity which would be required in the anticipated amphibious operations required.

The obvious answer lay in the deployment of small two-deckers, able to operate in the shallower waters of American estuaries and harbours, and able to bring fairly heavy batteries to bear upon coastal targets. The 50-gun ship in particular, now available for such colonial service in some quantities having abandoned its fleet role, enjoyed the additional advantage that its larger crew (compared to a frigate) provided an adequate reservoir of manpower which could be used to support land operations.

> You can have no idea of the number of men it takes to attend upon such an Army as this is; with the ships we have here (which is two thirds of those employed in America), when all the flatboats, galleys, gondolas, etc are manned, there is scarce enough men left on board many of the ships to move them. So that we really want six or eight line-of-battle ship; not so much perhaps for the use of the ships, as for their large complements of men for the purposes before mentioned.[32]

The American Revolutionary War, which began in July 1775 as a counter-insurgency action, mushroomed by the close of the decade as Britain found herself at war with France (13 February 1778), Spain (19 June 1779) and the Dutch (20 December 1780). The main theatre of the war, however, remained in North America, and it was the small two-deckers rather than the ships of the line which the Navy found to be in short supply. From 1775 to 1781, therefore,

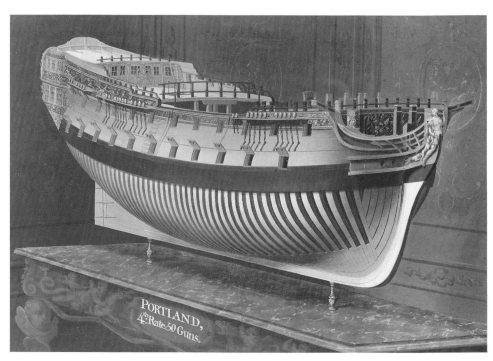

ten 50-gun ships – seven to the *Portland* design and three to lengthened designs in 1780 by a new Surveyor, Edward Hunt – and nineteen of the smaller 44-gun two-decker Fifth Rates were ordered.

As anticipated, the war in North America was essentially one of small ship actions, with few fleet contests. Britain lost the *Experiment* to a French squadron off Georgia in 1779, and in 1782 the *Hannibal* was similarly captured by Suffren's squadron off Sumatra. Around the close of that year the Navy also lost the brand new *Cato*, which disappeared en route from Brazil to India without trace of either ship or crew, including (the first) Vice-Admiral Sir Hyde Parker. During this war the only Fourth Rates taken by the British navy were two old Dutch ships – the *Prinses Carolina* (54 guns) and the *Rotterdam* (50 guns), captured by the *Bellona* and the *Warwick* respectively. Both vessels were coppered in June 1781 for further service (see Part II) but were hulked after a further two and three years respectively – the latter taking the former's name when the *Princess Caroline* was sunk in 1799.

Britain's opponents during the American war built relatively few 50s. France built none. Spain constructed a single 54-gun ship, the *Minho*, at Ferrol in 1779; this vessel lasted until broken up in 1814. Only the Dutch Admiralties, with their need for smaller vessels for trade protection duties, built a series of 54- or 56-gun ships – the *Prinses Louisa* (later renamed *Broederschap*, *Erf Prins*, *Piet Hein* and *Batavier* had been built at Amsterdam between 1769 and 1779 and the *Tromp* at Rotterdam from 1777 to 1779 – and these were followed by the *Brakel* and *Delft* at Rotterdam in 1782, *Ter Goes* at Vlissingen in 1782, and *Alkmaar* and *Beschermer* at Enkhuizen in 1783 and 1784.

In March 1778 Edward Hunt was appointed Joint

One of a series of oil paintings of models representing the latest types in the fleet of the 1770s commissioned by Lord Sandwich when First Lord of the Admiralty and presented to King George III. This one of the *Portland* shows the layout of the quarterdeck and of the roundhouse at its rear, as well as a three-dimensional view of the ship's frames, although they represent the traditional 'Navy Board' convention rather than real practice. (Science Museum photo B004590)

The 1748-built *Prinses Carolina* illustrates the considerable differences between the English and Dutch designs, particularly in internal layout. There is no orlop deck, merely a series of discontinuous platforms fitted in the hold. Among these is one for the galley, requiring an enormous chimney through two decks to ventilate it. The jeer capstan occupies the space under the forecastle, and there seems no provision for the cable tiers, the heavy, waterlogged hawsers apparently being stored directly in the hold. The sail room lies aft of the cockpit, and must have presented great difficulties in stowing and unstowing canvas. (NMM: DR6692)

The *Rotterdam*, although a more recent Dutch vessel than the *Prinses Carolina*, is laid out in a similar manner. The stern and quarter lights are much reduced on the later ship, which seems much less ornate. The *Rotterdam* was first defeated on 31 December 1780 by the *Isis*, but the latter failed to take possession of her (*Isis*'s captain was court-martialled for this), and it was to the *Warwick* that she struck in a fresh encounter five days later. (NMM: DR1661)

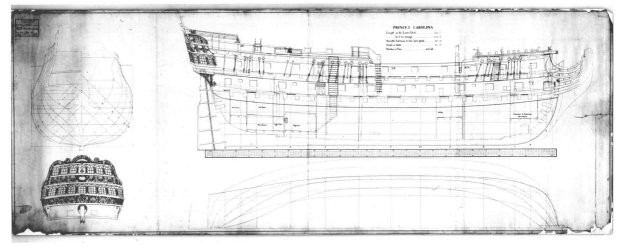

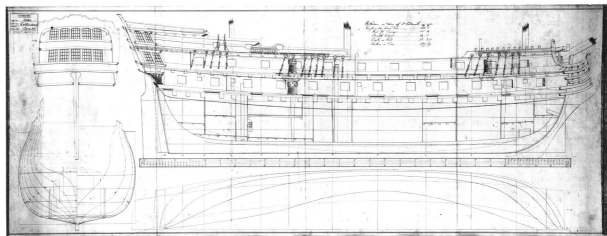

Surveyor with Williams, and when in 1780 replacements were required for lost or decaying Fourth Rates, he produced a new 50-gun design, stretching the gundeck by another 2ft beyond the *Portland* class. The new class were to be armed like the *Portland*s, and like them had eleven lower deck gunports and twelve on the upper deck. Like the *Experiment*, this design dispensed with the roundhouse and had no upper lights, and similarly had four pairs of quarterdeck ports.

Two vessels were quickly ordered to this design, but the second vessel – ordered at Gravesend – was given a substantial roundhouse with a full stern gallery, and only six gunports on the quarterdeck. Hunt's lines were then stretched by yet a further 2ft before the third order was placed at Bristol a month later. Approval for the amended design followed on 26 July for this final ship – the *Trusty* – which followed the Gravesend-built *Cato* in having a roundhouse, a structure which in the *Trusty*'s case was strong enough to have its roof barricaded with ports cut in for carronades to surmount the roundhouse by the time of her launch in 1782.

No change was made in the established armament and manning for these new vessels, but after the war the *Trusty* was re-armed, with fourteen 32pdr carronades (eight on the quarterdeck, six on the forecastle) replacing all her 6pdrs. Her complement, like those of other surviving 50s, was reduced from 350 to 343 men in 1794, her lower-deck 24pdrs being replaced by carronades.

The ranks of the 50-gun ships were also augmented by conversions during the war. During 1777 three antiquated 64-gun ships – the *Captain*, *Buckingham* and *Northumberland* – had been converted into storeships, retaining 30 guns apiece, and were renamed *Buffalo*, *Grampus* and *Leviathan* respectively (on

Table 75: Captured ships of the War of American Independence, 1776–83

Vessel	Builder	Built	Captured	Fate
Princess Caroline	Rotterdam	1747–48	31.12.1780	Fitted as receiving ship at Sheerness 12.8.1783 – 9.1783; sunk as a breakwater 1799
Rotterdam	Rotterdam	1760–61	5.1.1781	Fitted as sheer hulk and receiving ship 14.12.1784 – 8.4.1785; sold 17.7.1806 (for £1100)

Vessel	Gundeck	Keel	Beam	Depth	Tons	Keel/Beam Ratio
Princess Caroline	128 1	107 5	38 10	15 6	861 $^{60}/_{94}$	2.77 : 1
Rotterdam	134 4	111 4	38 6	15 3½	877 $^{73}/_{94}$	2.89 : 1

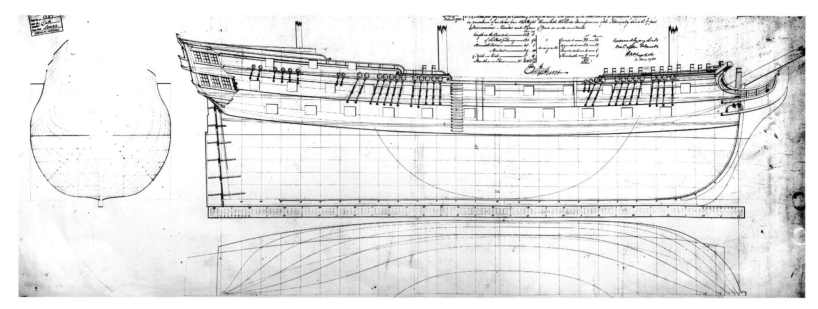

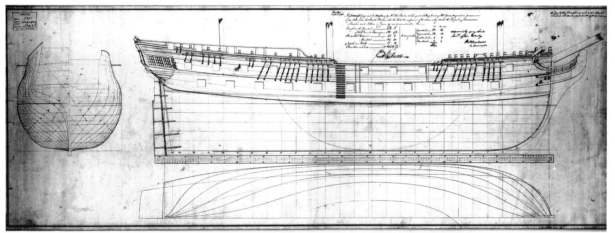

The *Cato*, although to the same specification as the *Grampus*, retained both the beakhead bulkhead and the quarterdeck roundhouse (with a stern gallery on this level) of earlier designs, as well as the built-up bulwarks along the quarterdeck instead of open rails. (NMM: DR1357)

Hunt's draught for the *Grampus* retained the gun layout of the *Portland*s but dispensed with the roundhouse, thus allowing the quarterdeck gunports to be moved aft. There was no beakhead bulkhead, but instead a fully built-up bow, with the forecastle extended to the stempost; this radical innovation, first introduced in sloops about 1732 and subsequently a standard feature of all but the first few frigates, was not repeated in other 50-gun ships (or applied to larger vessels) until the start of the next century. Gangways along each side now linked the forecastle to the quarterdeck, beginning the process of enclosing the waist. (NMM: DR1370)

7 February, 19 April and 13 September); but a year later it was decided to re-arm and re-class them as 50-gun ships.

The *Buffalo*, which had originally been built at Woolwich between 1740 to 1742 as a 70-gun vessel and reduced to 64 guns in 1760, was so converted in 1778, and served as a 50-gun ship until broken up in October 1783. In her new role she was re-armed to the same establishment of men and guns as the existing 50s, thus retaining twenty-two of her former twenty-six lower-deck 24pdrs, but exchanging her upper deck guns for twenty-two 12pdrs and her fourteen 9pdrs for the 50s' usual six 6pdrs.

The other pair were not so fortunate. Although somewhat more recent (they had been launched in 1750 and 1751 as 68-gun ships), both proved too frail to withstand the rigours of a North Atlantic winter. The *Grampus* foundered in November 1779 while returning home from Newfoundland, before she could be re-armed; the *Leviathan* received her conversion in 1779, but in February 1780 she likewise foundered while on passage home from Jamaica.

Most of the Navy's 50-gun ships were employed in North America during the war. The start of 1783 found five on that station – the *Chatham* (Rear-Admiral Robert Digby's flagship), *Centurion*, *Renown* and *Warwick*, plus the prize *Rotterdam*; the *Portland* was the station flagship at Newfoundland, the *Leander* was in the Leeward Islands and the *Jupiter* and *Preston* at Jamaica, while the *Bristol* and *Isis* were in the East Indies. Only the *Salisbury* and *Trusty* were in commission in home waters (at Portsmouth), while the remaining ships were still completing or otherwise out of commission – the *Romney*, *Grampus*, *Adamant*, *Assistance* and *Princess Caroline*.

Several of the 50s took part in fleet actions during this war. The *Renown* was in Keppel's fleet at Ushant on 27 July 1778. Two 50s were in action off Martinique in 1780 – the *Centurion* in the battle on 17 April and both *Centurion* and *Preston* in the lesser action in May. The *Preston* was also in action against the Dutch at the Dogger Bank on 5 August 1781. The *Adamant* was in action off Cape Henry on 16 March 1781 and at Chesapeake Bay on 5 September 1781, against the French. While no British 50 fought at the war's most famous action – the Saintes in April 1782 – the

Table 76: The *Grampus* class (Hunt design 1780) – construction history

Vessel	Builder	Ordered	Begun	Launched	Fate
Grampus	John Fisher, Liverpool	15.2.1780	3.1781	8.10.1782	BU 8.1794.
Cato	William Cleverley, Gravesend	17.2.1780	6.1780	29.5.1782	Presumed foundered l2.1782
Trusty	James Hillhouse, Bristol	28.3.1780	7.1781	9.10.1782	Troopship 8.1799; prison ship 5.1809; BU 4.1815*

* troopship August 1799 (reduced to 26 guns); reverted to 50 guns 1804; hulked as prison ship at Chatham May 1809.

Table 77: The *Grampus* class (Hunt design 1780) – dimensions in feet and inches

Vessel	Gundeck	Keel	Beam*	Depth	Tons	Keel/Beam Ratio
Design: (first pair)	148 0	121 9½	40 6	17 9	1062 $^{58}/_{94}$	3.01 : 1
(amended for *Trusty*)	150 0	123 9½	40 6	17 9	1080 $^{63}/_{94}$	3.06 : 1
Grampus	148 1	121 8	40 8	17 9½	1070 $^{25}/_{94}$	
Cato	147 10	121 5	40 8¾	17 9	1071 $^{32}/_{94}$	
Trusty	150 5½	124 0¾	40 7⅜	17 9¾	1088 $^{16}/_{94}$	

* beam outside the planking but inside the wales; extreme breadth was 5in more.

captured *Experiment* took part on the French side, together with her captor *Le Sagittaire*; both were also in the French line at Martinique in April 1781.

The *Isis* and *Jupiter* were in action at Porto Praya Bay on 16 April 1781, and *Isis* later fought as a unit of Sir Edward Hughes's squadron in all five of the hard-fought series of actions against the French under Pierre de Suffren in the Indian Ocean – off Sadras (on 17 February 1782), Providien (12 April 1782), Negapatam (6 July 1782), Trincomalee (3 September 1782) and Cuddalore (20 June 1783); the *Bristol* was also present at Cuddalore.

The introduction of the carronade during the war led to a number of experiments in re-arming ships with the new weapon. While the best-known example of this practice was the conversion of the 44-gun *Rainbow* in early 1782 to carry 48 carronades of mixed calibres, during the same year the 60-gun *Rippon* (built at Woolwich from 1752 to 1758) was refitted as a 54-gun ship with an all-carronade armament and with the masts and spars of a 50-gun ship. The close of the war in January 1783 put a temporary end to further experiments with the carronade. In 1788 the *Rippon* was hulked as a receiving ship at Plymouth and remained there until she was broken up in January 1808.

In July 1779 an Establishment was promulgated[33] under which the new carronades were allocated to each rate of vessel. The 50-gun ships were ordered to carry ten carronades; like all of the larger two-deckers they were to carry two 12pdr carronades on the forecastle, and another six on the poop (in the case of those 50s that had poops); unlike larger vessels, provision was also made for the 50s to mount two carronades on the quarterdeck, these being 24pdr weapons – the only carronades of this calibre to be provided under the Establishment (smaller vessels were allocated 18pdr or 12pdr weapons on their quarterdecks). By July 1782, nine 50s had been supplied with carronades, although none precisely matched the new Establishment.

At the end of the war in 1782, the British navy had thirteen 50-gun ships, while France still possessed seven and Spain three.[34] While the 50-gun ship had proved its continuing worth in its role in North America, Britain's loss of her colonies inclined her to give more consideration to future conflict in Europe, where the heavy guns of the battlefleet were the strategic reality. The remaining 50s were highly suitable for the overseas stations, and for wartime use in convoys and cruising, but this was seen as only a secondary requirement for the 1780s. Only limited replacement to maintain these lower levels of deployment were considered necessary.

The Henslow designs

Williams retired in 1784, being replaced by John Henslow, who became the sole Surveyor on Hunt's retirement two years later. In 1790 Henslow produced a revised design for the standard 50-gun ship. The length remained at that of the *Trusty*, and the

Hunt's third ship, the *Trusty*, extended the design of his earlier ships by 2ft. Like the *Cato*, the *Trusty* retained the beakhead bulkhead, roundhouse (with gallery, suggesting employment as a flagship) and solid bulwarks along the quarterdeck. The massive roundhouse was itself surmounted by further solid bulwarks into which a fourth tier of gunports was cut for the carronades mounted on the poop deck. The *Trusty* was completed with the mizzen channels moved up above the aftmost quarterdeck gunports. (NMM: DR1555)

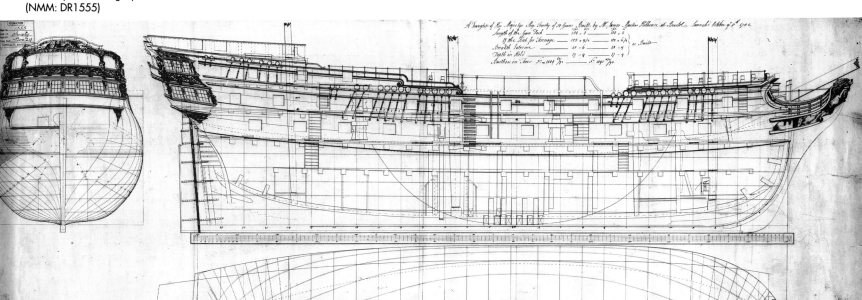

establishment – both of guns and of men – was un-altered, but the new ship was to be 6in broader. The design followed the *Cato* in having a substantial roundhouse with a stern gallery. A twelfth pair of gun-ports was introduced on the lower deck, but these were so far forwards that they could rarely have been utilised. One ship was ordered in February 1790 and two more in December of that year.

While the first ship – named *Antelope* after the ves-sel broken up at the close of the American War – was built to this 1790 design, Henslow produced a slightly lengthened version of the design a year later, and this was approved on 14 July 1791 with the two latter ships being laid down in 1792 to the revised draught. None of the trio was given priority in construction, and they were not to be completed until the closing stages of the French Revolutionary War.

Progress on all three was slow. Although prelimin-ary work on the *Antelope* was begun in June 1790, work on the solid model for her was reported as still in hand at the end of 1791, and her frames were still being moulded during 1793. The Progress Book re-ports her as actually 'begun' (*ie* keel laid down) in June 1794, but in November the Master Shipwright re-ported that from 18 August to 27 September all the dockyard hands were taken off her to expedite the fitting out of ships, reflecting the desperate need with the onset of war to work on fitting out existing vessels at the expense of new construction.[35]

Her framing was completed in June 1796, and was left to season, with little further work being undertaken for another year. In July 1797 the Dock-yard Commissioner, Captain Francis Hartwell, suggested that 'some shipwrights may be employed on her without prejudice to other services',[36] and the·

response indicates the Navy Board was agreeable only 'whenever the more urgent business of the port may permit'. Certainly they gave low priority to the ob-solete 50-gun ship!

Table 78: The *Antelope* class (Henslow design 1790) – construction history

Vessel	Builder	Ordered	Begun	Launched	Fate
Antelope	Sheerness Dyd	15.2.1790	6.1790	10.11.1802	Troopship 1817; convict ship 1.1824; BU 7.1845
Diomede	Deptford Dyd	9.12.1790	8.1792	17.1.1798	Troopship 9.1812; BU 8.1815
Grampus	Portsmouth Dyd	9.12.1790	10.1791	20.3.1802	Hospital ship* 7.1820; sold 1832

The *Antelope* was named by A.O. on 24 July 1790; she became a troopship in 1818, and was relegated to harbour service in January 1824 as a convict ship at Bermuda. The *Diomede* and *Grampus* were ordered and laid down under the names *Firm* and *Tiger* respectively, and were renamed on 29 December 1797 and 4 March 1802 respectively, each less than a month prior to its launch date.
* The *Grampus* was lent as a hospital ship to the Society for Distressed Seamen (under Admiralty Order of 13 January 1820), and refitted in July 1820 at Deptford for her new role; she was returned to the Admiralty on 20 October 1831.

Table 79: The *Antelope* class (Henslow design 1790) – dimensions in feet and inches

Vessel	Gundeck	Keel	Beam*	Depth	Tons	Keel/Beam Ratio
Design: (prototype)	150 0	123 8½	41 0	17 8	1106 7/94	3.02 : 1
(as amended 1791)	151 0	124 7½	41 0	17 8	1114 31/94	3.04 : 1
Antelope	150 0½	123 2½	41 1¼	17 8	1107 25/94	
Diomede	151 1½	124 7⅞	41 1¾	17 7	1122 52/94	
Grampus	151 0	124 7½	41 0	17 8	1114 31/94	

* beam outside the planking but inside the wales; extreme breadth was 5in more.

The *Antelope* was developed by Henslow along the lines of the *Trusty*, but broadened. There was also a twelfth lower deck gunport on the broadside. (NMM: DR1408)

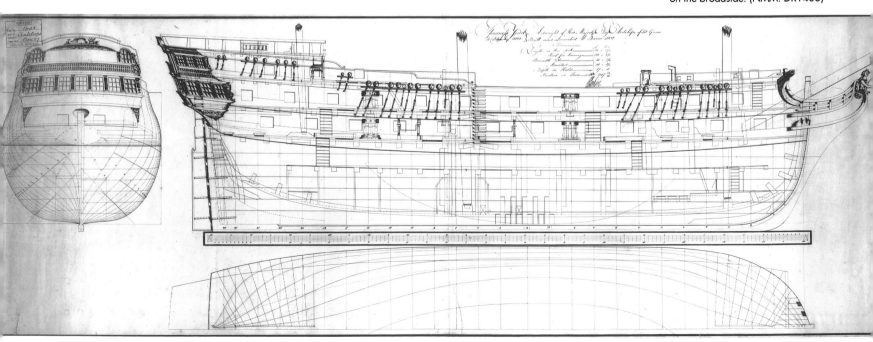

Few 50s remained in service by 1793, but those that did were still playing key roles as squadron flagships on overseas stations. The *Romney* was the flagship of the depleted Mediterranean Fleet. The *Trusty* was flagship on the Leeward Islands Station (the *Centurion* was also there), while the *Europa* fulfilled the same role at Jamaica and the *Assistance* at St Johns, Newfoundland. The *Leopard* was still in commission with the Channel Fleet (as was *Medusa*, reduced to a 44 and soon to become a receiving ship at Plymouth). The other nine surviving 50s were in ordinary – most in need of repair – but most were to be swiftly brought back into service within the first year of war. However, the *Grampus* was broken up in August 1794 and the *Renown* in December 1794.

Work on the three new ships ordered in 1790 proceeded slowly, with priority being given to other classes. The *Diomede* was not launched until early 1798, and the other two did not enter the water until 1802. However, further vessels were acquired from 1795 onwards. Nine Indiamen then in service or under construction on the Thames were taken into service. The *Ceres*, for example, was purchased from her builder at a cost of £10,800 for the hull only, and took the name of the *Grampus*. These vessels bore little relation to the traditional 50-gun ship, each having a principal battery consisting of fourteen 18pdrs a side on the lower deck, and with an upper deck armament of 32pdr carronades. The *Glatton*, however, was given an all-carronade armament, consisting of twenty-eight 68pdrs on the lower deck and an equal number of 42pdrs on the upper deck.

Although not much greater in dimensions than the purpose-built warships, these merchant hulls were much more capacious. Although they drew more water than the existing 50s (see Part II, Table 106) they had a freeboard of over 8ft when stored for Channel service, and little less even when on foreign service. They carried considerably more ballast than the 50s; the *Calcutta*, for example, had 200 tons of iron and 150 tons of shingle ballast (plus 600 tons of water), while the *Glatton* held 170 tons of iron and 470 tons of shingle ballast (plus 500 tons of water).

Few of these vessels lasted long as Fourth Rates. Two vessels – *Calcutta* and *Weymouth* – were turned over to the Transport Board on 5 January 1796 and struck from the Navy List (although the former was returned to the Navy in 1804); the *Coromandel* followed suit on 9 August 1796. Most of the remainder were also converted into storeships within a few years, a role for which their capacious holds made them eminently suitable. The *Grampus* was the first of these, being converted at Sheerness in November 1796 for her new role and reclassed at the start of February 1797. By the end of 1807 only the carronade-armed *Glatton* remained as a Fourth Rate.

Following the losses of the original *Malabar* in 1796 and *Hindostan* in 1804, two further, somewhat smaller vessels – originally built of teak in India – were purchased from the East India Company in May 1804, and commissioned as Fourth Rates, taking the same names. The *Malabar* was established with 310 men and 56 guns, comprising twenty-eight 18pdrs on the lower deck and the same number of 24pdr carronades on the upper deck; the *Hindostan* had 294 men and two fewer guns (of the same type) on each deck.

French revolutionary forces under Charles Pichegru overran the United Provinces of the Netherlands in December 1794 and captured the Dutch naval forces icebound off Texel. Following the creation of the Batavian Republic as an ally of France in February 1795, Dutch warships soon came into conflict with the Royal Navy. Of nine Dutch ships of 50 to 56 guns, seven were taken by the British between 1795 and 1799; and although one – the *Delft* – sank shortly after her capture, the other six were incorporated into the Royal Navy. As established as 54-gun ships in their new role, most differed little from the recent British 50s, except to carry an extra pair of 12pdrs on the upper deck and an additional pair of 6pdrs on the quarterdeck.

The *Brakel* and the *Delft* belonged to a larger variant of the Dutch 56-gun ship. Both had been built at Rotterdam for the Maas Admiralty in 1782, the *Brakel* in the naval ship yard by Pieter van Zwyndrecht, and the *Delft* at Delfshaven by de Hoog and de Wit; they were to a design measuring 160ft (Dutch) in length and 45ft in beam, with a depth in hold on 20½ft. The *Brakel* fell into British hands at an early date; on 19 January 1795 the Admiralty issued orders to seize all Dutch vessels in British waters, and the port-admiral at Plymouth accordingly detained the *Brakel* upon her arrival there on 5 February, although she was not taken possession of for the British navy until March 1796. Following a refit at Plymouth at the end of 1796 at a cost of £12,700, she was established in the Royal Navy as a guardship with 355 men and 54 guns, comprising twenty-two 24pdrs on the lower deck, twenty-four 12pdrs on the upper deck, and eight 6pdrs (six on the quarterdeck and two on the forecastle).

The other five captured 56-gun ships were to smaller designs. The earlier *Tromp* was taken (with other ships) by Rear-Admiral Keith Elphinston's squadron in Saldanha Bay on 17 August 1796; she was also built in Rotterdam as a 54-gun ship; her design measured 154ft (Dutch) in length, 43⁹⁄₁₁ft in beam and 19ft depth in the hold. The remaining four were to a common design measuring 154½ft (Dutch) in length, 43ft in beam and 20ft in the hold; the *Princes Louisa* (renamed *Broederschap* in 1795) and *Batavier* were 56-gun ships built in Amsterdam; the *Alkmaar* and *Beschermer* were rated as 50-gun ships when built for the Noorderkwartier (North Holland) Admiralty at Enkhuizen, but by 1795 both carried 56 guns.

Four 56s were among the fifteen Dutch ships of the line commanded by Vice-Admiral de Winter which was crushed by Adam Duncan's fleet off Camperdown on 11 October 1797, but of these the *Batavier* and *Beschermer* made good their escape, while the *Alkmaar* and *Delft* were both captured. The destruction of the Batavian fleet was completed in August 1799 by Mitchell's squadron (see below).

Service in the French Revolutionary and Napoleonic Wars

While the 50 had officially been relegated from its place in the line at the start of the Seven Years War, some still found a place during the major battles of the Napoleonic period. Two were in Duncan's fleet at Camperdown in October 1797 – the *Adamant* and *Isis*. Here four Dutch 'fifties' (actually mounting 56 guns each at capture – twenty-four 18pdrs, the same number of 12pdrs, and eight 8pdrs) were in action, and the *Alkmaar* and *Delft* were taken by the British. The *Delft* was so severely damaged that she sank in a storm three days later while in tow of the 64-gun *Veteran*, while the *Alkmaar* was incorporated in the Royal Navy.

The *Leander* took her place at the rear of the line at the Nile on 1 August 1798, and proved effective in that role; Nelson had no frigates or small craft so the ship was assigned to carry Nelson's despatches after the battle to Earl St Vincent at Cadiz, whither she sailed on 5 August – only to fall in with the French 74-gun *Le Généreux* thirteen days later. After six hours of close and bloody conflict, dismasted and with 35 dead and 57 wounded from among the 282 men and boys aboard at the start of the action, the Fourth Rate eventually surrendered to her vastly superior opponent. She was retaken by the Russians at the capture of Corfu on 3 March in the following year, and returned to the British.

In the summer of 1799 the British government decided to mount an expeditionary force to the northern Netherlands, which offered the prospect of capturing

Table 80: Converted Indiamen during French Revolutionary War, 1793–1802 – construction history

Vessel	Builder (as Former Name)	Launched	Purchased[1]	Fate
Calcutta	John Perry & Co, Blackwall as *Warley*	4.1795	9.3.1795	Transport 1796; taken by the French 26.9.1805
Grampus	John Perry & Co, Blackwall as *Ceres*	1795	9.3.1795	Storeship 2.1797; bilged 19.1.1799
Hindostan (i)	William Barnard, Deptford as *Born*	1795	9.3.1795	Storeship 6.5.1801; burnt 2.4.1804
Abergavenny	Thomas Pitcher, Northfleet as *Earl of Abergavenny*	1795	9.3.1795	Sold 1807
Malabar (i)	Thomas Pitcher, Northfleet as *Royal Charlotte*	1795	9.3.1795	Foundered 10.10.1796
Glatton	William Wells, Blackwall (kept same name)	1795	9.3.1795	Water depot ship 1814; sunk as breakwater 10.1830
Coromandel	John Perry & Co, Blackwall as *Winterton*	9.5.1795	20.5.1795	Transport 1796; storeship 1800; hulked 10.1807; sold 24.7.1813
Madras	William Wells, Rotherhithe as *Lascelles*	4.7.1795	20.5.1795	Storeship 1803; sold 1807
Weymouth	William Wells, Rotherhithe as *Earl Mansfield*	30.9.1795	28.5.1795	Transport 1796; wrecked 21.1.1800
Further purchases during Napoleonic War:				
Malabar (ii)[2]	Calcutta as *Cuvera*	1798	5.1804	Storeship (20 guns) 1805; convict ship 10.1827; BU 12.1853
Hindostan (ii)[3]	Calcutta as *Admiral Rainier*	1799	5.1804	Storeship (20 guns) 1811; convict ship 1824; sold 24.10.1855

[1] date of registration in the Royal Navy. [2] renamed *Coromandel* 7 March 1815. [3] renamed *Dolphin* 22 September 1819; renamed *Justitia* 1831.

the remainder of the Dutch fleet, a large part of which lay blockaded off Texel Island. The naval side of this force, under the command of Vice-Admiral Andrew Mitchell, comprised six 64-gun ships, the 54-gun *Glatton*, and two 50s – the *Romney* and the *Isis*, in the last of which Mitchell mounted his flag; there were also five frigates and two Russian ships of the line, the latter supplied under a recent Anglo-Russian treaty. On 28 August, the force took possession of thirteen Dutch ships (including the *Broederschap*) at anchor in

As a storeship, the captain complained, the *Hindostan* was crank, and at Chatham in November 1813 the roundhouse was removed. This required the revision of the the upper deck accommodation for this ship, providing cabins for the boatswain and carpenter and displacing their storerooms forward, as shown in this plan of 11 November 1813. (NMM: DR4094A)

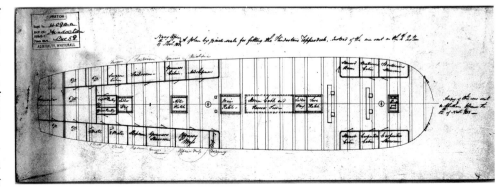

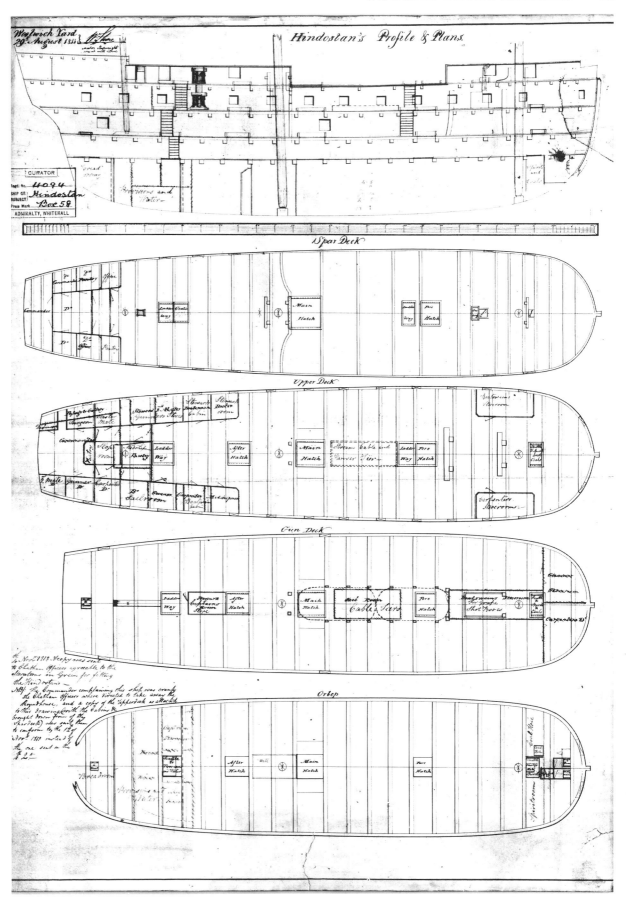

Typical of the design of ships purchased from the East India Company, with the square midship section common among merchantmen, the *Admiral Rainier* was unusual in that, being built at Calcutta, she was constructed from teak. Bought by the Navy in 1804, she served as the 52-gun *Hindostan* for seven years before being converted into a storeship. The profile and deck plans taken off at Woolwich in August 1811 reflect this new role, with the former thirteen gunports along each side of the gundeck reduced to a couple, and drastic changes made to her accommodation. The ship had a complete unbroken spar deck, with no visible waist. (NMM: DR4094)

the Nieueve Diep, at the Helder; and a further twelve vessels were surrendered two days later in the Vlieter (including the *Batavier* and *Beschermer*) without a shot being fired.

The first three 56s taken from the Dutch were soon employed as troopships; the final three Dutch prizes saw service as floating batteries before being hulked, the *Batavier* and *Beschermer* being converted at Chatham in July 1801 at a cost of £7831 and £7120 respectively, and the *Broaderscarp* at Sheerness in October 1803. For political reasons they had been taken over in the name of the deposed Prince of Orange, so none of the three was officially added to the Navy until some time after May 1803. Notably, while none of the Dutch prizes was considered suitable for front-line service, all of them were extensively employed as auxiliaries and then saw further service as harbour hulks; they thus outlasted most of the contemporary British 50s of pre-war construction. The last of them – the *Beschermer* – was lent to the East India Dock Company on 4 November 1806 and returned to the Navy in August 1838.

The last traditional 50-gun ships and the concept of the *razee*

Few Fourth Rates were lost by the British during the long years of war; of the ships built for the Navy, the only loss to enemy action was the *Leander* (see above), and she was later recaptured. Excluding the *Medusa*, bilged in 1798 while serving as a transport, four ships were lost by groundings – the *Salisbury* off Santo Domingo on 10 May 1796, the *Assistance* off Dunkirk on 29 March 1802, the *Romney* off Texel on 18 November 1804 (11 drowned) and the *Jupiter* in Vigo Bay on 10 December 1808; but this was a rate of attrition from natural causes no more than might have been expected during peacetime. There were further losses among the ex-Indiamen purchased in 1795 – the *Malabar* foundered in the Western Approaches on 11 October 1796 while escorting a homeward-bound convoy from the Caribbean. The Navy's only other loss to enemy action was the *Calcutta* on 26 September 1805, in a gallant defence against superior odds while escorting a convoy off the Scilly Isles; she served in the French navy until 12 April 1809, when she was retaken by Cochrane during Lord Gambier's attack on the Basque Roads before being destroyed by an explosion.

While no additions to the 50-gun class were made during the first decade of the new century, four new vessels were ordered soon after – two in mid-1810 (*Jupiter* and *Salisbury*) and a second pair almost a year later. The lines of this design were derived by Sir William Rule, the Surveyor since 1793, from those of the 80-gun Danish Third Rate *Christian VII*, captured at Copenhagen and added to the Royal Navy in 1807. Some 4ft longer than the Henslow design, and 6in greater in the beam, these ships had an enclosed bow

Table 81: Converted Indiamen during French Revolutionary War, 1793–1802 – dimensions in feet and inches

Vessel	Gundeck	Keel	Beam	Depth	Tons	Keel/Beam Ratio
Calcutta	156 11	129 7¾	41 3½	17 2	1175 ^{73}/94	3.14 : 1
Grampus	157 1	130 4	41 3	15 6	1165*	3.16 : 1
Hindostan (i)	160 3	132 0	42 1	17 1	1249*	3.14 : 1
Abergavenny	160 0	131 6	41 1½	17 0	1182 ^{93}/94	3.20 : 1
Malabar (i)	161 0	132 3¼	42 2¼	17 6	1252 ^{19}/94	3.14 : 1
Glatton	163 11¼	133 4¼	42 1	17 0	1256 ^{22}/94	3.17 : 1
Coromandel	169 0	139 3⅝	42 5¼	17 2	1340*	3.28 : 1
Madras	175 1½	144 0	43 1¾	17 6	1425 ^{83}/94	3.34 : 1
Weymouth	175 5	144 1	43 3	19 7	1433 ^{56}/94	3.33 : 1

Further purchases during Napoleonic War:

Malabar (ii)	168 6	127 4	37 2	?	935 ^{57}/94	3.43 : 1
Hindostan (ii)	158 6	121 9	37 0	?	886 ^{54}/94	3.29 : 1

* these tonnages are as quoted in Dimensions Books but do not correlate with dimensions given with them.

Table 82: Prizes taken (all from Dutch) during French Revolutionary War, 1793–1802 – construction history

Vessel	Builder	Built	Captured	Purchased	Fate
Brakel	Rotterdam Dyd	1782–84	4.3.1796	25.10.1796	Troopship 6.1799; receiving ship 1807; sold 29.9.1814
Tromp	Rotterdam Dyd	1777–79	17.8.1796		Troopship 1798; prison ship 1799; receiving ship 1811; sold 9.8.1815
Alkmaar	Enkhuizen Dyd	1783	11.10.1797		Troopship 1798; hospital ship 12.3.1801; storeship 1805; sold 30.11.1815
Broaderscarp (ex-*Broederschap*)	Amsterdam Dyd	1769	28.8.1799		Floating battery 10.1803; BU 10.1805
Batavier	Amsterdam Dyd	1779	30.8.1799		Floating battery 7.1801; laid up 1809; convict ship 9.1817; BU 3.1823
Beschermer	Enkhuizen Dyd	1784	30.8.1799		Floating battery 7.1801; lent as hulk 4.11.1806 to 8.1838; sold 9.1838

Table 83: Prizes taken (all from Dutch) during French Revolutionary War, 1793–1802 – dimensions (British measured) in feet and inches

Vessel	Gundeck	Keel	Beam	Depth	Tons	Keel/Beam Ratio
Brakel	148 3½	117 7	42 1½	17 2¾	1109 ^{81}/94	2.79 : 1
Tromp	143 10½	117 10	40 8¾	15 3	1039 ^{65}/94	2.89 : 1
Alkmaar	142 4	117 10⅛	40 9	15 6½	1040 ^{83}/94	2.89 : 1
Broaderscarp	140 1	114 11	41 8½	8 8½	1063 ^{32}/94	2.76 : 1
Batavier	144 7	118 1⅞	40 10	16 5	1047 ^{87}/94	2.89 : 1
Beschermer	145 1	118 7	40 10	16 4	1051 ^{67}/94	2.90 : 1

Table 84: *Jupiter* class (Rule design 1810) – construction history

Vessel	Builder	Ordered	Begun	Launched	Fate
Jupiter	Plymouth Dyd	30.6.1810	7.1810	22.11.1813	Troopship 11.1837; coal hulk 4.1846; BU 1.1870
Salisbury	Deptford Dyd	13.7.1810	1811	21.6.1814	Sold 1.1837
Romney	John Pelham, Frindsbury	13.5.1811	1811	24.2.1815	Troopship (30 guns) 1820; receiving ship 6.1837; sold 12.1845
Isis	Woolwich Dyd	13.5.1811	2.1816	5.10.1819	Coal hulk 3.1861; sold 3.1867

Table 85: *Jupiter* class (Rule design 1810) – dimensions in feet and inches

Vessel	Gundeck	Keel	Beam*	Depth	Tons	Keel/Beam Ratio
Design:	154 0	127 5⅜	41 6	18 0	1167 ⁴⁹⁄₉₄	3.07 : 1
(amended 1811)	154 0	127 3¾	41 11	17 6	1189 ⁷⁶⁄₉₄	3.04 : 1
Jupiter	150 0	127 3⅜	41 7½	18 0	1173 ⁴⁄₉₄	
Salisbury	154 4	127 3⅜	42 1	17 6	1199 ²⁄₉₄	
Romney	154 9	127 8	42 6	17 6	1226 ⁵⁵⁄₉₄	

* beam outside the planking but inside the wales; extreme breadth was 5in more.

Table 86: 58-gun vessels razeed from 74-gun Third Rates – conversion history

Vessel	Launched	Re-builder	Ordered	Re-launched	Fate
Majestic	1785	Robert Seppings, Chatham Dyd	12.2.1813	2.4.1813	BU 4.1816 after stranding
Goliath	1781	Robert Seppings, Chatham Dyd	12.2.1813	29.5.1813	BU 6.1815
Saturn	1786	Joseph Tucker, Plymouth Dyd	30.3.1813	28.7.1813	Lazarette 9.1825; receiving ship 1845; BU 1.1868
Elephant	1786	Nicholas Diddams, Portsmouth Dyd	1816	3.1818	BU 11.1830
Excellent	1787	Nicholas Diddams, Portsmouth Dyd	20.5.1820	6.1820	Gunnery training ship 1830; BU 10.1835

Table 87: 58-gun vessels razeed from 74-gun Third Rates – dimensions in feet and inches

Vessel	Gundeck	Keel	Beam	Depth	Tons	Keel/Beam Ratio
Designs: (*Majestic*)	170 0	140 5	46 7	20 6	1632 ³⁵⁄₉₄	3.01 : 1
(last four)	168 0	138 0	46 9	19 9	1604 ²⁷⁄₉₄	2.95 : 1
Majestic	170 6	141 0	46 9½	20 6	1642 ⁸⁄₉₄	
Goliath	168 0	138 0	46 9	19 9	1604 ²⁷⁄₉₄	
Saturn	168 2	138 1¼	46 11	19 10	1616 ⁹¹⁄₉₄	
Elephant	168 0	137 10⅞	46 11½	19 9½	1617 ⁵⁰⁄₉₄	
Excellent	168 0	138 0	46 11	19 9	1614 ⁸⁹⁄₉₄	

with a raked stem. After the first ship – the *Jupiter* – was begun, the design was modified somewhat, adding a further 5in to the breadth.

Compared with the preceding 50-gun ships, an additional pair of 12pdrs was provided for the upper deck, occupying the foremost pair of gunports previously left empty on this deck. To carry the hawsers, a further pair of hawse holes was cut forwards, where the round bows were now built up to the level of the forecastle deck. Since 1802 this built-in forecastle had increasingly supplanted the old-fashioned beakhead bulkhead in all two- (and three-) deckers. The forecastle deck was now itself barricaded like the quarterdeck, improving the protection for men working there and producing a drier and more seaworthy ship.

The four 6pdrs on the quarterdeck in earlier classes were deleted and in their place the new design provided for eight 24pdr carronades mounted on slides, while a further two of these carronades were added to the forecastle to supplement the two 'chase' 6pdrs there (the *Salisbury* was given 12pdr chase guns instead of 6pdrs). The roof of the roundhouse was barricaded, with two additional pairs of gunports cut in them, but there is no sign that carronades were ever mounted here. The weight of the broadside was thus raised from 414 to 522 pounds (528 pounds for the *Salisbury*), although the carronades were of course much restricted in range compared with the truck-mounted long guns.

Of the original second pair, the ship ordered from Woolwich was 'not proceeded with', but in its place a fresh order was placed on 10 September 1811 with the same dockyard. This vessel, the *Isis*, was begun in February 1816 as a conventional Fourth Rate, but while on the stocks she was lengthened by 11ft and converted to a 'frigate' before her launch on 5 October 1819. She was completed with thirty 24pdrs on the gundeck and twenty-eight 42pdr carronades on the continuous deck above formed by a 'spar' deck linking the forecastle to the quarterdeck. She was reduced to fifty guns in 1823 and then to forty-four guns in 1839. Her story, and that of the other 50-gun frigates that followed her, falls outside this account.

In 1813 three elderly 74-gun ships were converted to 58-gun Fourth Rates by cutting down ('razing' or 'razeeing') at forecastle and quarterdeck; two more were similarly adapted after the war. They became the last two-decker Fourth Rates to join the Navy. Four of these ships were of the *Arrogant* class, designed by Thomas Slade in 1758, while the *Majestic* was of Bately's contemporary *Canada* class, designed in 1759.

Each ship retained her gundeck battery of twenty-eight 32pdrs, but her upper deck 18pdrs were replaced by 42pdr carronades, while two 12pdrs were installed as bow-chasers to give each ship thirty guns on the flush upper deck and a broadside of 1048lbs. The

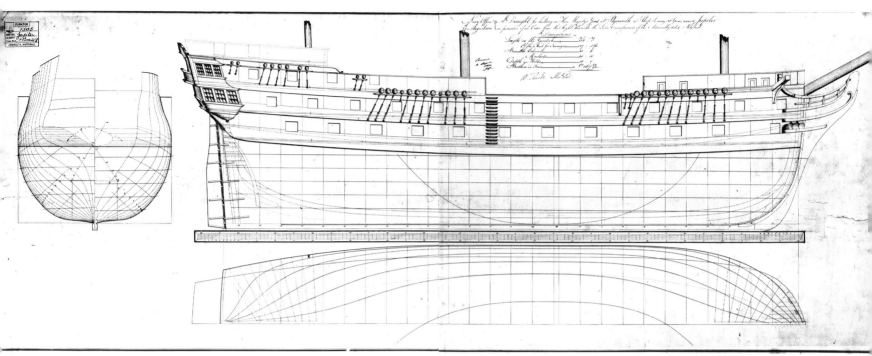

Above: The draught for the *Jupiter* illustrates the final appearance of the 50-gun two-decker. With the disappearance of the beakhead bulkhead, the forecastle now extends to the stempost, while proper chase ports are provided on both decks in the eyes of the ship. The widening of the gangways (now at the same level as the forecastle and quarterdeck) has created a continuous spar deck, with the waist reduced to an open hatchway, crossed by transverse beams on which the ship's boats are carried. (NMM: DR1505)

Below: The *Saturn*, like the other conversions from 74-gun ships of the line, bore no real resemblance to the standard 50-gun two-decker. These *razee* carried a much heavier armament than other Fourth Rates, retaining their lower deck 32pdrs but replacing their upper deck 18pdr long guns with 42pdr carronades. These conversions were ordered as an emergency counter to the large American frigates of the *Constitution* type, nominally 44-gun ships but actually (by English measurement) 1533-ton vessels mounting thirty 24pdrs on the gundeck, two more of the same on the forecastle, and twenty-four carronades (42pdrs), so no match for the *razees*. (NMM: DR1748)

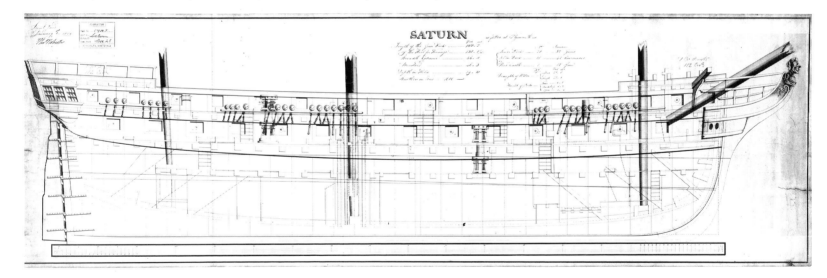

complement was set at 495 men and boys. The advantages secured from these conversions were 'superiority in sailing, an equal degree of force, and, with the aid of a black hammock-cloth thrown over the waist-barricade, such a disguised appearance as might induce the large American frigates to come down and engage'.[37]

The *Goliath* was broken up in 1815 and the *Majestic* a year later, leaving the *Saturn* as the only 58-gun ship to survive, along with the older 56-gun *Glatton*. Among the 50-gun ships, eight survived at the end of 1815, including the three new-built ships of the *Jupiter* class – the *Salisbury* still in commission, and the *Jupiter* and *Romney* in ordinary. Of the older vessels, only the *Antelope* was still in commission, while the *Batavier*, *Beschermer*, *Grampus* and *Hygeia* (the former *Leander*) remained as hulks in various forms of harbour service.

Under the new scheme of rating approved during 1816 and brought into force in February 1817, in which carronades were for the first time included in the official number of guns carried, the old category of 50-gun ship disappeared, with the creation of a new 50-gun category which covered the six 24pdr frigates previously rated as 40s. All the two-decker 50s were all now re-rated as 58-gun, except the *Antelope* which became a troopship, and the *Jupiter*, which was initially re-rated at 60 guns, but became a 58-gun ship in 1822.

Part II: The Ships

8. General Arrangement and Layout

The main feature of the development of each type of warship from 1650 to 1815 was a gradual increase in size, accompanied by incremental improvements in design rather than startling change. This is particularly true of the smaller two-decked ship such as the 50-gun ship, which emerged from the seventeenth century with its role seen as a compromise between the requirements for fleet action and those for the lighter duties of protecting British merchant trade and the sea-lanes that carried it.

It is said that the result was a failure to meet either role ideally – the fate of any compromise. The limited size of the 50-gun ship meant that it could not support the weight of ordnance to play a part in the line of battle equivalent to the larger Third Rates – particularly the 74-gun ship which eventually emerged as the ideal platform for fleet operation in terms of armament and strength of construction. Similarly the 50-gun ship was too costly – in terms of construction and manning – to operate in the convoy and cruising role when compared with her smaller and hence cheaper consorts.

The fleet role suffered particularly at times when there was a general escalation in the level of armaments. This was particularly true in the 1740s, when there was an 'up-gunning' of most of the rates in order to provide the heaviest (and consequently most damaging) amount of firepower that could be carried. The second quarter of the eighteenth century experienced an arms race which was dominated by France, which introduced remarkable improvements in design. Britain, in comparison, experienced a period of ingrained conservatism of which the various Establishments, a series of rigidly-enforced standards in the dimensions not only of the ships themselves, but of almost every facet of their construction, were a symptom rather than a cause.

With little scope for innovation, British ships fell behind those of her main competitor in both size and design flair. Even when this was recognised, and attempts made to alter the Establishment standards to allow upgrading, there was little willingness to provide the radical alterations that were by then required to close the gaps. Not only were the Surveyor and shipwrights unwilling to go against their own habits and experience, but their political masters were ill-equipped to understand the changes that were needed and thus unwilling to take the lead by approving major departures from practice, and, more importantly, the extra funding that enlarged vessels required.

Long years of peace contributed to the problem, when, as always, technological change languished. Between 1713 and 1744 the peace was broken only by brief conflicts with Spain, by then too weak a naval power to puncture British complacency. King and Parliament saw little reason to disturb the basic composition of the British Navy, and naval professionals were not prepared to risk disapproval by enlightening them. Only the arrival of France into the war as Spain's ally in 1744, with a navy capable of seriously disrupting Britain's maritime lifelines, secured a reappraisal of the situation that led to the abandonment of the Establishment system.

The extra weight of ordnance that resulted from the 1743 Establishment of Guns particularly affected the shorter vessels, both among the three-decker and two-decker types. British warships were less capable of safely carrying the extra weight than were their opponents. They were forced to sit deeper in the water, with a much-reduced freeboard. Not only were sailing qualities adversely affected, but in heavy weather the lowest tier of gunports could often not be opened for fear that water would wash in through them. Preference shifted away from the 44-gun and 50-gun two-deckers towards the larger Third Rates which could be relied upon to operate in almost any weather, and similarly among three-deckers the 80-gun ships were abandoned for the larger and more seaworthy 90s.

Under the inspired direction of Anson, the Navy underwent a transformation which concentrated on those types of warship best suited to the distinctive needs of the mid-eighteenth century – the 74-gun ship as the optimum two-decker with heavy armament for fleet work, and the single-decked frigate for convoys and cruising.

The chief function of the sailing warship in what we now call the Age of Sail was to be a mobile gun platform, capable of directing the maximum possible firepower upon its opponents commensurate with its size. The basic layout of the two-decker, therefore, was dictated by the need to provide space for two tiers of heavy cannon to bear on either side of the ship, and for this purpose two continuous decks were provided, superimposed one above the other, and both sufficiently high above the waterline for gunports through which the guns could fire, with enough freeboard at the lowest gunports to minimise the risk of admitting the sea in all but the worst weather.

For reasons of stability, this requirement for adequate freeboard was limited by the need to mount the guns and other equipment as low down in the ship as possible. Not only had the lower gun deck to be set as low down as safety permitted, but the upper gun deck had also to be kept as far down as possible, resulting in the lowest possible headroom in the space between the two decks.

Early gun-armed warships had often carried weapons at several different levels, but it was soon recognised that, to allow the swift movement of men and supplies from one end of the ship to the other, the main gun decks should be continuous. The early English frigates of the 1640s mounted most of their ordnance on the gundeck, a continuous deck running from bow to stern, on which the guns could be positioned as needed. This was the only continuous deck in these vessels, but further light guns could be mounted on the half-deck abaft the main mast, where the elevated structure served as the descendent of the after-castle that had been carried on medieval warships. Doubtless these early frigates proved very wet ships, with no protection for the crew from seas breaking over the bow, for by 1648 a light forecastle was already being constructed as a platform over that part of the gun deck forward of the fore mast. On some ships a small quarterdeck was also added, at first more to provide a better vantage point than to carry extra guns.

This simple structure, however, was soon enlarged on. There is a natural tendency in many fields to take a successful design and enlarge on it, even if the particular virtues of the original design depended on its small size. While the Commonwealth was still young, the later orders for frigates requested that the waists of this next batch be built over, joining the half-deck to the forecastle platform to produce a continuous upper deck. Thus the very features of the frigate – its low-built, narrow hull which sacrificed firepower for speed – were at least partly lost as the second generation of frigates were enlarged, given a higher structure and more heavily gunned.

At first, this upper deck did not carry guns along its whole length. But by the end of the Commonwealth the upper deck had become not only continuous but also largely closed in, and a new platform built over it forwards meant that the forecastle was re-emerging at

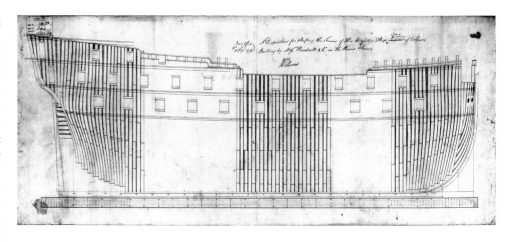

a high level – although this was not to carry ordnance until much later in the century. The quarterdeck above the upper deck was now a more solid structure, capable of carrying several light guns.

Gunports were cut along the length of this upper deck, at first on the part that had previously been the half-deck and forecastle, but soon along its whole length. Gunports were also cut in the beakhead and stern bulkheads, to provide for end-on fire during chases. Along each broadside the two-deckers had eventually eleven or twelve gunports positioned on the upper deck, usually the same allocation as on the lower deck although in some cases the lower deck had one extra port per side. The two Fourth Rates designed and built by William Castle in 1654 were exceptions, as Castle provided a thirteenth gunport along each side on the upper deck, one more than for the lower deck; Henry Johnson had a similar layout for the gunports of one ship he built at Deptford in this period, but it is likely that he used Castle's designs for this vessel.[38]

Whatever the layout of gunports, it is important to realise that guns were not stationed at every gunport. The actual ordnance carried by a warship altered significantly throughout the seventeenth century, as different layouts were used, worn guns were removed and newly-forged weapons brought aboard. The Establishment of Guns allocated to any ship altered regularly during her service, and even guns actually carried were not necessarily placed on the deck to which they were assigned in the official Establishment. Guns of varying force, length and calibre were

Two tiers of ordnance required substantial framing, as revealed in this draught for the *Jupiter* at Rotherhithe in 1776 (also used for her sister, *Isis*). Details of framing changed gradually throughout the wooden ship era, and up to about the middle of the eighteenth century, despite the Establishments, even varied between Dockyards. Thereafter, framing draughts of this nature are more common, indicating that the ship's structure has become as much a concern for the designer as the hull form and layout. The blank sections repeated the pattern demonstrated amidships, and was probably intended to save on draughting effort as the building programmes were expanded for the American War. (NMM: DR1482)

This plan view of a Navy Board model of a 50-gun ship of the 1706 Establishment (dated about 1715) shows the structure of the the transverse beams supporting the upper deck, quarterdeck and poop (roundhouse roof). The 'aerodynamic' shaping of the quarter galleries is most evident. (NMM: 2402)

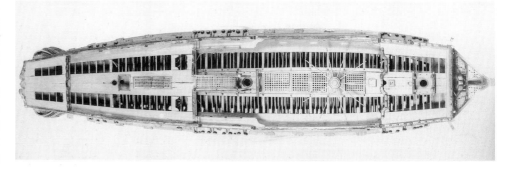

Table 88: Dimensions of the 1706 Establishment for 50-gun ships – dimensions in feet and inches

Length on the gundeck	130 0	Breadth overall	35 0	Height in hold	14 0
Length on the keel	108 0	Breadth of the transom	20 8	Height of orlop	5 10
Length of the forecastle	25 0	Tumblehome	3 7		
Length of the waist	56 8			Draught forward	14 6
Length of the quarterdeck	51 6	Number of ports on a tier	12	Draught abaft	16 0
Length of the roundhouse	14 0	Distance between ports	7 6		

Height of LD ports from water (midships)		4 6	Height of LD ports from the beam	2 2
Height of forecastle from the UD	fwd	5 6	LD ports length × height	2 9 × 2 5
	aft	5 6	Height of UD ports from the beam	1 6
Height of QD from the UD	fwd	5 10	UD ports length × height	2 3 × 2 1
	aft	6 5	Height of QD ports to the sill	1 2
Height of Lower Deck at the side	fwd	6 5	QD ports length × height	2 0 × 1 10
	mid	6 5		
	aft	6 8		

Source: NMM PNS/1 (Shipbuilder's Notebook, 1706–16).

Various internal changes took place to the 50-gun layout during the 1720s, as is shown by the *Lichfield* following her rebuilding. The main magazine, its structure previously supported on a separate platform just a few feet lower than the orlop deck, has been lowered several feet and has now become part of the hold. The gap between the two platforms that form the cockpit and the cable tiers has narrowed, and on their way to merge into a single orlop deck. (NMM: DR1458)

carried in an assortment on each deck, and it was not until later in the century that the Admiralty began to impose order and rationalise the layout of guns to insure that weapons of one rating and calibre were mounted on the same deck, and to match the number of gunports to the guns on that deck. At the same time, as the number of guns carried by Fourth Rates was increased, the easiest procedure was clearly to station them in the gunports initially left vacant.

The size of gunports was laid down in the Establishments and – like other dimensions – altered over the years. The largest guns required the larger ports. Table 88 shows the size of the ports fixed for each class of gun in 1706, and these dimensions were gradually enlarged later in the century.

Layout of the decks

By the start of the Hanoverian period (1714), therefore, the basic features of the 50-gun ship had settled down, and it is necessary to consider a layout which was to survive with minor modifications (and gradual enlargements) over the next hundred years. Apart

from the elm keel, the timber used in the construction was usually oak – English was preferred, but from 1677 increasing use was made of supplies from the Baltic, and in 1787 permission was given for other types of wood to be used for some of the less vital parts of the ship.[39] Internally, thick strakes and knees were added to provide support for the deck beams, which were securely bolted to the frames at the sides. The two decks which ran the full length of the ship, from stempost to sternpost, were the upper deck and the lower or gundeck. The latter retained its name from its origins as the only continuous deck to carry guns. Below it a further deck – the *orlop* – did not run the entire length of the ship because of the narrowness of the bow and stern structures, but provided a partial deck or platform which allowed additional space for storage below the waterline. By about 1800 this platform was continuous from almost the stempost to aft of the mizzen.

As the orlop deck did not have to bear the massive weight of guns and their carriages, it was of lighter construction than those above it, and for a similar reason had less headroom than the decks where space was required to work the guns. It carried the anchor cables, and provided permanent storerooms for much of the ship's equipment as well as sleeping areas for some of the warrant and petty officers. The carpenter, boatswain and gunner each had storerooms forward on this deck, and the sailroom was also found here, midships between the cable tiers. Many of the petty officers of the ship were content to berth here, away from the inconveniences of the gundeck above.

Aft of the cables was the cockpit, flanked by additional storerooms for the captain's and lieutenants' belongings, for clothing and other purser's stores, and cabins for some warrant officers such as the purser and surgeon. The cockpit itself served as quarters where the midshipmen and master's and surgeon's mates were berthed. In action, the cockpit was taken over by the surgeon and used as his operating theatre. While

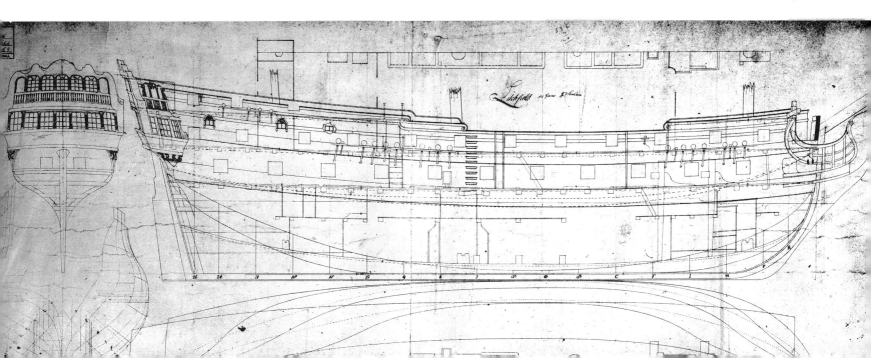

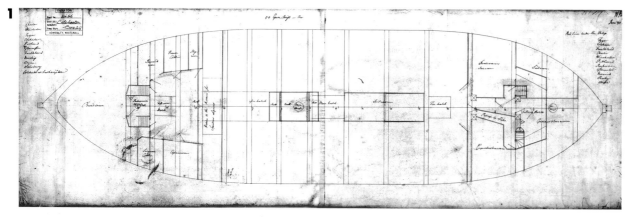

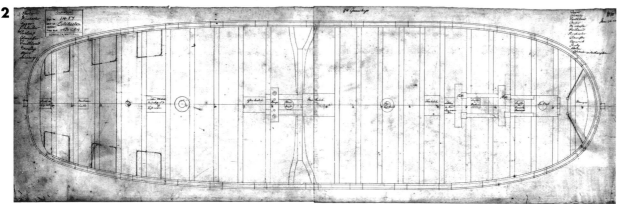

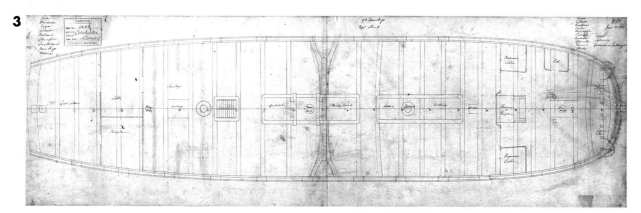

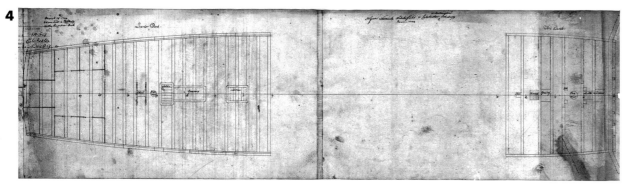

1. This traditional layout for the orlop deck, retained for the 1741 Establishment designs, shows the accommodation aft for the surgeon and purser, plus various storerooms, clustering around the cockpit. The cable tiers occupy the main part of this deck – on either side of the sailroom and the hatchways along the centreline – and are flanked by walkways (not shown) kept clear for the carpenter and his mates to gain access to any leaks along the waterline. (NMM: DR1486)

2. The 1741 Establishment gundeck shows the temporary cabins. Other than the low walls of the manger forwards, where livestock were secured, little permanent structure interfered with the operation of the main battery in the space along both sides of the centreline hatches, but the majority of seamen and marines were required to berth here, and with little sunlight or ventilation (the gunports, only a few feet above the waterline here, were required to be secured tightly while at sea – other than in action), the air was always fetid and fume-ridden. (NMM: DR1487)

3. The captain's accommodation in the 50-gun ship remained on the upper deck until the 1750s; it comprised the after half of the area under the quarterdeck, and was divided into the Great Cabin right aft (with its stern lights providing good illumination) and the captain's dining area (or lobby) and bedplace forwards of this. The area sheltering under the quarterdeck extended forward to the after hatch, including the main companionway to the lower deck. Under the forecastle, the cook-room included not only the galley firehearth but also accommodation for the cook, while separate access through the forecastle bulkhead was to the carpenter's and boatswain's cabins. (NMM: DR1488)

4. The 1741 Establishment design for the quarterdeck and forecastle shows few changes from previous decades. The wheel remains aft of the mizzen mast, and the lieutenants' accommodation is still in the roundhouse; the latter has, however, been greatly enlarged by additional cabins and the four gunports a side have been shifted forwards to make room for this. (NMM: DR1489)

lacking any form of natural light and ventilation except that which crept down through companionways and hatches, the orlop deck had the advantage that its contents did not have to be stowed away when the guns were cleared for action, while – being below the waterline – it was relatively safe from enemy fire.

Below the orlop, the floor of the hold provided the bulk of the storage space for ballast and the provisions and stores required for a protracted voyage. Pigs of iron ballast were laid down on either side of the keelson, and shingle ballast was laid on top of this. Casks of water and spirits were stowed in the shingle, and other supplies were added. Separate areas of the hold were partitioned off to create specialist storage areas.

This midships section through the *Jupiter* (1813) shows the latest structural developments of this period, the chocks, flat iron knees and iron plate knees that increasingly replaced wooden hanging and lodging knees in the role of transverse fastenings. These improvements were partly an attempt to strengthen the larger and longer ships of the time, but also a response to acute shortages of natural 'grown' knees. These twin pressures were eventually to produce Seppings' diagonal system. (NMM: DR1508)

Most secure among these was the main magazine and its adjacent filling room, just aft of the fore mast; forwards of this lay the *fore-peak*, used to store wood and coal for the galley stove. Below the cockpit were separate rooms for fish (because of its smell) and spirits (for reasons of security) as well as the after powder room and, right aft, the bread room.

Above the orlop deck, the *gundeck* was more massively constructed to take the weight of the ship's principal battery. The 50-gun ship usually carried its twenty-two heaviest guns here, and in action virtually the whole of this space had to be cleared of obstructions. The after section was the *gunroom*, originally the home of the gunner but by the eighteenth century shared with other warrant officers including the chaplain and marine lieutenants. In the early years cabins here were permanent, although bulkheads could not interfere with the movement of the tiller. In 1757 it was instructed that this area had to be kept clear, so that only temporary cabins, which could be rapidly dismantled for action, were allowed here. In the gunroom also, those boys aspiring to become midshipmen found a home. But the bulk of the ship's complement were required to sling their hammocks and lay out their mess tables in the restricted spaces above and between the monster weapons they served during battle.

One deck above, the *upper deck* was organised on similar lines, although the scantlings which bore its weight could be somewhat less and the space between the guns fractionally more, as the weapons here were a little smaller than on the gundeck. Until the 1757 reforms, the area at the stern, under the quarterdeck, was occupied by the relatively spacious accommodation for the captain, while his lieutenants and the master were accommodated in the roundhouse on the quarterdeck above; after 1757, the positions were reversed, with the lieutenants establishing themselves on the upper deck around the area that became known as the *wardroom*. Forward along this deck, cabins were placed for the boatswain and carpenter on opposite sides of the ship by the bulkhead of the forecastle, while the space forward of this bulkhead was occupied by the galley.

Under the 1745 Establishment, the 50-gun ship reached the dimensions that the 60-gun ship had enjoyed before the war. All dimensions were enlarged in proportion; for example, the breadth of the transom was now 25ft. The gunports, now required to carry the larger ordnance of the 1743 Establishment, measured 3ft 3in long by 2ft 7in high on the lower deck, and were now 2ft 3in above the beam; the ports on the upper deck and quarterdeck were now 2ft 8in by 2ft 7in and 2ft 5in by 2ft 4in respectively, the former being 20in above the beam and the latter measuring 18in in height to the sill. Internally the headroom also improved, with the height on the orlop deck and on the upper deck each becoming 6ft 8½in between plank and plank; the gundeck had an additional ½in.

In the 1750s it required over 100,000 cubic ft of timber to construct the hull of an average 50-gun ship. Large amounts of wood were measured in *loads*, a precise term equal to fifty cubic ft. Table 89 illustrates the amounts required for the 1745 Establishment *Falmouth* and the *Romney* (of a design modified from this Establishment), both launched in 1752. By the close of the 1780s, the amount required was estimated at over 140,000 cubic ft.

Table 89: Timber required to build the *Falmouth* and *Romney* (both 1752) in loads and cubic feet

	Falmouth		Romney	
	Loads	Cu ft	Loads	Cu ft
Straight oak timber	813	34	318	45
Compass ditto	810	17	1065	13
Elm timber	69	41	28	15
Fir timber	108	22	1412	23
Knees. square	47	46	76	49
Raking	105	45	56	46
'Thick stuff' (*) of 10in	0	22	78	43
of 9in	0	49	0	42
of 8in	3	14	4	30
of 7½in	42	7	18	10
of 7in	38	17	7	15
of 6½in	27	9	39	20
of 6in	25	12	19	10
of 5½in	28	19	45	35
of 5in	33	41	32	5
English oak plank of 4in	94	17	75	10
of 3in	45	22	95	13
of 2½in	0	30	45	43
of 2in	0	0	8	21
Danzig oak of 4in	106	31	114	22
of 3in	12	22	11	35
Elm plank of 4in	9	42	5	42
of 3in	0	10	0	10
Total	2425	19	2151	18

Source: Charnock, *History of Marine Architecture*. Note one load equals 50 cubic feet.
* heavy pieces of longitudinal planking in the hold, nailed internally over the joins in the futtocks.

Decoration

The elaborate decoration of English warships by woodcarving, gilding and painting began during the Tudor period but developed enormously around the start of the seventeenth century. The Stuart monarchs enthusiastically ensured that virtually every external (and many internal) surface of a King's ship above the waterline was lavishly decorated, and on inheriting their Navy in 1649 the Commonwealth leaders did not let their Puritan attitudes interfere with the continuation of the practice, although the iconography changed to reflect different political ideals. Models and portraits surviving from this era show extensive carving of the stern, head and broadside on vessels of every size, though the greatest care and expense was lavished on the larger ships.

The Restoration saw the replacement of the Commonwealth emblems adorning all vessels by royal regalia. The Stuart coat of arms was returned to the counter. The next forty years saw the most baroque ornamentation, in English as in foreign warships, as monarchs vied for the status they believed bestowed by such brilliantly intricate work.[40]

In 1700 the Admiralty took the first steps towards curbing the excessive carving and painting which added so much to the cost of a warship, and in June 1703 a more detailed Order reduced the carving to a lion figurehead (usually gilded) and trailboard, taffrail and two quarter pieces, with mouldings replacing

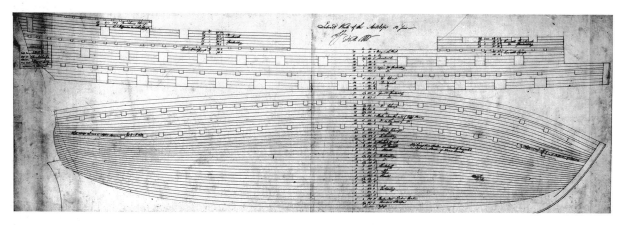

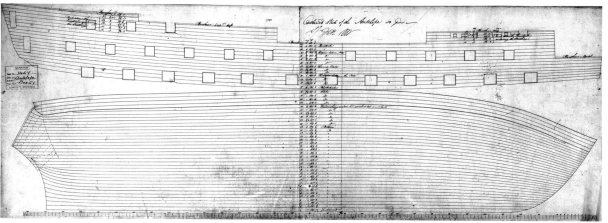

The planking expansions – for inboard work and for outboard – for the *Antelope* of 1802 are deliberately distorted to reflect the length and relative position as well as the width of each of the strakes of planking from the garboard (faired into the keel) up to the top of the roundhouse. Internally there were 50 strakes – 42 up to the quarterdeck and forecastle beams (*ie* to the waist) and 8 more for the upperworks; externally there were 55 strakes – the first 49 to the waist, of which levels 33 to 36 were the 'thick stuff' of 7¼in material which formed the main wales, and levels 41 to 43 were of 4½in thickness to form the channel or upper wales. (NMM: DR1406 and 1407)

carved brackets both around the head and the stern galleries; the remainder of the elaborate carvings, including the port wreaths, were abolished.[41] After a few years, a newer and less lavish form of decoration began to emerge.

From the 1740s permission was granted for ships to have more individual figureheads, usually relevant to the ship's name, instead of the standard lion; from the 1760s these were painted in various colours rather than in gilt, and a decade later there was a general move towards simpler, smaller figureheads; a later attempt in the 1790s to replace carved figureheads with wooden scrolls proved highly unpopular and was abandoned. Uniformity of colour was likewise not achieved; notwithstanding the impression often given that all ships were painted black with horizontal strakes of 'yellow' (in effect the yellow ochre used was closer to a modern beige), as specified by an Admiralty Order of 1780 in practice many variations persisted.

The practice of displaying a ship's name on her stern – specifically, on her second counter (the one directly below the stern lights on the upper deck) – although common to most Continental navies since the early seventeenth century, was not adopted by the Royal Navy until 1771. Initially, all names were to be in 12in high letters, enclosed in a 'surround' or box, but a year later the requirement for the surround was dropped, and the letters were ordered to be made as large as the counter would permit.

Underwater protection

Even when their activities were confined to the cooler waters around Europe, the durability and performance of British warships – like the ships of other countries – had been hampered by the growth of weed and barnacles, cutting their effective speed until such time as their underwater hull could be cleaned. As a consequence every ship had to be periodically docked or careened and the infestations scraped off. The marine growth would also speed up the decay of the ship's hull underwater, shortening its life (the average age of most wooden ships in the age of sail was under twenty years) and requiring periodic repair.

A variety of means were used to clean the hull. *Caulking* the hull with oakum forced between the seams to ensure watertight joints was done during construction, sometimes renewed when the ship was dry-docked or careened. *Tallowing* – coating the hull with a mixture of tallow and soap – was sometimes employed. The most common action in service was *graving*, using various combination of anti-fouling compounds, known by different names in the dockyards. During the seventeenth century *white stuff* was a mixture of fish or whale oil, pine-tree rosin and brimstone (sulphur); the less expensive *black stuff* which replaced it early in the eighteenth century was composed of tar and pitch; and in the 1740s *brown stuff* was introduced as a compromise between the other types, made of brimstone mixed in with black stuff.

When the Navy began to voyage into the warmer waters of the Caribbean and other semi-tropical zones, a more serious danger to the ship was the spread of the shipworm *teredo navalis*, and similar crustacean borers like *limnoria* (gribble), whose voracious burrowing rapidly weakened a ship's underwater planking. The two problems were related but required different means of countering them, and more than a century of experimentation were required before effective solutions were found.

Until the last quarter of the eighteenth century, the most common means of protecting the hull from worm was by wooden sheathing, that is, by coating the hull with a mixture of tar and hair, covered and held in place by a thin layer of planking. Various compositions were tried to deter the growth of marine life, but no coating proved very effective. In the late seventeenth century Anthony Deane attempted the sheathing of the lower hull with lead, but electrolytic reaction between the lead, seawater and the iron bolts fastening the lead to the timbers caused rapid decay.

Experiments with both lead and copper sheathing continued intermittently for nearly a century. Copper

For a short period in the 1770s, builders were instructed to supply the Navy Board with draughts of each ship 'as completed'. These often included very detailed depictions of the decorative work at bow and stern, an excellent example being this draught of the *Isis* – although the annotation suggests it is a design draught. Note the name shown prominently on the lower counter and the carving on the trailboards below the figurehead. (NMM: DR1481)

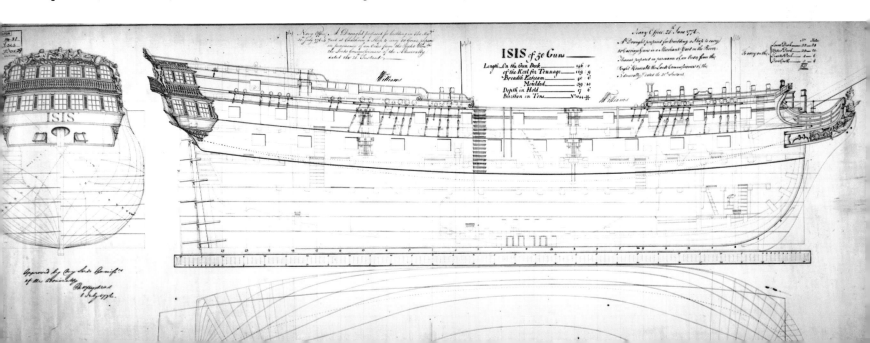

proved more durable than lead, but the problem of electrolysis continued until it was realised that replacing the iron bolts and nails by copper ones would minimise the problem. Nevertheless, the high cost of replacing iron nails by copper ones put off the Admiralty from adopting this radical solution until the late 1770s.[42]

The need to expand the Navy rapidly to meet the requirements of the North American emergency led the Navy Board to review any means of extending ships' lives and reducing the proportion of time they had to spend in dock. Notwithstanding the high cost of replacing iron bolts throughout the fleet with copper ones (at least, where seawater could reach), the Navy introduced copper sheathing and bolting for a substantial part of the fleet. To protect the fittings on the hull, the Navy also introduced a layer of thick brown paper between the hull planking and the copper plates which served to insulate the hull fittings from the effects of the copper. During the war, the step proved so cost-effective in extending the seatime of ships of every class, and improving their speed, that by 1783 the Navy was well on its way to having such work done on all its ships.

Ships were not coppered during the actual process of construction, but after launch, whether from a dockyard slipway or by a merchant builder; they were towed into a dockyard's dry-dock where the sheathing could be added while other items of the ship's fitting out were also effected. The sheathing process was not permanent, but had to be renewed – sometimes several times – during a ship's life, as the copper plates tended to wear away or suffer from underwater knocks and scrapes. This renewal was the most important part of the ship's periodic dockyard maintenance, amounting sometimes to a simple patching of damaged plating but at other times requiring a complete and costly removal of the existing covering and its replacement by new plating.

The copper was installed in the form of plates each measuring 4ft long and 14in deep, with varying grades of thickness depending upon the wear they were intended to face. The thickest plates (graded as 32oz of metal per square foot covered) were in the bows, the middle grade (28oz per square foot) in the section of hull behind the bows, and the thinnest (22oz) covered the rest of the hull. Initially plating ceased about a foot below the waterline, but in 1783 it was ordered that the plating should be extended to cover up to 16in above the waterline.[43] The plates were bolted onto the

Table 90: Coppering of selected 50-gun ships 1780–1802

Vessel	Built at	Launched	Sailed	Coppered* at	from – to	Sailed
Hannibal	Bucklers Hard	26.12.1779	1.1780	Portsmouth Dyd	6.1.1780–?	22.2.1780
Adamant	Liverpool	24.1.1780	6.1780	Plymouth Dyd	1.7–17.7.1780	12.8.1780
Leander	Chatham Dyd	1.7.1780	–	Chatham Dyd	?	21.8.1780
Pr.Caroline	Rotterdam	(1748)	(prize)	Woolwich Dyd	9.3–19.6.1781	25.8.1781
Rotterdam	Rotterdam	(1761)	(prize)	Portsmouth Dyd	24.4–9.6.1781	14.9.1781
Assistance	Liverpool	12.3.1781		Plymouth Dyd	19.10–1.11.1781	31.12.1781
Cato	Gravesend	29.5.1782	5.1782	Woolwich Dyd	1.6–12.6.1782	10.8.1782
Trusty	Bristol	9.10.1782	–	Bristol	?	7.1.1783
Grampus	Liverpool	8.10.1782	7.1.1783	Plymouth Dyd	?	18.3.1783
Europa	Woolwich Dyd	19.4.1783	–	Woolwich Dyd	?	10.9.1783
Leopard	Sheerness Dyd	24.4.1790	26.5.90	Chatham Dyd	28.5–1.6.1790	3.6.1790
Diomede	Deptford Dyd	17.1.1798	–	Deptford Dyd	17.1–2.3.1798	11.5.1798
Grampus	Portsmouth Dyd	20.3.1802	–	Portsmouth Dyd	20.3–23.3.1802	11.4.1803
Antelope	Sheerness Dyd	10.11.1802	–	Sheerness Dyd	10–24.11.1802	15.3.1803

* fitted for sea at same dockyard before sailing, except *Leopard* which returned to Sheerness for fitting on 3 June, finally sailing thence on 9 July 1790. This table excludes the smaller *Experiment* and *Medusa*, and also the prizes and purchases of 1795–1802.

wood with 4in copper nails, allowing a small overlap of neighbouring plates to prevent the penetration of crustacea. At first the plates were only nailed to the planking around each's edges, but in time it was found that the plate was sealed more tightly to the wood if nails were spaced across its surface as well.

Over 2000 copper plates were need to cover the hull of a 50-gun ship. Table 91 shows the amounts and costs used for the new *Hannibal* in 1780.[44] A Navy Board Establishment issued shortly after provided a standard allowance at a slightly higher level, with a further £1103 added for providing and fixing the copper bolts.

Normally considered as part of the sheathing process was the fabrication of the gudgeons (or braces) and pintles (originally 'pintails') used to hinge the rudder. Originally these were made of iron and subject to rapid deterioration, but by 1768 they were manufactured of a copper alloy by a single specialist contracting firm, William Forbes of Deptford. The 50-gun ship had four of each item, typically weighing about 23¾cwt (see Table 91 below).

Table 91: Materials used in sheathing the *Hannibal* (1780) with copper, together with the weight of each article and the value of materials and workmanship.

2010 copper sheets, weighing 6 ton 12cwt	Value of all materials	£1032
40½ cwt of copper nails (4in length)	Value of workmanship	£67
4 braces and pintles weighing 23¾cwt	Total	£1099

9. Manpower and Accommodation

Throughout its history, the small two-decker was the most cramped for accommodation of all ship types except the small brigs lacking a continuous lower deck. Virtually all the ratings were berthed on the lower deck, sharing their accommodation with the ship's battery of largest guns. A minority, essentially selected petty officers and idlers, were allowed to berth in the cable tier or occasionally in the hold. Whereas on a frigate the unarmed lower deck could be largely given over to sleeping and messing area for the seamen, marines and servants (except aft, reserved for the officers), in the two-decker the men had to find what space they could between the guns. There were two mitigating factors: the headroom on the lower deck had to be sufficient to work the guns without severe discomfort, so designers, while never generous, ensured that the height to the bottom of the beams above was almost never less than 5½ft; and they had light and air through the gunports when weather allowed these to be opened, in addition to the small amount received through the gratings in the upper deck.

By the middle of the seventeenth century the hammock, adopted from the traditional *hammacoes* of the Caribbean indigenous inhabitants (the original name remained the more common usage throughout the era of sail), had come into general use, supplanting the straw-filled palliasses or mattresses of Elizabethan times. Constructed from a piece of hempen cloth, 6ft long and 3ft wide, gathered together at each end by a clew or arrangements of small lines of rope and slung from hooks in the deck beams above, each hammock had its own numbered place which was carefully marked out on the deckhead; inside the hammock each seaman had his bedding, consisting of a bed or mattress of dry rag flocks or wool, a bolster or pillow, a blanket, and a *coverlet* or second blanket. While the hammocks were provided by the Navy, and issued by the boatswain on loan, one to each man (by the end of the eighteenth century, two were allowed to each man), the bedding was the property of the seaman, who had to buy it from the purser if he did not bring his own aboard.

With certain privileged exceptions, all petty officers and ratings slung their hammocks from the deckhead beams in a fore-and-aft position. Throughout the era of sail, each seaman was allowed no more than 14in of width for this, although it must be remembered that when at sea, with a proportion of the crew being on watch at any time, the space actually occupied by the hammocks of those men asleep could be up to twice the width. In harbour the congestion must have been horrendous, eased perhaps by arranging for alternative hammocks to be slung at slightly different levels. Petty officers were each allowed 28in, twice the allocation for a seaman.

Upon change of watch, those rising had to lash up their hammocks to make room for those coming off watch; each morning, all hammocks except for those men excused as sick had to be tightly lashed, with all bedding stowed out of sight inside them, and (from the middle of the eighteenth century) brought up on the upper deck and stowed in netting racks provided along the bulwarks of the ship.

While commissioned and senior warrant officers were able to have the privacy of their own cabins in most cases, such cabins were rarely permanent structures except in the case of the captain, who throughout the period had as much advantage over his officers as they had over the ordinary ratings. Apart from the captain's Great Cabin aft, and a few dank places below the waterline on the orlop deck, all cabins had to be cleared away in action, as most were shared by its human occupants with a carriage gun around which the officer would have to arrange himself. The occupants of most cabins slept in their own cots, a box-like frame with canvas stretched over the sides, containing their bedding and suspended from the beams above.

The *Mordaunt* was built as a private venture in early 1681, and was purchased by the Navy two years later. The numerous figures give a good sense of the smallness of these ships and the relative crowding on board. (NMM: VV598)

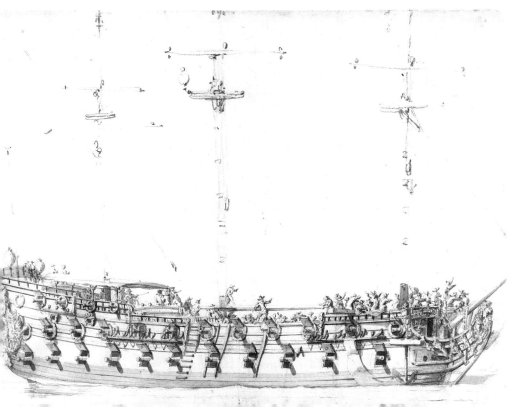

Traditionally, the captain was accommodated in the stern on the upper deck. Indeed, his accommodation occupied virtually the whole area here below the quarterdeck, on top of which were the cabins for his lieutenants, his clerk and the sailing master. From early times, the captain's Great Cabin spanned the width of the ship, and here he worked, ate and slept. Forward of this, and separated from it by a permanent transverse bulkhead, was the steerage, where prior to the introduction of the wheel the helmsman controlled the whipstaff to govern the movement of the rudder.

In the early years of the eighteenth century the development of the wheel enabled the helmsman to be moved to the quarterdeck, the change being introduced to the Fourth Rates during the last few years of Queen Anne's reign. This enabled the captain to fully take over the steerage area (which retained its name) for his own greater comfort. It was divided into two areas separated by a fore-and-aft bulkhead into a larger compartment to larboard usually called the coach (used as office accommodation or dining area) and a smaller one to starboard into which the captain could now move his sleeping area or bedplace.

The Established complement and their pay

The Commonwealth, faced with a massive expansion in the size of the fleet, took the first steps to regularise both pay and conditions in the Navy. Following the Civil War, the new Navy Commissioners drew up revised pay scales for both officers and men. From the start of 1653, able seamen were paid 24/- a month, ordinary seamen 19/-, 'gromets' (an intermediate class at this period) 14/3d and boys 9/6d. For Fourth Rates, the captain was to receive £10 a month (unchanged since 1647) and his lieutenant 70/-. The (sailing) master was paid 86/2d a month and his mate 47/10d, while midshipmen had 33/9d; the other principal warrant officers – boatswain, carpenter, gunner, surgeon and purser – each received 50/-, and their deputies – the boatswain's and gunner's mates, quartermaster and corporal – 30/- (the carpenter's mate slightly more at 34/-). Among the other petty officers, quartermaster's mates had 28/- and master trumpeters 25/-, as did cooks. These rates, in an age when inflation was not thought of, were with certain exceptions to remain unchanged for 144 years. In total, the first establishment of officers and men for Fourth Rates was fixed at 130 (compared with 140 for Third Rates). By the Restoration this had already been raised to 150 (160 for Third Rates).

Early in the Second Dutch War, it began to be appreciated that the existing level of manning was seriously underestimating the needs of the wartime service. In July 1666, a great many ships were granted temporary increases to last for the duration of the war. Most of the Fourth Rates immediately before this time had complements established at between 170 and 200 – the smaller 40- or 44-gun ships had fewer, and the larger or newer ships reached 220 (for the *Princess*, *Saint David* and *Saint Patrick*) and an exceptional 250 (for *Leopard*) or 260 (for *Greenwich*), at which latter figure it matched that of some of the Third Rates.

These figures are in each case the highest establishment of men, that allocated for war service in the near seas. For foreign service in war, a somewhat lower complement was fixed, while each ship had also a third figure, the lowest, which was for the complement allowed in peacetime. In 1666 the 'war abroad' figure for each Fourth Rate was from 120 to 145 men (a few of the larger ships had more) and the peacetime figure ranged from 100 to 120 men. When 'peacetime' levels were re-attained after the war, these were already in excess of the levels that had been assigned for wartime service previously.

In July 1673, Pepys presented to the Navy Board proposals for an Establishment of cabins.[45] These set out, among other types, that Fourth Rates should be provided with the following:

On the poop – trumpeters' cabins (2 cabins).
The round house (if divided) – the master and lieutenant (2 cabins).
In the cuddy – 2 mates.
Bulkhead of the steerage – the carpenter (on the starboard side) and the boatswain (on the larboard side).
In the steerage – a land officer and a midshipman.
Pantry for the captain.
Forecastle bulkhead – the cook (on the starboard side) and the boatswain's mate (on the larboard side).
In the gunroom bulkhead – the gunner and the surgeon.
Between decks:
In the cockpit – the purser, the steward, and the surgeon's mate.

The 1706 Establishment model from the stern. The captain's gallery on the upper deck and its closed quarter galleries are prominent, while the ordinary windows of the roundhouse above illuminate the lieutenant's quarters. Note the stern frames just visible behind the transoms. This was the traditional arrangement of officers' accommodation until the middle of the century. (NMM: A9952)

Table 92: Complements of Fourth Rates, 1666 and 1670

Vessel	1666	1670	Vessel	1666	1670	Vessel	1666	1670
Pre-1649 types:			Assistance	170	170	Crown	170	180
Expedition	140	–	Centurion	180	170			
Providence	140	–				Broad-beam		
			Diamond	180	170	type:		
Cons't Warwick	150	170	Ruby	170	180	Newcastle	200	240
Assurance	150	160				Yarmouth	200	180
Adventure	150	150	1652 Group:			Happy Return	190	180
Dragon	160	160	Kent	170	180	Leopard	250	250
Tiger	160	160	Hampshire	160	170	Princess	220	180
Elizabeth	160	–	Portland	180	180			
			Bristol	200	180	1663-1667:		
1649 Group:			Swallow	180	170	Bonaventure	180	180
Portsmouth	160	180	Antelope	190	180	(RB)		
Sapphire	160	160	Jersey	190	180	Greenwich	260	250
Reserve	180	180	Mary Rose	190	170	St David	220	?
Advice	180	180	Dover	170	170	St Patrick	220	–
Foresight	170	170						

The 1666 complement of men is taken from a document dated April 1666 preserved in the British Museum (Add 9302). Frank Fox, who reproduces it in *The Great Ships*, points out that these complements soon proved inadequate, and in July numerous ships were granted wartime increases. The 1670 figure is taken from Deane's *Doctrine of Naval Architecture*, with ships having reverted to peacetime levels.

The above table excludes the various prizes taken during up to the end of the Second Dutch War, which had all gone by 1670; in April 1666 of these the *Matthias* had 250 men, the *Charles V* 200 men, the *Convertine* and *Seven Oaks* each 190 men, the *Mars, Maria Sancta, West Friesland, Black Spread Eagle* and *Guilder de Ruyter* each 180 men, the *Hope* and *Golden Lion* each 170 men, the *Marmaduke, Saint Paul, Black Bull, Delfe* and *Zealand* each 160 men, and the *Amity, Guinea, Unity, Welcome* and *Young Prince* each 150 men.

Captain's storeroom.

In the forecastle – the carpenter's mate and a midshipman.

In February 1686 the Navy Board proposed a new Establishment of Wages, which *reduced* some warrant and petty officers' pay and included details of the numbers of officers of every type in each rate of ship. For the Fourth Rate, these comprised:

1 captain (paid £10 a month)
1 lieutenant (70/- per month)
6 warrant officers – master (77/6), boatswain (45/-), gunner (45/-), purser (45/-), carpenter (45/-), surgeon (50/-)
5 gunroom officers – 2 master's mates (42/- each), 3 midshipmen (30/- each)
Lesser warrant officers and petty officers, graded by monthly wage rate:
1 on 32/- (carpenter's mate)
3 on 30/- each (yeoman of the powder, surgeon's mate, captain's clerk)
5 on 28/- each (2 quartermasters, 1 boatswain's mate, 1 corporal, 1 gunner's mate)
4 on 26/- each (yeoman of the sheets, coxswain, 2 quartermasters' mates)
6 on 25/- each (cook, master trumpeter, 2 quarter

gunners, 2 ordinary carpenters)
2 on 24/- each (coxswain's mate, armourer)
1 on 20/8 (steward)

With the addition of the sailmaker (paid 4/- a month 'above what he receives in another quality') this produced a total of 2 commissioned and 34 warrant and petty officers. Thus in the 230 wartime manning total for the 48-gun ship, there were 194 'ratings', among which able seamen (including the cook's mate, cooper and swabber) received 24/- per month and the ordinary seamen 19/- per month. The total included ratings of lower status ('gromets'), boys and servants; each of the commissioned and warrant officers had a couple of servants – the captain being able to appoint a dozen although, apart from one or two personal servants, these would all be young boys being 'bred to the sea' (what we would now call 'cadets') and appointed by the captain as distinct from the higher-status midshipmen.

The manpower, of course, was related to the ordnance established for each ship. For example, the 24pdr was allotted five men per gun, the culverin and 12pdr were allotted four men per gun, and the demi-culverin, saker and minion had three men per gun, with two men per 3pdr; in practice, these numbers were doubled, as each gun crew managed a pair of guns, one on either beam. Thus the 54-gun *Leopard* was given 210 men for her guns (with 70 for all other purposes, including filling and carrying powder and shot, handling the sails, etc), and the 42-gun *Nonsuch* was given 126 men for her guns (and 54 for all other purposes).

By 1685 the situation had, with a few exceptions, crystallised into the following:

54/46 gun ships: 280/240/185 men.
50/44 gun ships: 240/210/155 men.
48/42 gun ships: 230/200/150 men.
46/40 gun ships: 220/185/140 men.

At this stage there is still only one lieutenant accommodated (although all higher rates by now had two or more). However, the table of pay rates adopted in June 1686 provided for Fourth Rates to carry *two* lieutenants and seven midshipmen.[46] The role of the lieutenant having become more defined during the preceding century, a number of lieutenants was established for each rate, with two lieutenants being included for each Third or Fourth Rate (a third lieutenant was added for Fourth Rates early in the eighteenth century, and a fourth Lieutenant in 1794). The 1686 Schedules of Wages also provided for up to seven midshipmen for a Fourth Rate, with most of the warrant and petty officers being established in the pattern that would exist throughout the next century. An exception lay in the function of trumpeter; in 1685 a master trumpeter and five ordinary trumpeters were established for every ship of the Fourth Rate and above, whereas by the close of the eighteenth century a single trumpeter remained on the establishment for each ship.

In 1693 the pay of captains was more than doubled, from £10 per month (of 28 days) to 15/- per day. At the same time the monthly pay of lieutenants, masters and surgeons were precisely doubled, going to £7, £8-12-4d and £5 respectively. This was a blatant attempt to improve the questionably loyalties of many officers, some of whom retained Jacobite sympathies, with the constant fear of treachery present.[47] It would be some years before the reforms instituted by the admirals of the last Stuarts would create the disciplined and trained naval officers of the Nelsonic age. In 1700, however, the pay of all but the surgeons was cut again, the captain coming down to 10/- a day, the lieutenants to 4/- a day and masters reduced to £5-12-0d a month. The new rates were to remain in force for the whole eighteenth century. Pay rates for other warrant officers, and all ratings, remained at the levels that had come into force in 1653.

The establishment became the common one for all the Fourth Rates other than the 60-gun ships; and with the abolition of the 48/42-gun class in 1704, the 280/240/185 complement became virtually universal. The transformation – initially on paper only – of the 54-gun Third Rate into the 50-gun ship with significantly heavier ordnance did not effect the manning levels, with 280 remaining the norm (the highest level or 'war abroad' category increasingly being the only figure quoted – although the lower levels of manpower in peacetime, or on home service in wartime, undoubtedly remained in use). The complements were not, in fact, raised again until the proposed 1733 Establishment, when it was raised to 300. This figure was to remain unchanged when the next Establishment was enacted in 1741.

The next increase in the established complement of the 50-gun ship took place in 1745, when it was raised to 350 (including 7 'widows' men') in order to provide for the increased gun crews required by the supplanting of 18pdr and 9pdr guns by heavier weapons. Although the highest complement was that universally quoted, in peacetime service ships were allocated a 'lowest' complement which amounted to 280 for a 50-gun ship. Tables of stores and victuals carried are included elsewhere in this volume, showing the volumes required for different conditions.

While the captain's entitlement of servants was increased from 12 to 14 (ie remaining at 4 per cent of the total complement), all the other additions were to the seamen in the crew, adding a man to the crew of every gun except the 6pdrs on the upperworks. The authorised complement was to remain at this level for the rest of the service life of the traditional 50-gun ship,

except for a minor reduction to 343 in 1794. The 1745 total included

4 commissioned sea officers (the Captain and three lieutenants), plus two lieutenants of marines;
6 warrant sea officers (master, boatswain, gunner, carpenter, surgeon and purser);
8 lesser warrant officers (chaplain, cook, schoolmaster, sailmaker, armourer, two surgeon's mates, master-at-arms);
2 master's mates;
10 midshipmen;
34 petty officers (captain's clerk, four quartermasters, four quartermasters' mates, two boatswain's mates, two yeomen of the sheets) coxswain, sailmaker's mate, gunner's mate, yeoman of the powder room, 12 quarter gunners, carpenter's mate, steward, two corporals, one 'trumpeter');
2 sailmaker's crew, 6 carpenter's crew, steward's mate, (26-)28 servants, (6-)7 widows' men, (137-)184 seamen (figures in parentheses show pre-1745 levels);
55 marine 'other ranks' (2 sergeants, 2 corporals, a drummer and 50 privates);
(by 1801 the number of privates fell to 43, but rose again to 52 by 1808).

In 1745 the captain's accommodation still occupied the after end of the upper deck, while cabins for the lieutenants and some warrant officers were in the roundhouse on the quarterdeck, with their roof forming the poop. Under the 1745 Establishment this remained unchanged, with the Order in Council confirming:

> That 50-gun ships have two cabins under the poop for the First Lieutenant and Master, and – as some of them will admit of two, and other of four, other cabins under the poop clear of all the guns on the quarterdeck, and a good passage left to the stern – that the said cabins be put up, where the ship will admit thereof.
>
> That 50 and 44 gun ships have two cabins on the gundeck, on the transom where there is room to put them up clear of the after guns, and two cabins in the forecastle for the boatswain and carpenter.
>
> That all the aforesaid cabins be put up with deal panels to slide in grooves, with battens on the deck instead of cants, so as to be taken down in a moment, in case there is occasion to make use of the stern ports.[48]

This clearly left certain officers without accommodation, and a subsequent Order provided that 'the other officers, who would not have cabins by the above regulation, be allowed double hammacoes and canvas curtains properly contrived to fall before them . . . in the gunroom on board 50- and 44-gun ships.'[49]

In June 1757 a significant change was agreed in this

internal layout, which was introduced for the newly-built *Chatham* and for the two new 50-gun ships ordered during the war. For some years captains had been increasingly envious of the more desirable location above them, and it was agreed that in future that the captain's accommodation – consisting of great cabin, *coach* (or dining room) and *bedplace* (sleeping cabin) – should occupy the roundhouse above while the lieutenants would be moved down to the upper deck, with their cabins grouped around a shared central area that became the wardroom. This change in layout was retro-fitted to the ships of the 1745 Establishment as the opportunity arose,[50] and probably also to the older *Centurion* and *Deptford* which, as former 60s, had been built to similar large dimensions.

That ships of 50 guns built by the Establishment of 1745 (or of dimensions equal thereto) to be fitted with a great cabin, bedplace and coach for the captain upon the quarterdeck; cabins for the carpenter and boatswain under the forecastle, for the purser and surgeon on the after platform, and to have their ward and gun rooms prepared for the accommodation of such other officers in the same manner as directed for the 74-, 70- and 60-gun ships. And for such ships of 50 guns as are of inferior dimensions, or may be already fitted with a great cabin, bedplace and coach for the captain *under* the quarterdeck, they are to continue so, but as the main capstan is now made with a double

barrel to heave on the upper deck, the foremost bulkhead of the coach is to be disposed of at such a distance abaft it so as to give sufficient room for the sweep there of the bars, and to have no other bulkhead before it.

And as most of this class of ships, though of small dimensions, have a roundhouse, there is to be parted off under the same for the first and second lieutenants (or master) – with a passage in the middle between them to the stern light – one cabin on each side before those for two other officers, and a small coach between them to be in common to all; and for such officers as were allowed cabins upon the quarterdeck; the gunroom is to be fitted with canvas berths for their accommodation, as directed on board the foregoing classes.[51]

In 1794 the established complement of the 50-gun ship (as well as those of other classes) – unchanged since 1745 – was revised from 350 to 343.[52] The total continued to include 5 'widow's men' (a theoretical number of dead men retained on the muster roll so that widows could receive pay) and 21 boys, of whom 'a fifth was to consist of young gentlemen volunteers, intended for officers',[53] but the number of officers' servants was cut by 8, while the only increase was the addition of a fourth lieutenant.

The organisation of the crew

Precise Establishments were laid down, as with most aspects of shipboard life, for the organisation of the crew when undertaking different duties. The allocation of seamen while working ship, for example, is set out in Table 93. Similar regulations were set out for most of the other conditions which ships regularly met (see Table 107 for the stations for mooring/unmooring ship).

The ratings were split between a number of equal-sized divisions for administrative purposes; these divisions, equal in number to the total of lieutenants, comprised all the ship's company except for the marines. Each lieutenant was responsible for the health and welfare of the men in his division, and exercised discipline through the master's mates or midshipmen in charge of the squads into which each division was sub-divided. Each division comprised men from the different parts of the ship and different stations, mixed in roughly equal numbers.

Excluding the officers, marines, servants and idlers, those who were required to stand their watch amounted to 251 of the 350 complement. This total included 33 petty officers, leaving 218 seamen. Each watch (most captains maintained a two-watch system) was divided into several 'parts of the ship' which allocated the watch-keeping men in it to different stations during normal sailing operations. There were essentially five 'parts' for this purpose; the fore top (28

This internal layout for 50-gun ships is dated 29 December 1756, six months before the decision to move the captain's accommodation to the quarterdeck – and to move the lieutenants and other wardroom officers down onto the upper deck. (NMM: DR8022a)

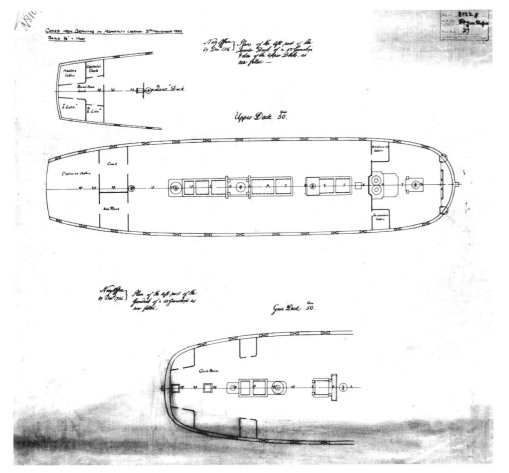

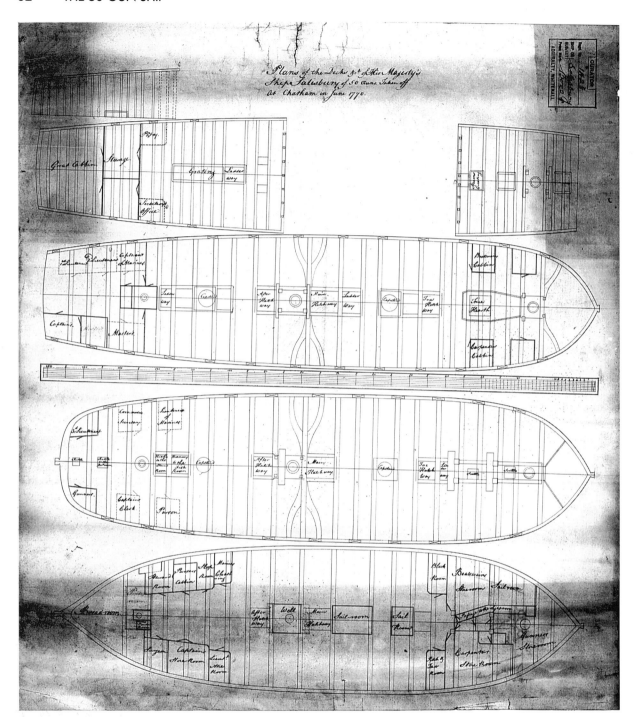

The deck plans of the *Salisbury* show the new layout of accommodation following the removal of the Great Cabin to the quarterdeck. Note this plan, taken off in June 1770, shows the Captain occupying a cabin on the upper deck, with the accommodation above obviously fitted out for a flag officer – a temporary cabin on the gundeck has been provided for a 'commodore's secretary'. (NMM: DR1428)

seamen in a 50-gun ship) and the main top (30 seamen) were generally the most skilled of the able seamen; the forecastle (32 men) were generally older seamen, as their work would not generally require them to go aloft; the afterguard (44 men) included the mizzen topmen, but was otherwise not generally expected to go aloft; finally the waist (84 men) included the least skilled of the seamen and the landsmen. Each 'part' was under the command of a petty officer termed the 'captain' of that part; since most ships were composed of two watches, this means ten of these petty officers, who held status but received (until 1806) no extra pay for their responsibilities.

In action, most of the crew were stationed at the ship's guns. The majority of the men (including warrant officers and servants) were allocated to individual gun crews, each manning this meant a pair of guns, one on each side of the ship. On the lower deck of the 50-gun ship during the 1780s, for example, there were 121 men comprising eleven crews for each pair of 24pdrs, while on the upper deck 96 men comprised twelve crews for each pair of 12pdrs, and the four 6pdrs on the quarterdeck had 12 men forming two crews. Another 50 men were equipped with small arms and stationed where they could direct their fire upon enemy personnel; 18 were allocated to the poop, 8 to the forecastle, another 18 in the tops (8 in the main top, 6 in the fore top and 4 in the mizzen top)

Table 93: Stations for working ship or performing other manoeuvres for a 50-gun ship (c1787)

Allocation of 265 seamen (i.e. excluding boys and idlers)			*15 Selected petty officers*
50 on forecastle	6 on the gangways	40 on quarterdeck	4 quartermasters (poop)
4 fore chains	4 main chains	53 on poop	4 quartermasters (deck)
8 in fore top	8 in main top	4 in mizzen top	4 boatswain's mates
	88 on the main deck (waist)		3 sergeant & corporals

Source: NMM SPB/15, p74.

while the other 6 were in the rigging (2 each in the fore, main and mizzen rigging); these men were also responsible for working the sails in action.

The various officers, of course, also had stations when the ship went into action. The captain's post was naturally on the quarterdeck, accompanied by the first lieutenant and the master, the captain's clerk (to keep a written record of instructions) and two midshipmen 'to pass the word'. One lieutenant (with a master's mate and two midshipmen) was posted on the upper deck, and another lieutenant (with three midshipmen) on the lower deck, where they had tactical control of the guns on those decks under the overall command of the captain. The captain of marines and one of his subalterns were stationed on the poop, while the other marine lieutenant was on the forecastle with the boatswain and the other master's mate. The remaining three midshipmen were allocated to the three lower tops, to take charge of the men there.

Below decks, the surgeon awaited casualties in the cockpit – along with his mates, the purser and the chaplain; the carpenter and his crew were stationed in the well of the hold and the wings (the passageways along the sides of the cable tiers), ready to patch any holes made 'between wind and water' by enemy shot. The cook took charge of the light room. Finally the yeomen for the three standing warrant officers were posted in their respective storerooms, to ensure that neither pilferage nor cowardice went unnoticed in the heat of battle.

Even in action, most seamen were also allocated subsidiary duties. Individual members of each gun crew (except for the two gun captains for that pair of guns) had to be ready to be called away to form boarding parties, to help trim the sails, or to operate the pumps if the ship was holed. For each of these duties, two men in each gun crew were earmarked, while one man was appointed to join the fire party if the ship was set alight, and another to fetch and hold a lantern in the event of night action. All this organisation required careful planning and training, and a knowledge of the abilities of every man aboard; the quarter bill for the ship was an invaluable document which named every man and set out all his responsibilities.

Off watch, the men were allowed some latitude to organise themselves. They were divided into 'messes' of up to a dozen men – this being the maximum number who could reasonably gather around the wooden tables around which each mess ate – but the seamen could choose their own messmates, subject to prescriptions on the maximum and minimum numbers each mess could include. There were mess tables interspersed between each pair of lower deck guns, along both sides of the ship.

Each table, constructed by the carpenter to match the space between two guns, could be pivoted up to the level of the deck beams when not required; in use, it was lowered to a horizontal position, with one end supported by a batten against the side planking and the other suspended from the deckhead beams. Removable benches ran along each side of the table, for the men to sit on, and their plates and utensils were also stored in a rack hung from the side of the ship. Each seaman also had a *ditty bag*, containing his bedding and spare clothing, which hung in the mess; his other belongings were kept below in wooden sea-chests, normally one of which was provided for every eight men.

The *Centurion*'s deck plans, more detailed than *Salisbury*'s, show the transverse beams below each deck, together with the structural members between them. (NMM: DR1369)

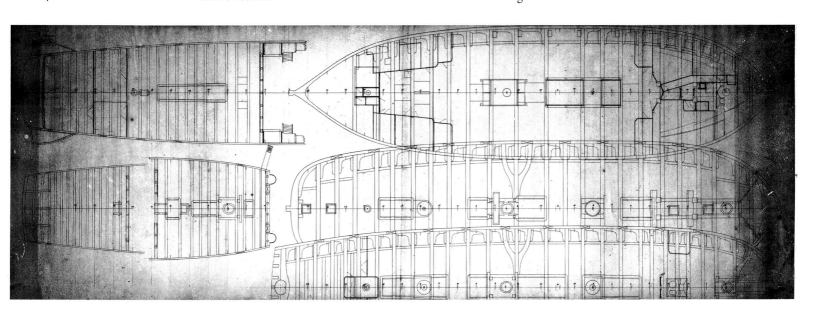

10. Masting and Rigging

All Fourth Rates – indeed, all rated ships – were three-masted vessels carrying square sails on the fore and main masts, and square topsails above a fore-and-aft sail set on the mizzen mast. Some early warships of the Elizabethan and early Stuart period had carried a fourth mast, the bonaventure mizzen, but by the middle of the seventeenth century this had disappeared. In addition, square 'sprit' sails were also carried on the bowsprit, while a variety of fore-and-aft sails were set between the masts and bowsprit. Late in the seventeenth century, extra 'stunsails' were introduced which when extra canvas was required could be set on extensions or booms to the yards that carried the square sails.

This simplistic picture masks an extraordinary array of specialist sails and rigging of enormous complexity which was used to set and control the sails. While several centuries of earlier development meant that further alterations during the last two centuries of the sailing era were incremental and evolutionary, there was a gradual process whereby the efficiency of the sails as a means of propulsion was refined, with additional topgallant yards and sails being introduced above the existing topsails as mast heights increased, the fitting of a spritsail topmast above the bowsprit, the increase in fore-and-aft rigged staysails between the masts, and in the eighteenth century the replacement of the three-sided lateen sail on the mizzen mast by a four-sided gaff sail, also rigged fore-and-aft but set between a gaff and boom, both spars being attached at their ends to the mast, instead of from one long yard suspended diagonally across it.

For a full discussion of the 'top hamper' of the three-masted ship of war, the reader is referred to such specialist works as James Lees' *The Masting and Rigging of English Ships of War 1625–1860*. The present book can only summarise the main features in so far as they relate to the 50-gun ship.

Masts

The construction of masts and yards was a highly specialised business, with the timber procured mainly from New England or the Baltic through commercial sources which lay largely outside the control of the Navy Board. Master mastmakers at each Royal Dockyard supervised the finishing of the spars where construction was carried out, usually after the launch of the completed hull which was then towed into position. Specialised vessels, 'sheer hulks', largely consisting of decommissioned former ships of the line specially rigged with 'sheers' or legs for the task of lifting the weighty and awkward masts and yards into position, were employed for the final fitting out of the new vessels, or for the refit of ships dismasted by heavy weather or enemy action.

Masts and bowsprit were strengthened by wolding and iron bands wound around the masts. The woldings were comprised of rope wound tightly around the masts, with enough turns to create a band about as deep as the diameter of the mast; the iron bands fastened above and below each wolding held it in place.

Each mast served a different function. The main mast, whose sails would take most of the stress of the wind, was much the largest, and was situated just aft of the mid-point of the hull, usually just aft of the break in the quarterdeck. It was usually raked slightly backwards, so that the shrouds which held it remained in tension and held it more firmly in place. Over the years the position of the main mast moved gradually forward, so that by the nineteenth century it had moved forwards of the mid-point of the gundeck, being about five-ninths of the gundeck's length from the sternpost.

The fore mast was usually raked very slightly forward, although occasionally it was practically vertical. When the wind was aft it provided most of the driving power of the ship, and its situation well forward of the centre of the ship gave it the prime role in keeping the ship on course. Thus it was initially set as far forward as possible, usually with its foot mounted over the rake of the stem rather than over the keel. In practice this interfered with the balance of the rig when the wind was other than from aft, and in the eighteenth century it was gradually moved aft, to finish about a ninth of

While most Van de Velde portraits of English warships are drawings, this detailed painting in oils by Van de Velde the Elder shows the *Woolwich* (1675) before a light breeze. It displays all the main features of the contemporary rig: sprit topmast at the end of the bowsprit, mizzen lateen, no mizzen topgallants, and no royals on any mast. The pre-1707 ensign flies from her stern, while on the sprit topmast the Union is fulfilling its proper role of jack. The high degree of giltwork and ornate carving typify a late seventeenth century warship. (NMM: BHC3732)

Table 94: Rope used for wolding masts for ships of 50 guns, as established 1764

Mast	Size (in)	Length (fathoms)	Weight Cwt lbs	Value £ -s -d
Fore mast, main mast & bowsprit	3	420	9 38¼	14-0-3¼
Mizzenmast	2	75	1 20½	1-15-5¾

Source: NMM SPB/15, p30. Note this Establishment gave 44-gun ships and 36-gun frigates the same allowance as 50-gun ships.

Table 95: Length and diameters of masts and yards for a Fourth Rate, 1670 (Deane's *Doctrine of Naval Architecture*)

Spar	Length defined as	Ft & ins	Diameter defined as	Ft & ins
Bowsprit	⅔ of main mast	58 6	Same as that of main mast	2 2
Sprit topmast	⅓ × main topmast	15 0	$^{15}/_{16}$" per 3ft of length	0 4⅔
Fore (lower) mast	$^9/_{10}$ × main mast	78 4	$^{15}/_{16}$" per 3ft of length	2 0½
Fore topmast	$^{17}/_{31}$ × main mast	45 0	$^{15}/_{16}$" per 3ft of length	1 2
Fore topgallant mast	$^{17}/_{31}$ × main mast	18 0	$^{15}/_{16}$" per 3ft of length	0 5⅝
Main (lower) mast	(⅗[K+Br+D]) – (Br–27ft)	87 0	$^{15}/_{16}$" per 3ft of length	2 3
Main topmast	$^{19}/_{31}$ × main mast	51 0	$^{15}/_{16}$" per 3ft of length	1 4
Main topgallant mast	$^8/_{31}$ × main mast	21 0	$^{15}/_{16}$" per 3ft of length	0 6½
Mizzen (lower) mast	⅔ × main mast	69 5	⅔" per 3ft of length	1 4
Mizzen topmast	½ × main topmast	27 0	⅔" per 3ft of length	0 6
Spritsail yard	$^{17}/_{31}$ × main mast	45 0	⅝" per 3ft of length	0 9⅜
Spritsail topsail yard	$^{17}/_{62}$ × main mast	22 6	⅝" per 3ft of length	0 4⅔
Fore yard	$^{25}/_{31}$ × main mast	66 4	⅝" per 3ft of length	1 1¾
Fore topsail yard	$^{13}/_{31}$ × main mast	36 4	⅝" per 3ft of length	0 7½
Fore topgallant yard	$^{13}/_{62}$ × main mast	18 2	⅝" per 3ft of length	0 3¾
Main yard	$^{28}/_{31}$ × main mast	78 10	⅝" per 3ft of length	1 4½
Main topsail yard	$^{16}/_{31}$ × main mast	43 0	⅝" per 3ft of length	0 9
Main topgallant yard	$^{17}/_{62}$ × main mast	22 6	⅝" per 3ft of length	0 4⅔
Mizzen yard	$^{25}/_{31}$ × main mast	66 4	½" per 3ft of length	0 11
Mizzen topsail yard	$^{17}/_{62}$ × main mast	22 6	⅝" per 3ft of length	0 4⅔
Crossjack yard	$^{17}/_{31}$ × main mast	45 0	$^8/_{13}$" per 3ft of length	0 9¼

NB: Diameter given above is that measured at the partners; diameter at the mast top was about two-thirds that at the partners (except in the case of the bowsprit, where the diameter at the top was half that at the partners). For explanation of the length of the main mast, see the text.

the gundeck's length abaft the foot of the stempost. Its length was about 90 per cent that of the main mast throughout the late seventeenth and eighteenth century, and its diameter was in proportion to that of the main mast.

The mizzen mast, like the main, was raked backwards, but not so far that its fore-and-aft sail would overhang the stern. Like the fore mast, it was introduced to help in steering more than to increase propulsive power, and the mizzen course, originally the only sail carried on this mast, provided mainly lateral thrust. The mizzen yard, and the course it carried, were originally lateen rigged, but in the latter half of the eighteenth century that part of the boom and course projecting forward of the mast were removed, turning the sail into a gaff rig, with the addition of a boom added below the course to provide extra support and control over the sail. The mizzen mast was about two-thirds of the length of the main mast in the mid-seventeenth century, but as topmasts and topgallants were added in the eighteenth century it increased to about five-sixths of the main mast's length, and its diameter became somewhat narrower in proportion.

In theory, the length of the main (lower) mast was calculated from a variety of other dimensions including the length and breadth of the hull, while the length of all other spars was determined as a known fraction of that main mast length, with similar predetermined fractions governing the diameters of each mast and yard. The main mast length – the primary length from which all other mast and spar dimensions were derived, was arrived at via various formulas, the most common in the late seventeenth century being three-fifths of the sum of three of the ship's principal dimensions (the keel length, breadth and depth in hold); where the breadth exceeded 27ft – as it would for every Fourth Rate except some pre–1647 ships and a couple of small prizes – this excess was then deducted from the preceding total. While different designers would use a variety of formulas, the end of the seventeenth century saw the adoption of a simpler calculation for that given above; the main mast length became half the sum of the gun-deck length and the keel. Finally the 1719 Establishment replaced this calculation by one which reduced the main mast length to the product of a fixed constant and the breadth of the ship. For 50-gun ships this constant was at first 2.36, but the 1745 Establishment altered it to 2.22.

In practice, the bowsprit served as a fourth mast, angled upwards and forwards from its seat at an angle of some 30 degrees from the horizontal in 1670. This angle grew to about 33 degrees by the end of the century as the stem knee was rounded up, and during the eighteenth century increased even further. It braced the fore mast and provided a base to secure the bowlines that held forward the edges of the fore course and those sails above it. It carried its own course (called the *spritsail*), on a yard slung below the bowsprit, and until about 1720 even had its own topsail, mounted on a topmast which rose vertically from the cap at the end of the bowsprit.

The lower ends of all the lower masts and the bowsprit were firmly seated in the hull of the ship. The base of the fore and main masts were fixed to the keel of the ship in a step, a massive block of wood designed to take the tension in the masts caused by the pressure of wind, and as they rose through each deck they were secured to that deck's beams by further timbers called *partners*. The greatest circumference of each lower mast was at the point where it emerged through the partners into the daylight, and from that point each mast was tapered both upwards to the caps and downwards to the step. The lower mizzen mast was similarly constructed, except that it was sometimes stepped in the orlop deck rather than on the keel. The bowsprit was stepped on the upper deck, and above the stempost was supported by the knightheads, extensions of the bow structure which rose vertically on either side to prevent lateral movement of the spar.

Tables of the proportions and measurements of

Table 96: Actual length and diameters of masts and yards for the *Mary Rose*, a typical 50-gun ship, 1685

Spar	Length Ft & ins	Diameter Ft & ins
Bowsprit	55 6	1 11
Sprit topmast	19 6	0 5¾
Fore (lower) mast	72 0	1 9
Fore topmast	47 0	1 1
Fore topgallant mast	18 0	0 5¼
Main (lower) mast	84 0	2 0½
Main topmast	54 0	1 2
Main topgallant mast	21 0	0 5⅔
Mizzen (lower) mast	67 0	1 3
Mizzen topmast	24 0	0 6
Spritsail yard	45 0	0 10
Spritsail topsail yard	21 0	0 5
Fore yard	62 0	1 2
Fore topsail yard	36 0	0 8½
Fore topgallant yard	18 0	0 4
Main yard	72 0	1 4½
Main topsail yard	39 0	0 10
Main topgallant yard	20 0	0 4½
Mizzen yard	64 6	0 10½
Mizzen topsail yard	16 6	0 4½
Crossjack yard	38 0	0 6

Table 97: Length and diameters of masts and yards for 50-gun ship, 1711 (for ships built to 1706 dimensions)

Spar	Length defined as	Ft & ins	Diameter defined as	Ft & ins
Bowsprit	⅔ × main mast	55 0	⁹⁄₁₀ the main mast's diameter	1 9⅝
Sprit topmast	⁸⁄₄₅ × main mast	14 8	¹⁵⁄₁₆" per 3ft of length	0 4½
Fore (lower) mast	⁹⁄₁₀ × main mast	74 3	⅞" per 3ft of length	1 9⅝
Fore topmast	²⁴⁄₄₅ × main mast	44 0	¹⁵⁄₁₆" per 3ft of length	1 1¾
Fore topgallant mast	⁴⁄₁₅ × main mast	22 0	¹⁵⁄₁₆" per 3ft of length	0 6⅞
Main (lower) mast	½ × (gundeck+breadth)	82 6	⅞" per 3ft of length	2 0
Main topmast	⅗ × main mast	49 6	¹⁵⁄₁₆" per 3ft of length	1 3½
Main topgallant mast	³⁄₁₀ × main mast	24 9	¹⁵⁄₁₆" per 3ft of length	0 7¾
Mizzen (lower) mast	⁶⁄₇ × main mast	70 9	⅔" per 3ft of length	1 3¾
Mizzen topmast	³⁄₇ × main mast	35 4	⅔" per 3ft of length	0 7⅞
Spritsail yard	⅝ × main yard	45 1	⅝" per 3ft of length	0 9⅜
Spritsail topsail yard	½ × spritsail yard	22 7	⅝" per 3ft of length	0 4¾
Fore yard	⅞ × main yard	63 2	¾" per 3ft of length	1 3¾
Fore topsail yard	⁵⁄₉ × fore yard	35 1	⅝" per 3ft of length	0 7⅜
Fore topgallant yard	½ × fore topsail yard	17 7	⅝" per 3ft of length	0 3⅝
Main yard	⅞ × main mast	72 2	¾" per 3ft of length	1 6
Main topsail yard	⁵⁄₉ × main yard	40 1	⅝" per 3ft of length	0 8⅜
Main topgallant yard	½ × main topsail yard	20 1	⅝" per 3ft of length	0 4¼
Mizzen yard	⅞ × main yard	63 2	½" per 3ft of length	0 10½
Mizzen topsail yard	⅓ × mizzen yard	21 1	⅝" per 3ft of length	0 4⅜
Crossjack	56% of the main yard	40 5	⁸⁄₁₃" per 3ft of length	0 8¼

masts are published in a variety of specialist volumes such as James Lees' aforementioned book. However, the actual spar dimensions of seventeenth-century Fourth Rates differ considerably from the figures calculated from these fractions. Throughout these tables the term main mast, fore mast or mizzen mast implies the lower mast in these positions.

The most noticeable differences from later dimensions are that seventeenth-century ships bore not only fewer spars, but that the length of the upper masts and yards was proportionally much less than in the eighteenth century.

From about 1779 the fore and main topgallant masts began to be extended ('long-headed') so that a further sail, known as a topgallant royal sail from its surmounting location, could be set flying above. In 1794 a further tier was added to the fore and main mast structures, with the addition of a separate royal mast above the topgallant masts; these then carried their own yards from which the royals (as the name became shortened to for the topmast canvas) were set.

In the same year an extension to the jibboom was added, known as the flying jibboom (confusingly, this name was originally the full name of the jibboom itself in the early 1700s).[54] At the same time the Navy officially adopted the martingale, a short vertical spar projecting downwards from the lower end of the bowsprit cap and used to stabilise the jibboom; first introduced unofficially in the 1780s, this spar later became known as the dolphin striker, with the term 'martingales' being used for the stays which connected the spar's lower end to the flying jibboom.

Table 98: Length and diameters of masts and yards for 50-gun ship, 1719 Establishment

Spar	Length defined as	Ft & ins	Diameter defined as	Ft & ins
Bowsprit	¹⁹⁄₃₂ × main lower mast	50 5*	1½" per 3ft of length	2 0
Jibboom	⁷⁄₂₀ × main lower mast	30 0	⅞" per 3ft of length	0 8¾
Fore (lower) mast	⁹⁄₁₀ × main mast	76 6	¹⁵⁄₁₆" per 3ft of length	1 10⅞
Fore topmast	²⁴⁄₄₅ × main lower mast	46 1	⁹⁄₁₀" per 3ft of length	1 2⅝
Fore topgallant mast	⁴⁄₁₅ × main lower mast	23 2	1" per 3ft of length	0 7⅝
Main (lower) mast	2.36 × ship's breadth	85 0	¹⁵⁄₁₆" per 3ft of length	2 1½
Main topmast	⅗ × main lower mast	49 3	⁹⁄₁₀" per 3ft of length	1 2⅜
Main topgallant mast	³⁄₁₀ × main lower mast	24 2	1' per 3ft of length	0 8⅛
Mizzen (lower) mast	¹¹⁄₁₃ × main lower mast	71 10	⅔" per 3ft of length	1 4
Mizzen topmast	²⁄₇ × main lower mast	34 6	⅝" per 3ft of length	0 9⅝
Spritsail yard	63.6% of main yard	48 8	⅝" per 3ft of length	0 10⅛
Spritsail topsail yard	⅔ × spritsail yard	32 5	⅗" per 3ft of length	0 6⅜
Fore yard	⅞ of main yard	66 11	⅗" per 3ft of length	1 3⅜
Fore topsail yard	63.6% of main yard	48 8	⅝" per 3ft of length	0 10⅛
Fore topgallant yard	½ × fore topsail yard	28 4	⅗" per 3ft of length	0 5⅝
Main yard	57.1% of gundeck length	76 6	¾" per 3ft of length	1 5⅞
Main topsail yard	72.7% of main yard	55 7	⅝" per 3ft of length	0 11⅝
Main topgallant yard	½ × main topsail yard	32 6	⅗" per 3ft of length	0 6½
Mizzen yard	⅚ of main yard	63 5	⁷⁄₁₃" per 3ft of length	0 11⅜
Mizzen topsail yard	¾ of crossjack yard	36 6	⅝" per 3ft of length	0 7¼
Crossjack yard	63.6% of main yard	48 8	⁸⁄₁₃" per 3ft of length	0 10
Stunsail booms (calculations by the author):				
Fore Lower St. boom	⁶⁄₁₃ × fore yard	30 10⅝	⅝" per 3ft of length	0 6½
Fore Topmast St. boom	⁵⁄₉ × fore topsail yard	27 0½	⅝" per 3ft of length	0 5⅝
Main Lower St. boom	⁶⁄₁₃ × main yard	35 3¾	⅝" per 3ft of length	0 7⅜
Main Topmast St. boom	⁵⁄₉ × main topsail yard	30 11¼	⅝" per 3ft of length	0 6½

* of which 39ft 5in was before the stem. Note lengths were rounded off to nearest inch (*eg* fore yard should be 66ft 11¼in).

Each lower mast tapered upwards to the trestletrees at its summit, where it overlapped with the base of the topmast. Here, the trestletrees – two fore-and-aft timbers, one on each side of the mast – and three crosstrees at right angles to them, supported a stout

Table 99: Length and diameters of masts and yards for 50-gun ship, 1745 Establishment

Spar	*Length defined as*	*Ft & ins*	*Diameter defined as*	*Ft & ins*
Bowsprit	63% × main mast	55 9 *	1 3/7" per 3ft of length	2 ⅜
Jibboom	70% × bowsprit	41 0	⅞" per 3ft of length	1 0
Fore (lower) mast	90% × main mast	82 0	15/16" per 3ft of length	2 2⅜
Fore topmast	54% × main mast	50 2	1" per 3ft of length	1 4½
Fore topgallant mast	4/15 × main mast	25 4	1" per 3ft of length	0 8½
Main (lower) mast	2.22 × ship's breadth	91 0	1" per 3ft of length	2 5¼
Main topmast	⅗ × main mast	55 1	9/10" per 3ft of length	1 4½
Main topgallant mast	3/10 × main mast	28 0	1" per 3ft of length	0 9¼
Mizzen (lower) mast	11/13 × main mast	78 10	⅔" per 3ft of length	1 5⅞
Mizzen topmast	2/7 × main mast	39 6	⅚" per 3ft of length	0 11
Spritsail yard	0.72 × fore yard	52 1	⅝' per 3ft of length	0 11
Spritsail topsail yard	⅔ × spritsail yard	35 11	⅗" per 3ft of length	0 7⅜
Fore yard	⅞ × main yard	72 10	¾" per 3ft of length	1 5¼
Fore topsail yard	0.72 × fore yard	52 1	⅝" per 3ft of length	0 11
Fore topgallant yard	⅔ × fore topsail yard	35 11	⅗" per 3ft of length	0 7⅜
Main yard	9/10 × main mast	82 10	¾" per 3ft of length	1 7⅝
Main topsail yard	0.72 × main yard	59 7	⅝" per 3ft of length	1 0¾
Main topgallant yard	½ × main yard	41 2	⅗ per 3ft of length	0 8½
Mizzen yard	⅚ × main yard	67 11	7/13" per 3ft of length	1 0½
Mizzen topsail yard	½ × mizzen yard	39 1	⅝" per 3ft of length	0 8
Crossjack yard	0.72 × fore yard	52 1	8/13" per 3ft of length	0 11

* of which 40ft 3in was before the stem.

Table 100: Length and diameters of masts and yards for 50-gun ship, 1773 Establishment

Spar	*Length defined as*	*Ft & ins*	*Diameter defined as*	*Ft & ins*
Bowsprit	19/32 of main mast	56 1*	13/7" per 3ft of length	2 4½
Jibboom	43% of main mast	39 8	⅞" per 3ft of length	0 11⅞
Fore (lower) mast	90% of main mast	81 6	⅞" per 3ft of length	2 2⅜
Fore topmast	54% of main mast	48 2	1" per 3ft of length	1 4
Fore topgallant mast	27% of main mast	24 1	1" per 3ft of length	0 8⅛
Main (lower) mast	2.23 × ship's breadth	92 0	⅞" per 3ft of length	2 5
Main topmast	60% of main mast	53 3	9/10" per 3ft of length	1 4
Main topgallant mast	30% of main mast	26 6	1" per 3ft of length	0 8⅞
Mizzen (lower) mast	11/13 × main lower mast	78 3	1" per 3ft of length	1 6⅜
Mizzen topmast	42% of main mast	39 10	7/10" per 3ft of length	0 11⅛
Mizzen topgallant mast	21% of main mast	19 10½	1" per 3ft of length	0 6⅜
Spritsail yard	'as fore topsail yard'[1]	52 1	⅝ per 3ft of length	0 11⅝
Spritsail topsail yard	'as fore topgallant yard'[1]	35 11	⅗" per 3ft of length	0 6¼
Fore yard	⅞ × main yard	72 5	7/10" per 3ft of length	1 4⅞
Fore topsail yard	63.6% of main yard	52 8	⅝" per 3ft of length	0 11⅝
Fore topgallant yard	⅗ of fore topsail yard	31 6	⅗" per 3ft of length	0 6¼
Main yard	9/10 × main mast	82 2[2]	7/10" per 3ft of length	1 7¼
Main topsail yard	72% of main yard	60 9	⅝ per 3ft of length	1 1½
Main topgallant yard	⅗ of main topsail yard	36 8	⅗" per 3ft of length	0 7⅜
Mizzen yard	9/10 of main yard	74 6	7/13" per 3ft of length	1 1⅜
Mizzen topsail yard	¾ of crossjack yard	39 3	⅝ per 3ft of length	0 8¼
Mizzen topgallant yard	⅗ of mizzen topsail yard	28 0	⅗" per 3ft of length	0 5⅞
Crossjack yard	63.6% of main yard	52 8	8/13" per 3ft of length	0 11⅝
Stunsail booms and yards (calculations by the author):				
Fore Tm St. boom	½ × fore topsail yard	26 4	⅝" per 3ft of length	0 5½
Fore Tm St. yard	4/7 × fore topmast st. boom	15 0	⅝" per 3ft of length	0 3⅛
Fore Tm St. boom	½ × fore topgallant yard	15 9	⅝" per 3ft of length	0 3¼
Fore Tgt St. yard	4/7 × fore t'gallant st. boom	9 0	⅝" per 3ft of length	0 1⅞
Main Lower St. boom	5/9 × main yard	46 0	⅝" per 3ft of length	0 9½
Main Lower St. yard	4/7 × main lower st. boom	26 3	⅝" per 3ft of length	0 5½
Main Tm St. boom	½ × main topsail yard	30 4	⅝" per 3ft of length	0 6¼
Main Tm St. yard	4/7 × main topmast st. boom	17 4	⅝" per 3ft of length	0 3⅝
Main Tg St. boom	½ × main topgallant yard	18 4	⅝" per 3ft of length	0 3¾
Main Tg St. yard	4/7 × main t'gallant st. boom	10 6	⅝" per 3ft of length	0 2¼

* of which 40ft 3in was before the stem. [1] clearly untrue! [2] this figure would appear wrong, and correct value should be 82ft 9in.

platform which when planked over provided a secure working area for lookouts, sharpshooters when in action, and for men working on the upper yards; they also served as spreaders for the shrouds supporting the upper masts. The head of the topmast similarly overlapped with the bottom of the topgallant mast, and again trestletrees were provided to strengthen the join, but without the need for a working platform.

The mizzen mast differed in that after about 1690 it was stepped, not into the keelson, but on the lower deck, and was raked backwards at a slightly greater angle than the main mast, while early Fourth Rates lacked a topgallant mizzen mast; it was at its widest where it emerged through the poop deck.

The bowsprit served not only to carry the bowlines which held the edges of the fore sails when sailing close to the wind, but also functioned as a mast in its own right, carrying its own sails; it was similarly to carry its own topmast, rising vertically from the end of the bowsprit, although by 1720 in two-deckers this was superseded by the jibboom, an extension of the bowsprit itself.

In the early seventeenth century bowsprits were immensely long, sometimes as long as the fore mast and thus 80 per cent or more of the length of the main mast, with a maximum diameter of 28 per cent of its length (or an inch per yard of length). By the 1680s the length had reduced to some 74 per cent of the fore mast, and the diameter reduced to 26 per cent of the length (15/16th inch per yard). The outboard proportion of the bowsprit was reduced from two-thirds of its length in 1650 to about 60 per cent in 1670. Thereafter the proportions remained constant, but the angle to the horizontal increased to about 35 degrees by 1700 as the stem knee became rounded up.

The lower sails, or courses, were suspended from yards fastened just below the crosstrees. These massive spars were long enough to be truly rectangular to maximise the area taking the wind. The upper yards were shorter and narrower than the lower yards, to reduce topweight. The topsail yard was originally half the length of the lower yard, although during the later Stuart era it rose to reach 72 per cent of the lower yard's length (for each mast) by 1719, a proportion maintained for the remainder of the eighteenth century. This shorter length meant that the topsails were trapezium in shape instead of rectangular, although during the seventeenth century the height of the topmast, and hence of the topsail, gradually increased so that the latter's effective area was almost equal to that of the course. The topgallant yards and sails were similarly scaled down in proportion.

The 1773 Establishment, as in earlier periods, only made provision for topmasts and topgallant masts with their yards (and sails) above the lower main and fore masts. In 1779, as noted earlier, the continued demand for more canvas to be spread led to the introduction of

HMS *Leopard* 1790

Drawings by John McKay

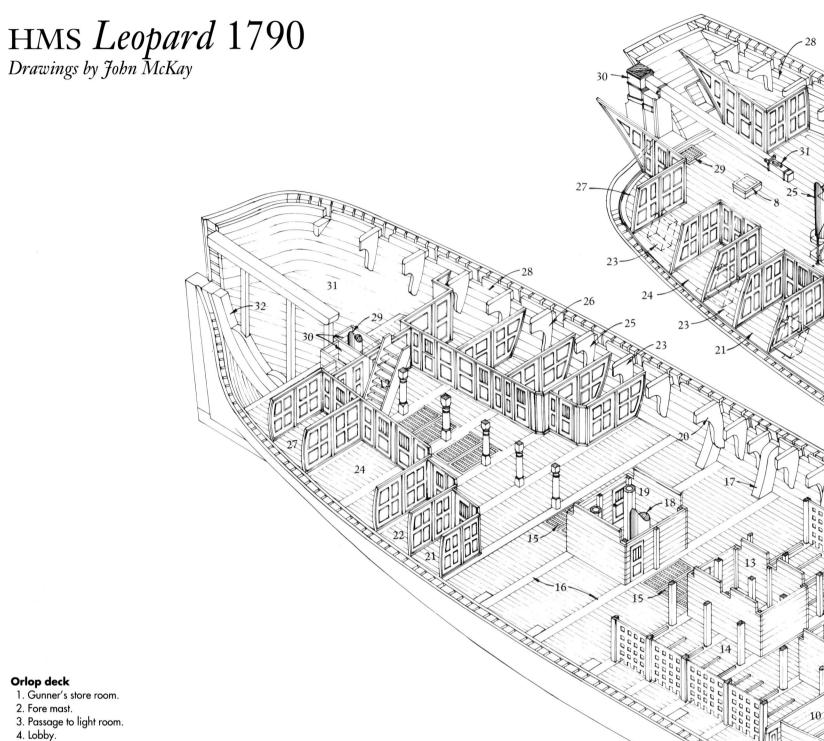

Orlop deck

1. Gunner's store room.
2. Fore mast.
3. Passage to light room.
4. Lobby.
5. Sail room.
6. Wing.
7. Riding bitts.
8. Carpenter's store room.
9. Hanging knee.
10. Pitch room.
11. Block room (with Boatswain's store forward of it).
12. Ladder.
13. Sail room.
14. Cable tier.
15. Hatch.
16. Orlop deck beams.
17. Rider.
18. Main mast.
19. Pump room.
20. Hanging knee.

21. Lieutenant's store room.
22. Captain's store room.
23. Marine clothing.
24. Commodore's store room.
25. Slop room.
26. Purser's cabin.
27. Surgeon's cabin.
28. Steward's room.
29. Mizzen mast.
30. Compartments containing hatch to after powderoom (nearest mizzen mast) and dispensary (adjoining Surgeon's cabin).
31. Bread room.
32. Keelson.

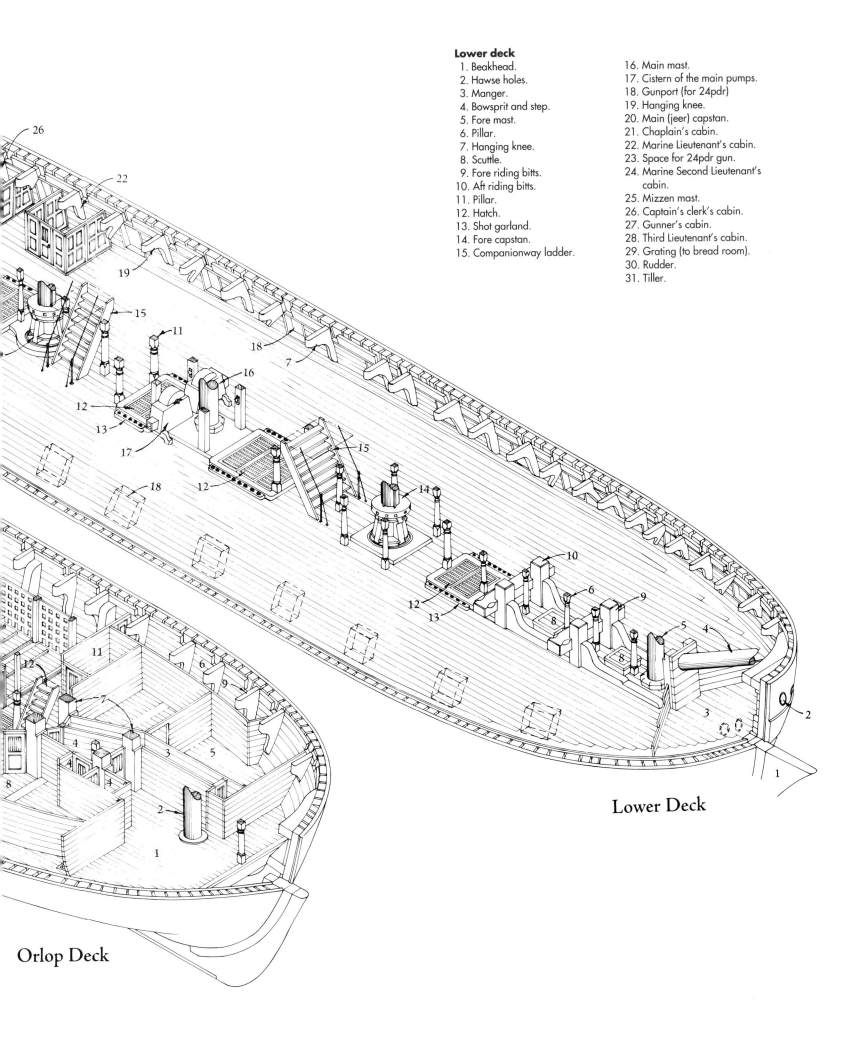

Lower deck
1. Beakhead.
2. Hawse holes.
3. Manger.
4. Bowsprit and step.
5. Fore mast.
6. Pillar.
7. Hanging knee.
8. Scuttle.
9. Fore riding bitts.
10. Aft riding bitts.
11. Pillar.
12. Hatch.
13. Shot garland.
14. Fore capstan.
15. Companionway ladder.
16. Main mast.
17. Cistern of the main pumps.
18. Gunport (for 24pdr)
19. Hanging knee.
20. Main (jeer) capstan.
21. Chaplain's cabin.
22. Marine Lieutenant's cabin.
23. Space for 24pdr gun.
24. Marine Second Lieutenant's cabin.
25. Mizzen mast.
26. Captain's clerk's cabin.
27. Gunner's cabin.
28. Third Lieutenant's cabin.
29. Grating (to bread room).
30. Rudder.
31. Tiller.

Lower Deck

Orlop Deck

Table 101: Length and diameters of masts and yards for 50-gun ship, 1794 Establishment

Spar	*Length defined as*	*Ft & ins*	*Diameter defined as*	*Ft & ins*
Bowsprit	⅗ × main mast	57 4	Same as main mast	2 4⅝
Jibboom	0.715 × bowsprit	41 0	⅞" per 3ft of length	1 0
Fore (lower) mast	8/9 × main mast	84 11	0.9' per 3ft of length	2 1½
Fore topmast	24/45 × main mast	50 11	1" per 3ft of length	1 5
Fore topgallant mast	4/15 × main mast	25 6	1" per 3ft of length	0 8½
Fore royal mast	7/10 × fore topgallant mast	17 10	⅔ × fore topgallant mast	0 6
Main (lower) mast	½ × (gundeck+breadth)	95 6	0.9' per 3ft of length	2 4⅝
Main topmast	⅗ × main mast	57 4	1" per 3ft of length	1 7⅛
Main topgallant mast	3/10 × main mast	28 8	1" per 3ft of length	0 9½
Main royal mast	7/10 × main topgallant mast	20 1	⅔ × main topgallant mast	0 6¼
Mizzen (lower) mast	11/13 × main mast	80 9	⅔" per 3ft of length	1 6
Mizzen topmast	3/7 × main mast	40 11	7/10" per 3ft of length	0 9½
Mizzen topgallant mast	3/14 × main mast	20 6	1" per 3ft of length	0 6⅞
Spritsail yard	⅝ × main yard	53 1	⅝" per 3ft of length	0 11
Spritsail topsail yard	19/40 × main yard	40 4	⅝ per 3ft of length	0 8½
Fore yard	7/9 × main mast	74 3	7/10" per 3ft of length	1 5¼
Fore topsail yard	⅝ × main yard	53 1	⅝" per 3ft of length	0 11
Fore topgallant yard	19/40 × main yard	40 4	⅗" per 3ft of length	0 8
Fore royal yard	½ × fore topgallant yard	20 2	⅝" per 3ft of length	0 4¼
Main yard	8/9 × main mast	84 11	7/10" per 3ft of length	1 7¾
Main topsail yard	5/7 × main yard	60 8	⅝ per 3ft of length	1 0⅝
Main topgallant yard	3/7 × main yard	36 4	⅗ per 3ft of length	0 7¼
Main royal yard	½ × main topgallant yard	18 2	⅝" per 3ft of length	0 3¾
Mizzen boom	5/7 × main yard	60 8	⅔ per 3ft of length	1 1½
Mizzen gaff	3/7 × main yard	36 4	7/10xb' per 3ft of length	0 9½
Mizzen topsail yard	⅔ × main topsail yard	40 6	⅝" per 3ft of length	0 8½
Mizzen topgallant yard	⅗ × mizzen topsail yard	24 4	⅗ per 3ft of length	0 4⅞
Crossjack yard	⅝ × main yard	53 1	⅝" per 3ft of length	0 11
Stunsail booms:				
Fore Tmt St. boom	½ × fore topsail yard	26 7	1" per 5 ft of length	0 5¼
Fore Tg St. boom	½ × fore t'gallant yard	20 2	1" per 5 ft of length	0 4
Main Lower St. boom	½ × main yard	42 6	1" per 5 ft of length	0 8½
Main Tmt St. boom	½ × main topsail yard	30 4	1" per 5 ft of length	0 6
Main Tg St. boom	½ × main t'gallant yard	18 2	1" per 5 ft of length	0 3⅝

Note that stunsail yards were each 4/7 of the length and diameter of their respective boom. The figures are calculated for the *Antelope* class (1790).

Table 102: Dimensions (in feet and inches) of caps, tops and trees for 50-gun ship, 1788

		Length	*Breadth*	*Depth*
CAPS:				
Lower:	Fore	5 4	2 8	1 2¼
	Main	5 4	2 8	1 2¼
	Mizzen	3 8½	1 10¼	0 9¼
Topmast:	Fore	2 8½	1 4¼	0 6½
	Main	2 11½	1 5¾	0 7⅛
	Mizzen	2 3	1 1½	0 5⅜
TOPS:	Fore	16 0⅝	12 0½	
	Main	17 8⅝	13 3½	
	Mizzen	13 3⅜	9 11½	
HOLE IN TOPS:	Fore	4 8	5 0¼	
	Main	5 1¾	5 6½	
	Mizzen	3 10¼	4 1¾	
TRESTLETREES:				
Lower	Fore	11 4½	1 0¾	0 8½
	Main	12 7½	1 2⅛	0 9⅜
	Mizzen	9 4½	0 9⅜	0 6¼
Topmast	Fore	5 10	0 8	0 4⅜
	Main	5 10	0 8	0 4⅜
	Mizzen	4 4¾	0 5⅞	0 3¼
CROSS TREES:				*Thickness*
Lower	Fore	16 11	0 8⅜	0 5⅝
	Main	17 0⅝	0 9¼	0 6⅛
	Mizzen	12 8⅜	0 6⅜	0 4¼
Topmast	Fore	12 0½	0 4	0 3¼
	Main	13 3½	0 4⅜	0 3⅝
	Mizzen	9 11½	0 3¼	0 2¾

Source: NMM SPB/15. * The 'lubbers hole', whose *after* edge was one-fifth of the top's length from the top's own after edge.

main and fore royal masts, with their own set of yards and sails; the provision of royals was extended to mizzen masts in 1790.

Standing rigging

The standing rigging was that which remained permanently in position to support the masts and bowsprit, easing the strain put on them by the force on the wind upon the sails they carried and by the motion of the ship. Tarred or 'blacked down' to protect it against the action of wind and seawater, the standing rigging comprised the shrouds, backstays and forestays.

The lower shrouds, which provided lateral support to the lower masts, fanned from the hounds of each lower mast down to the channels, small platforms projecting out from each side of the ship, with each pair set slightly aft of the mast to which it gave support. The topmast shrouds ran from the sides of the top around the lower mast, up to the hounds of the topmast, while the topgallant shrouds were similarly spread by the edge of the topmast crosstrees and ran up to the hounds of the topgallant mast.

Shrouds were made of four-stranded rope, put on in pairs over the masthead and set up with a system of deadeyes and lanyards to enable them to be tightened or loosened according to need. Deane's *Doctrine* in 1670 established that the main (lower) shrouds' circumference should be a quarter of the diameter of the main mast at its partners, *ie* 6¾in. In 1711 the main lower mast of a 50-gun ship usually had seven shrouds per side, each still of 6¾in circumference, while the fore lower mast had one fewer pair and the mizzen lower mast about half the number. By the 1794 Establishment, both the fore and main lower masts had seven pairs of shrouds, now of 8½in circumference, while the mizzen lower mast had five pairs each of 5½in. The topmast shrouds were each about half the circumference of the lower shrouds for that mast, and the topgallant shrouds about half of the appropriate topmast shrouds.

From the edges of both the top and the topmast

crosstrees, shorter 'futtock' shrouds led downwards and inwards to connect with the shrouds of the mast below. Horizontal ropes called catharpins were secured laterally at the connection point to apply a contrary force to the effect of the futtock shrouds in pulling the shrouds outwards. Lower, upper and futtock shrouds were all fitted with ratlines, crossing the shrouds horizontally at regular intervals, and in effect forming a rope-ladder up which men could climb to the tops and yards.

Backstays performed a similar function to the shrouds, but ran from the channels direct to the hounds of the upper masts. Most began from the aft end of the channels and thus gave backwards as well as lateral support, but some were connected at the forward end of the channel, almost abreast of the mast and were thus called breast-backstays, giving only lateral support.

The principal stays (fore stay, main stay and mizzen stay) ran forward from each mast, in a fore-and-aft line descending at an angle of about 45 degrees. Each had a circumference equal to half the diameter of the mast they supported. The lower mast stays connected the hounds of each lower mast to the deck at the partners of the mast ahead, or (in the case of the fore mast's stays) to the bowsprit. Topmast stays connected the hounds of the upper masts to the mast ahead (again to the bowsprit or jibboom in the case of those descending from the upper fore masts). Staysails could be hoisted on each of the various stays to provide a greater area of canvas. Most stays were doubled by an auxiliary or 'preventer' stay to take part of the strain; these were usually of about two-thirds the diameter of the stay they assisted.

To give the shrouds and backstays maximum lateral force, their lower ends had to be attached to the hull as far out from the centreline as possible. In practice, they had to be secured outboard of the hull, and for this purpose broad thick planks called channels (originally 'chain-wales') were attached along the ship's sides, and the shrouds fastened by deadeyes to a chain plate mounted on these rather than direct to the hull. In the seventeenth century these channels were fixed to the higher of the two upper wales, which ran along the ship's side directly below the upper deck gunports, with the chain attached to a plate on the lower of the upper wales; they were secured to the ship's side below by curved iron spurs or brackets. They were sufficiently broad to enable the shroud to clear the ship's rail, and in depth were roughly half the thickness of the upper wales. In the early eighteenth century, as the low position of the channels on the hull made them vulnerable to damage by heavy seas, they were moved up to above the upper deck guns.

Running rigging

The running rigging, which consisted of those ropes and lines which supported and controlled the yards and sails, was by definition required to move to manoeuvre the ship, and thus could not be tarred. It was divided into that rigging which operated the yards, and that which controlled the sails.

In the middle of the seventeenth century, all the yards were still hoisted into place by *halyards* connected to the yard and passing directly over blocks set in the head of each section of mast, and was then secured in place against the mast with *trusses*. This system was to remain largely unaltered for the upper yards, but the system changed for the lower yards around 1660, with the halyards being replaced by *jeers*, thick ropes passing through large blocks attached just below the top. The trusses for the lower yards were replaced around the same date by *slings* and *parrels*, consisting of frameworks of rope and wooden ribs and beads against which the yard could move, either to be raised up and down the mast or to pivot around the mast.

In the eighteenth century it became the practice for the lower yards to remain virtually permanently aloft, where they were held in position by the slings (now usually of chain rather than rope, particularly during

Although this model of a 50-gun ship of about 1685 cannot be identified with a particular ship, the rigging is believed to be almost entirely original, so is a reliable source of information on even the most minute aspects of top hamper during this period. (NMM: B9914)

Table 103: Cordage required for Fourth Rate of 1670

Type of cordage	Size (in)	Length (fathoms)	Weight (cwt – lbs)
Main mast stay	13½	14	4–109
Fore mast stay	11	11	2–62
Collar of the main mast stay	10	7	1–44
Collar of the fore mast stay	7	3	0–42
Main shrouds, buoy ropes, etc.	6¼	216½	20–34
Fore shrouds, main topsail sheets, etc.	6	168½	12–104
Main jeers, fore tacks, seizing for blocks, etc.	5¾	253	18–76
Wolding for bowsprit, main sheets, etc.	5½	137	6–96
Fore jeers, fore topmast sheets, etc.	5⅛	176	13–10
Blocks, fore sheets, cat ropes, etc.	4½	193	9–38
Main topmast standing backstays, etc.	3¾	255	5–52
Fore topmast standing backstays, etc.	3½	188	5–9
Mizzen shrouds, main bowlines, etc.	3½	96	2–61
Fore topmast shrouds, fore bowlines, etc.	3¼	200	5–1
Main tackles falls, main topmast bowlines, etc.	3⅛	309	7–38
Fore tackles falls, main lifts, etc.	2¾	789	13–14
Mizzen bridles, main topmast lifts, etc.	2⅛	714	9–91
Fore buntlines, fore topsail lifts, etc.	2	417	3–106
Fore clewlines, rattling for shrouds, etc.	1¼	1088	5–101
Robins and earrings & clew seizings.	1⅛	670	3–63
Total cordage		5905	141–60

Note the first column indicates (except for the first four lines) only the *primary* uses for rope of the size specified.
Source: Deane's *Doctrine of Naval Architecture*, 1670.

wartime). The system of halyards and trusses remained for the upper yards.

Lifts were ropes employed to keep the yards horizontal and prevent stress on the yardarms. The lifts were attached to a block fixed at each yardarm, and passed over a block at the masthead and then down to the deck. Also attached to the yardarms were *braces*, used to alter the angle of the yard to the ship's heading, and passed through blocks mounted either aft or forward of the yard to the deck below.

Square sails were held to the yard by *robbands* (ie 'rope-bands'), which passed through holes in the sail's upper edge and were fastened over the top of the yard.

The lower corners of the sails were controlled by *sheets*, ropes which led to blocks on the yard and then to other blocks secured to the sides of the hull. The sails themselves were furled or unfurled with the help of *clewlines* and *buntlines*.

Fore-and-aft sails, particularly the staysails, were set from the stays. One of the staysail's lower corners was guided by one of two sheets (attached one to each side of the ship); the other lower corner was controlled by a *tack*, a rope which was attached to the mast forwards of the staysail. The jibs, being triangular sails compared with the basic quadrilateral shaped of the staysails, had no need for a tack.

As the size of spars and the area of canvas rose, rigging grew in proportion. The ratio between the diameter of a rope and that of the masts remained constant throughout the sailing era, other than for a few minor items.[55] Lengths of rigging also increased to cope with the growth in the length of masts and spars, with extra masts being introduced, and with further pieces of rigging being added to improve control over sails. The rigging required under the 1706 Establishment for a 50-gun ship weighed 13 tons 17 cwt. A comparison between Deane's lists and the 1773 Establishment of Rigging (see Table 104) illustrates how much additional rigging was being used by the latter date.

In British practice, masting and rigging details were usually determined by elaborate warrants and lists of dimensions sent to the yards, so draughts were rarely regarded as necessary. However, a small number do survive, including a set associated with the 1719 Establishment, showing a vessel of each Rate. That for the 50-gun ship is usually identified with the *Oxford* of 1727 and shows the masts and yards provided in the 1719 Establishment, and probably the sails set out in the 1728 Establishment. Stunsails have been excluded for simplicity. Compared with earlier sail plans, the most obvious difference is the disappearance of the spritsail topmast, abolished (for all but three-deckers) in 1720; but the rig is notably 'squarer', with sails wider in relation to their height. (NMM: DR6196)

Table 104: Rigging Establishment of 30 July 1773, weights of cordage required for small two-deckers

Ship Type	Hawser laid ton-cwt-lb	Cable laid ton-cwt-lb	White rope ton-cwt-lb	Total worn ton-cwt-lb	Grand total ton-cwt-lb
70-gun & 64-gun	27-4-104	13-19-85	0-0-83	2-0-31	43-5-81
60-gun	23-6-110	11-9-38	0-0-83	1-2-8	35-19-6
50-gun	19-17-36	9-2-57	0-0-60	1-14-16	30-14-57
'small 50' & 44-gun	17-8-22	5-16-48	0-0-55	1-6-53	24-11-66

Source: NMM SPB/15, p39.

Table 105: Dimensions and value of sails (Establishment of 30 July 1773) for 50-gun ship

	Cloths at: Head	Feet	Yards deep	Lining	Total in sq. yards	(Qty)	Class and cost/yard	Value/sail £-s-d
Spritsail course	26	26	7	8½	190½	(1)	2 @ 20½d	16-5-5½
topsail	14½	25	8		158	(1)	6 @ 17d	11-3-10
Flying jib	0	23	22	2	255	(2)	6 @ 17d	18-1-2½
Fore course	35	35	11¼	51¾	445½	(2)	1 @ 20½d	38-4-2½
topsail	23	36	14¾	31	466	(2)	2 @ 20½d	40-9-1½
lining					34¾		5 @ 14¼d	2-1-3
topgallant sail	14½	23	7¼		136	(2)	6 @ 17d	9-12-8
Main course	42	42	13	61½	607½	(2)	1 @ 20½d	53-5-1¼
topsail	27	41½	16½	26½	591½	(2)	2 @ 20½d	51-6-0½
lining					41½		5 @ 14¼d	2-9-3¼
topgallant sail	17	26½	8		174	(1)	6 @ 17d	12-6-6
Mizzen course	13	14	15½/9	17	182½	(2)	2 @ 20½d	15-11-9¼
topsail	18	26	12	16½	280½	(2)	4	23-5-9
lining					26½		6 @ 13½d	1-9-9¾
topgallant sail	13	18	6		93	(1)	7 @ 15¾d	6-2-0
Driver	15	23	15½		294½	(1)	6 @ 17d	20-17-4
Fore staysail	18	11½	2		105½	(2)	2 @ 20½d	9-0-2¾
topmast staysail		17	15	2	129½	(1)	6 @ 17d	9-3-5¾
Main staysail		26	13	2	171	(1)	2 @ 20½d	14-12-1½
topmast staysail	21	23	21¾/8¾	1	336½	(2)	6 @ 17d	23-7-6
topgallant staysail	17	17	13½/4½	5¾	158¾	(1)	7 @ 15¾d	10-8-4
Middle staysail	20	20	13/5½	6	191	(1)	6 @ 17d	13-10-7
Mizzen staysail	18	20	11/7	5½	176½	(1)	2 @ 20½d	14-11-6¼
topmast staysail	15	16	13/4½	3½	139	(1)	6 @ 17d	9-16-11
Fore stunsail	11	15	13		169	(1)	6 @ 17d	11-19-5
top stunsail	9	12	15¾		165½	(2)	6 @ 17d	11-15-4½
topgallant stunsail	6	9	7¾		58	(1)	7 @ 15¾d	3-16-1½
Main stunsail	12	16	15½		219½	(2)	6 @ 17d	15-10-11½
top stunsail	10	13	17¼		200½	(2)	6 @ 17d	14-4-0
topgallant stunsail	7	10	8½		72¼	(2)	7 @ 15¾d	4-14-10

Source: NMM SPB/15, p47, with amendments from other documents.
The area of lining (doubling) calculated by author from difference between length of sail (average of columns 2 and 3) multiplied by depth of sail (column 4) and the total area quoted in square yards (column 6). Quantity and cost per yard do not appear on original.

Sails

English canvas was made up into sails using material of different thickness and strength according to the use to which that sail would be put (and hence the stress of wind that it would have to withstand). In the mid-seventeenth century various names were used for these different types, but by the eighteenth century they were defined in eight grades, numbered from One (the thickest) to Eight (the lightest). The thickest was used for the fore and main courses, and the next for the strongest of the topsails which would be set in storms; the stunsails and topgallants, hoisted only

when the wind was light, were of the thinnest material (see Table 105).

Sailmaking techniques altered little over the centuries. Strips of canvas, usually 18in wide and categorised as *cloths*, were sewn together by sailmakers working in large sail lofts ashore, situated in the major Royal Dockyards. Using large needles and triple-threaded English twine, they assembled sails of a variety of numbers and lengths of cloths, tailored to the size of ship.

To provide extra strength in those areas of the sail subject to particular stress or chafing, reinforcing pieces of canvas, called *lining* or *doubling*, were sewn into the canvas, and the whole sail's edges were protected by a *bolt rope* sewn around it. Various loops of rope were sewn in at different points along the bolt rope; at the upper corners were the *earrings* whereby the sail could be lashed to the yardarms, while at the lower corners were *clews* used to fix the various sheets and tacks for furling or controlling the sails.

The shapes of sails varied to suit their function. While those sails set transversely across the ship were called 'square', the name was a misnomer. The main and four courses were roughly rectangular, but were much wider than tall, and with a strong *gore* (or uplift of the centre) along the lower edge. The topsails, topgallants and royals were trapezium in shape, with their sides (or *leeches*) sloping inwards, since their heads were invariably attached to a shorter spar than their clews were.

The mizzen course was initially a triangular lateen sail, carried on a yard suspended across the mast. When the fore part of this yard was left off in the eighteenth century, the lateen was replaced by a gaff sail of four unequal sides. The staysails, arrayed fore-and-aft between the masts, were similarly four-sided, while the jib sails rigged on the stays between the fore mast and the bowsprit, were triangular.

Vast amount of canvas were required for a major warship, and this amount grew substantially during the eighteenth century. Among the Fourth Rates covered by Deane's 1670 *Doctrine* (see full list in Table 109), each supplied with twenty-four distinct sails, the majority were allocated 3826 (square) yards of canvas. The largest pair, the *Greenwich* and *Leopard*, each had 5258 yards, while four (the *Advice, Bristol, Centurion* and *Happy Return*) required 4072 yards apiece. Moreover, it would appear that Deane excluded staysails and stunsails from his calculations.[56]

A century later, a First Rate like the *Victory* had 16,619 square yards (almost three and a half *acres*) of sail,[57] and by the end of the 1780s even the 50-gun ship carried about 10,500 square yards (or 2.17 acres). This comprised forty-one distinct sails, of which twelve were spares stored in the sailroom, which was situated midships on the orlop deck, between the cable tiers.

Stunsails and driver

In very light winds, the width of canvas on the lower and top masts could be extended to catch every conceivable portion of the air by studding sails, usually called 'stunsails', which were spread between yards and booms extending outwards from the yardarms. Stunsails in the Royal Navy originated in the early Stuart era, as triangular sails which could be spread on booms and set on either side of the fore and main courses. They were officially added to the ship's complement of sails during the Commonwealth period. Later in the century, the principle was extended to the topsail yards, with main topmast stunsails appearing about 1675 and fore topmast stunsails a decade later.

No specification for the lengths of stunsail booms and yards seems to have been set officially until the 1780s, at which time the main lower stunsail booms measured $\frac{5}{9}$ of the length of the main yard (there were none on the fore yard), while the topmast stunsail booms were half the length of the topsail yard on which they were mounted. In 1794 every boom measured half the length of the yard on which it was set. The stunsail yards were always $\frac{4}{7}$ of the lengths of the equivalent booms. The diameter of each of these booms and yards was an inch for every 5ft of their length; this diameter was constant for the inner third of their length, but then tapered down to two-thirds of this at the end. Stunsails were not carried on the topgallant masts until after 1773, and never officially on the royal masts.

While stunsails could not be fitted to the fore-and-aft rigged lower mizzen sail, the equivalent here was the 'driver', by which this sail was extended – in effect replaced, since to rig the driver meant that the mizzen sail was lowered and the extra-wide driver hoisted in its place. To carry the extended head of this sail, a short yard was lashed to the head of the mizzen yard, and the foot was sheeted to a boom. The driver yard was of the same length and diameter as the fore topgallant yard of the same ship.

Flags and flagstaffs

While not contributing to a ship's propulsion as did the masts, sails and rigging, spars to carry the multiplicity of ensigns and flags formed part of its top hamper. Flagstaffs to carry the ship's ensigns and signal flags were fitted above the fore and main topgallant masts from towards the end of the seventeenth century; they were not mentioned in Deane's *Doctrine* in 1670. Where they were separate pieces from the topgallant masts, each was fitted to the top of that topgallant mast (or royal, when that appeared) and held in place with a pair of shrouds attached, via the topgallant crosstrees, to the head of the topgallant shrouds; the staff itself was surmounted by a rounded head or truck. Often, however, they were simply parts of the topgallant mast that stood up above the shrouds. A mizzen staff was similarly mounted above the mizzen topmast and, while the spritsail topmast existed, a jack staff was mounted above that in like manner, set up as if it were a spritsail topgallant mast.

In addition, an ensign staff was set up on the centre of the taffrail, raked backwards. At the end of the seventeenth century, the length of this projecting above the taffrail was between 35 per cent and 40 per cent of the length of the main mast, although during the eighteenth century this dropped to about one-third of the main mast's length, with a diameter of $\frac{1}{2}$in per 3ft of length. The staffs above the three principal masts were of roughly similar size, while the jackstaff was half the length of the ensign staff and had a diameter of $\frac{3}{4}$in per 3ft of length.

The ensigns and jacks carried on these staffs were of massive size, for maximum visibility at long range. For the 50-gun ship the 1706 Establishment stipulated an ensign 36ft long and 20ft high, while the jack was 15ft by 9ft; her commissioning pendant was to have a length of 72ft.

Besides the Navy's ensign, bent to the ensign staff, and the pendant used to identify the rank of a flag officer or commodore, each ship carried a full set of national ensigns, jacks and pendants used for signalling purposes. Initially, few were designed specially for signalling, and messages were communicated largely by the position in which existing flags were hoisted. From early in the eighteenth century, these flags were stored in a flag locker, fitted on the poop just inside the taffrail. The introduction of a special set of signal flags was formulated by Hawke in the middle of the century, and other commanders developed the system to arrange a complex system of messages that were recorded in a standard signal book.

This anonymous print, identified as the *Experiment* from her ten-gunport lower battery but two-level quarter lights, illustrates the masting and rigging of the 50-gun ship by the 1770s. The main development is the tendency to shorten the mizzen course, which is cut off and lashed to the mizzen lower mast, although the full length of the lateen yard is retained; ten years later this arrangement began to be superseded by a gaff-and-boom spanker. (NMM: PAI2613)

Table 106: Sailing Reports – draught and freeboard (1742–95)

	Draught fwd	Draught aft	Midship port above water	Date of Report	Source
1706 Establishment					
Winchester	15 ft 3in	15 ft 2in	2 ft 7in	28.2.1742/3	ADM 95/27
1719 Establishment					
Chatham	16 ft 6in	16 ft 8in	?	16.1.1747	ADM 95/23
Argyll	16 ft 8in	17 ft 4in	4 ft 3in	21.1.1742	ADM 95/27
Romney	?	?	4 ft 6in	Mid–1740s	ADM 95/27
Oxford	16 ft 10in	17 ft 3in	4 ft 11in	Mid–1740s	ADM 95/23
Falmouth	17 ft 0in	17 ft 4in	4 ft 4in	24.10.1746	ADM 95/23
1733 Establishment					
Guernsey	17 ft 10in	17 ft 2in	4 ft 10in	20.10.1748	ADM 95/24
Antelope	17 ft 0in	(unreadable)	4 ft 10in	6.11.1748	ADM 95/24
Sutherland	17 ft 2in	17 ft 0in	4 ft 2in	8.9.1748	ADM 95/23
1741 Establishment					
Harwich	18ft 0in	18ft 10in	5ft 5in	16.5.1750	ADM 95/24
Falkland	16ft 11in	17ft 11in	6ft 5in	20.4.1744	ADM 95/27
Chester	17ft 10in	18ft 4in	5ft 1in	9.7.1744	ADM 95/27
Portland	18ft 8in	19ft 6in	4ft 9in	7.7.1748	ADM 95/23
Norwich	18ft 10in	18ft 8in	5ft 10in	23.3.1748/9	ADM 95/23
Ruby	15ft 8in	16ft 4in	3ft 4in	19.8.1748	ADM 95/27
Colchester (ii)	18ft 7in	19ft 0in	4ft 8in	25.11.1748	ADM 95/23
Modified 1741 Establishment					
*Rochester**	18ft 3in	19ft 4in	4ft 3in	9.1757	ADM 95/65
1745 Establishment					
Tavistock	18ft 0in	18ft 6in	6ft 0in	6.10.1752	ADM 95/25
Post-Establishment					
Preston	18ft 2in	19ft 6in	4ft 4in		RUSI/74
Salisbury	18ft 8in	19ft 7in	4ft 7½in	14.7.1770	ADM 95/66
"	18ft 9in	19ft 9in	4ft 2ft	Mid–1780s	ADM 95/36
Centurion	18ft 3in	19ft 6in	4ft 6in	27.7.1792	ADM 95/38
Bristol	18ft 4in	19ft 8in	3ft 10in		RUSI/74
Adamant	18ft 2in	19ft 8in	5ft 0in	15.9.1786	ADM 95/36
Assistance	18ft 6in	20ft 2in	4ft 10in	15.8.1786	ADM 95/36
Leander	18ft 3in	19ft 6in	5ft 7in	3.9.1788	ADM 95/36
Isis	17ft 10in	19ft 8in	5ft 0in		RUSI/74
Europa	19ft 0in	20ft 2in	4ft 8in	14.9.1795	ADM 95/38
Leopard	17ft 10in	20ft 0in	4ft 8in	Mid–1790s	ADM 95/38
Medusa	17ft 6in	18ft 6in	4ft 3in	9.10.1792	ADM 95/38
Grampus	19ft 9in	20ft 7in	3ft 9in	3.5.1786	ADM 95/36
Trusty	19ft 2in	19ft 8in	6ft 2in	6.8.1793	ADM 95/38
"	19ft 0in	20ft 5in	4ft 0in	31.5.1795	ADM 95/38
Acquisitions 1795–1804					
Calcutta	18ft 10in	19ft 0in	8ft 3in		RUSI/74
Glatton	21ft 6in	20ft 2in	8ft 9in		RUSI/74
Coromandel	22ft 0in	21ft 1in	8ft 6in		RUSI/74
Tromp	19ft 0in	20ft 7in	4ft 7½in		RUSI/74
Alkmaar	21ft 0in	20ft 6in			RUSI/74
Batavier	19ft 6in	20ft 6in			RUSI/74
Hindostan (ii)	23ft 0in	23ft 3in	10ft 4in		RUSI/74

* stored for 4 months. Note that several of the forms are undated and the approximate period given above is an estimate of origin.

Performance under sail

Apart from some unquantified and anecdotal comment, there is little evidence on the performance of the earliest ships covered by this study, although speed under sail was an important requirement in the first 'frigates'. As they became genuine two-deckers, one may speculate that firepower became a more important criterion, and performance probably suffered. However, the Navy began to keep standard performance records called Sailing Quality Reports from at least the 1740s (although there is some evidence that some information began to be collected in a less formal way earlier), to provide some documentation of the behaviour under sail of later 50-gun ships.

These Sailing Quality Report Forms, retained from the 1740s until the end of the sailing era and recorded in the PRO series ADM95, also give the best sailing draught of water, and the crucial matter of freeboard (the height of the upper edge of the sill of the lowest gundeck port above the waterline) for each ship when victualled and stored for Channel service (three months). The Sailing Report information is supplemented from the Navy lists for the early nineteenth century in RUSI/74 in the NMM.

However, these reports need to be considered with some caution. They were usually filled out by captains at the end of a commission or cruise, and although they asked the same questions, they were answered with varying degrees of detail and candour. They were necessarily confined to the particular experience of that captain – who may, for example, never have encountered a gale in that ship – and they usually reported the best achievements of the ship rather than the average. A captain had nothing to gain from an outright lie, but the reports were subjective and most officers tend to bias in favour of their command. For generalisations to carry any weight, they need as many reports as possible on the same ship or those of the same design. This poses a problem for the first half of the eighteenth century for – contrary to popular opinion – the Establishments did not fix the hull form before 1745, so some variation in performance is to be expected.

One apparently objective set of statistics relate to the best sailing draughts of water and its crucially important result, the freeboard of the lowest gunport sill with the ship upright (on most points of sailing the ship would be heeled over, so on the leeward side the freeboard would be much reduced). The distance between the lower sill of the gunport and the waterline (when victualled and stored for three months Channel service) was a measure of a warship's seaworthiness; if it was too small, then the ship would not be able to open her lower ports, and hence employ her heaviest battery, in all but the calmest conditions. It should be stated, however, that this disadvantage could be eased if the ship could approach to leeward of her opponent; not only would the protagonist be heeled over away from her adversary, so that her windward battery ports be raised higher from the waterline, but the extra elevation would somewhat increase the range of her guns (against this, of course, the smoke from the discharge would unhappily blow back in the gunners' faces).

The freeboard measurements, detailed in Table 106, show a steady rise for the first half of the century, but – allowing for self-evident anomalies in the figures – settle down at a little less than 5ft thereafter. Assuming *Winchester*'s 31in is not unusual for the 1706 Establishment, this demonstrates a significant improvement in the fighting efficiency of the 50-gun ship; but, to put this into context, it compares poorly with the 7ft most frigates could boast by the 1780s. This could put the 50-gun ship at a disadvantage and lead to incidents like the action in 1799 between the *Jupiter* and the French 12pdr frigate *La Preneuse*, when the latter was able to escape because the 50-gun ship could not open her lower deck ports in the heavy swell running.

1706 Establishment. The report on the *Winchester* was made shortly before her withdrawal from service. Her low freeboard (noted above) was reduced another 6in when she was victualled for six months. She did not carry topgallant masts (presumably to save strain on an aged hull), and was not very fast or weatherly – 5 or 6 knots close-hauled being the best reported – and she was always bested by the *Mary Galley*, a 40-gun ship of the same Establishment, and by the *Chatham*, a 50 to the 1719 dimensions. She had once reached 10 knots in a gale under main topsail and foresail, but her best feature was a sea-kindly hull, her captain calling her 'as easy a ship in the sea as ever was built by man'.

Most ships of this Establishment had gone by the time that regular Reports started in the 1740s, and those that exist are inevitably for elderly hulls, so it is unfair to use this standard to judge the 1706 Establishment vessels as they were in their early years. There is some evidence that these ships were designed to provide a somewhat greater freeboard (see Table 88), but anecdotal evidence indicates that they were always more 'comfortable' than speedy in service.

1719 Establishment. It is possible to discern some improvements over the earlier ship in terms of speed on most points of sailing. Before the wind, these may be described as 9- to 10-knot (occasionally 11-knot) ships, and close-hauled as generally 7- to 8-knot, although the *Oxford* and *Falmouth* were a little faster and slower, respectively, than the average. Despite a higher nominal gunport freeboard, in practice this meant that for *Falmouth* the leeward sills touched the water in a topgallant gale (a wind in which topgallants could be set), were half the port's depth underwater in a topsail gale,

and were nearly submerged entirely in double-reefed topsail weather. In fact, all seem to have been better fair-weather performers than in heavy conditions, speed falling off dramatically in a seaway and leeway increasing similarly. They were generally easy seaboats, but *Falmouth* (which was very sharp forwards) was prone to pitching. No captain complained about their handling; tacking, wearing ship and steering were all performed satisfactorily.

1733 Establishment. The only real change in dimensions over the 1719 ships was a 7 per cent increase in beam, which should have made the new vessels more stable – presumably in response to complaints about ships like *Oxford* and *Falmouth* being crank. If anything, the available reports suggest a slight drop in speed on each point of sailing, and non-committal remarks like 'sails as well as most when clean' (from the captain of the *Antelope*) imply that they were nothing special under sail. On the other hand, Acworth, the Surveyor, claimed he had received a report from Captain Thomas Lymeburner ('a good manager of ships') of the great character of the *Hampshire*, and he expected that the contract-built ships which were to the same draught should sail as well.[58] One of these ships, the *Sutherland*, was said in a moderate blow to have gained three miles in four hours on the *Leopard* (another merchant-built ship), *Lyme* and *Biddeford* (24s of the same Establishment). There are hints that the heavy weather performance continued to be a weak spot, but the *Guernsey* was 'a dry ship' when lying to.

1741 Establishment. Under this revision, the 50-gun ships were accorded by far the biggest proportionate increase in size – some 13½ per cent in tonnage terms – but all this and more was necessary to carry the vastly heavier armament, under which 18- and 9pdrs were to be replaced by 24- and 12pdrs (see Table 112). They all appear to have achieved a creditable gunport freeboard, and in terms of the power to stand under sail only, the *Ruby* was said to be 'somewhat tender'. Close-hauled, they seem to have gone some way to regaining the speed of the 1719 ships, and were possibly faster before the wind; the *Portland* claimed to have once reached 13 knots (highly unlikely, given her waterline length) in a stiff gale, but the captain admitted that, by contrast, on a wind 'she will not forereach on middling-sailing ships'. Although they could take strong winds, like their predecessors they were much affected by heavy seas, losing speed and increasing leeway.

1745 Establishment. The 1741 dimensions were soon found wanting and another increase was formalised in 1745, but the new Establishment also introduced the idea of a standard draught for each Rate. The best feature of the new design was to achieve 6ft of freeboard for the gunports, but – judging by the *Tavistock* – the new vessels were not as good on a wind as their immediate predecessors; however, 11 to 12 knots with a quartering wind made them as fast off the wind. They were also easy seaboats, and the *Tavistock* at least did not suffer from an unresponsive helm like so many of the 1745 designs were said to do.

Salisbury class, 1766. The vessels of this generation were more heavily laden – with extra boats, carronades and so forth offset by more ballast – and this resulted in greater draught and reduced gunport freeboard. If anything, Slade's design for this class was even more affected by heavy weather; the *Salisbury* distinctly lost advantage of both speed and weatherliness as the wind and sea increased. For small two-deckers, they were very fast in light conditions – 10 to 12 knots off the wind and 7 to 10 knots close-hauled carrying all plain sail.

Portland class, 1767. Like the *Salisbury*, this design was no larger than the 1745 Establishment, and suffered the same heavier lading and consequent reduction in gunport freeboard. They did not possess quite the fair-weather speed of Slade's *Salisbury* – remarks like 'a good company keeper' (*Adamant*) and 'forereaches equal to the generality of other ships' (*Europa*) suggest average performance only – but they were better in heavier conditions, the captain of *Leander*, for example, claiming an advantage 'especially in a fresh gale'. They seem to have handled well, and there are no adverse comments on their seakeeping.

Experiment class, 1772. If these small and lightly-built ships were designed to test an alternative to the new single-decked frigates, then in terms of speed they were successful. The *Medusa* was capable of 9 to 10 knots close-hauled, and claimed to have managed 13 knots with the wind over the quarter, which would match the best frigates. However, a two-decker could not have been as weatherly as a frigate, and would have lost out in a chase to windward; on this point the Report is silent. The design was confined to two ships and was not repeated, so must have been seen as a failure – one near-certain reason being the small freeboard (3ft 10in, stored for Foreign Service) compared with around 6ft for a contemporary frigate. Otherwise, they were satisfactory ships.

Trusty, 1780. A longer, narrower design than the norm, presumably aiming for speed. This is borne out by two Reports, which claim her to be 'remarkable fast' close-hauled, translating as 9 knots in a topsail gale. She also handled very well, being quick on tacking and wearing, but was not so good before the wind. The figures for midship gunport heights at the stated draughts of water quoted in two Reports for this ship indicate how difficult it is to reconcile much of the data in these Reports. The higher figures seem unlikely and may have been measured to a port further forward or aft, where the sheer of the deck produced more freeboard (the *Grampus*, a ship 2ft shorter than the *Trusty* but otherwise similar, gives a figure lower than even the 4ft of the second Report).

A drawing by John Hood of the *Sutherland* (probably the 1741 ship) in heavy weather. It is easy to see why the freeboard of the lower deck gunports was a crucial indicator of the seaworthiness of warships. The ship has reduced sail to the courses, whereas later practice would probably favour close-reefed topsails only in these circumstances. (NMM: PU8497)

11. Fittings

This chapter covers a whole range of ships' equipment such as pumps, steering gear and cooking facilities.

Ground tackle

The sailing warship was fitted with a complex system of ground tackle, a generic term for the equipment used to moor the ship to the 'ground' (*ie* sea-bed), consisting of a range of large or small anchors, the three-strand hemp cables attached to them, and the capstans used to haul in or veer out the cables. For a large warship the effort required to move this equipment was of fearsome proportions, requiring the muscle power of large numbers of seamen.

Each ship carried a number of principal anchors. In the middle of the seventeenth century most Fourth Rates carried five, but by the 1680s this had reduced in almost all cases to four, and remained this quantity into the nineteenth century. Two of these anchors, kept ready in the bows of the ship, were logically called the 'bowers'. The larger of these anchors, the best bower, was carried on the port side, ready for use during a storm, while its slightly smaller mate, the second bower, hung on the starboard side and like its mate was kept ready for prompt use. When not required for immediate use, each would be 'fished', or swung up through a right angle so the shank was horizontal and fastened against the fore channels.

The largest of the four, the sheet anchor, was secured aft of the best bower, but without a cable attached to it. It was held in reserve, and was regarded as a last resort, to be used only in the direst emergency. A fourth anchor, slightly smaller than the other three, was kept as a spare. Besides these four principal anchors, the 50-gun ship carried two smaller ones. The stream anchor was for light work, being designed to hold the ship in light weather and against very weak currents. Even smaller was the kedge, which could be carried by the longboat or pinnace, and dropped to provide a mooring point to which the ship could haul herself by use of her capstan when there was no wind.

In 1670 these six anchors together weighed between 4.9 and 5.0 tons for most of the Fourth Rates (except for a huge 6.15 tons in the case of the *Greenwich* and *Leopard*, and only 4.6 tons in the case of the *Assurance* and *Constant Warwick* and 4.5 tons for the *Adventure*).[59] Until the end of the seventeenth century, the weights of all the anchors tended to increase; after that growth was only proportional to the increase in size of the ships themselves, but the differences between the sizes of the principal anchors on a ship

tended to reduce, although their different names and roles were retained for most of the eighteenth century. In 1706 the sheet anchor weighed 33cwt, and the combined weight of all the anchors totalled 99½ tons. The 1719 Establishment provided that the bower anchors of the 50-gun ship be of 39½cwt, with cables of 17½in circumference (5½in diameter).

By 1780 the differences between the sizes of the four main anchors had disappeared. In that year the weights for the larger 50s were raised to 49cwt each, for which cables of 19in circumference (diameter 6in) were specified; the two smaller anchors were to be of 11cwt and 5¼cwt respectively. The smaller 50s were assigned four main anchors of 46cwt, with a stream anchor of 10½cwt and a kedge anchor of 5¼cwt.

The cable – exclusively used for mooring purposes – consisted of a three-strand hemp rope measuring 120 fathoms or 720ft in length; indeed, the 'cable' became a standard measurement in the Imperial system of weights and measures. In 1670 most Fourth Rates carried seven main cables (except the *Greenwich* and *Leopard*, with eight apiece); but in the eighteenth century almost all 50-gun ships had eight main cables, or two per anchor. This allowed for replacement of cables worn out through frequent use, or for the doubling or joining together of cables for use when the ship had to moor in deep water of more than about 40 fathoms, since three times the depth of water was considered the minimum length required if the cable was not to be too near vertical, particularly when the ship was pitching in a heavy swell.

Cables of smaller circumference were carried for the stream and kedge anchors; for the kedge, these were classed as hawsers, small cables of up to 8in or 9in around, used also for warping or towing the ship,

Although unidentified – but probably of the *Portland* (see page 27) – this model of a 50 from the 1690s is rich in detail. The drumhead capstan includes bars and swifter, while the ground tackle includes a full complement of anchors – and there is even an anchor buoy lashed in the fore channels. Note at this time the difference in the size of anchors. (United States Naval Academy Museum, Annapolis model No 33)

mooring alongside, or as 'springs' – an auxiliary line from the after end of the ship to her main cable when at anchor which allowed the ship some manoeuvrability by hauling or veering the spring.

All these cables weighed a massive amount, particularly those which were waterlogged through long use, and they also occupied a vast volume of space, which had to be set aside for their storage. They were packed in vast coils on the cable tiers, platform areas (running for some 40 per cent of the ship's total length) on the orlop deck, from which water could drain off into the bilges. The cable tiers stretched along both sides of the deck, leaving just a space along the centreline where were the masts, companionways and storage areas such as sailrooms, separated from the cables by stanchions and light bulkheads.

The main cables entered the ship via the hawse holes, four of which (one for each main anchor) were placed in the bows just above the lower deck and thus well above the waterline to prevent the seas entering during heavy weather. The heavy timbers or hawse pieces around the holes, which measured perhaps 2½ times the diameters of the largest cable to be passed through it, were fitted parallel to the keel to enable the cables to be drawn over them, and by the late eighteenth century were lined with iron to prevent excess wearing. The lower edge of the hawse hole was rounded-off to prevent wear on the cables. The gap between the cable and the hawse hole was filled, when the cable was not being worked, by oakum-stuffed canvas 'hawse bags'; as inrushing seas still penetrated the hull at the holes, a barrier was fitted on the lower deck inside to limit the spread of water; this removable barrier, usually just under 4ft in height, enclosed a space known as the manger, used for the livestock carried for dietary purposes.

The cables were handled by one of two capstans, a device that came into general use in the middle of the fifteenth century. The early type, known as the crab, lacked a separate head to hold the four bars, which were passed through holes bored right through the upper part of the cylinder so that one man on each end

Table 107: Crew stations for mooring and unmooring a 50-gun ship (1788) – total 240 (leaving 20 seamen for other services)

12 on the forecastle	3 to take off the nippers
42 on the heaving tier	10 to carry forward and hold on to the nippers
36 on the veering tier	2 to pay the cable down the hatchway
14 light round the messenger	8 to fish jack and buoy
14 to hold onto the messenger	72 on the capstan bars
3 nipper men	24 to pull on the swifters

could apply horizontal leverage to turn the cylinder, although as each bar traversed the hub of the capstan at a different height at least six of the crew were forced to stoop or stretch. In the late seventeenth century a new type was invented by Sir Samuel Morland, and was introduced into the Royal Navy around the turn of the century. A large, broad wheel of timber – the drumhead – was attached to the top of the cylinder, with its wide circumference bored with up to twelve holes; the bars inserted into these no longer passed through the hub of the capstan but radiated like bicycle spokes at the same height, allowing a larger number of men to operate it more comfortably and effectively. Up to six men could push on each bar, allowing seventy-two around the drumhead, while another twenty-four could pull on the swifters – ropes tied between the ends of the bars.

The 50-gun ship had two of these drumhead capstans, each a double capstan, with heads on both the upper and lower decks, and with the heel of its spindle stepped on the orlop deck. There was a similar wheel – the trundlehead – fitted around the cylinder on the lower deck, and this could take a further set of bars to allow even more men to employ their efforts. The primary role of the main capstan, situated on the centreline about halfway between the main and mizzen masts, was for hauling in and letting out the anchor cables. This laborious task required the efforts of most of the seamen aboard, with a total of 240 assigned stations during this operation, as shown in Table 107.

The cable itself, being heavy and unmanageable, could not be wound directly on the capstan, but instead was indirectly connected through a lighter 'endless' rope called the messenger which led from the capstan alongside the cable and via a block forward back to the capstan again. Light lines called nippers were used to temporarily fasten the messenger to the section of anchor cable currently passing over the upper deck, and the capstan then employed to wind on the messenger.

Besides mooring and unmooring, the main capstan was also used for other purposes, such as lifting the

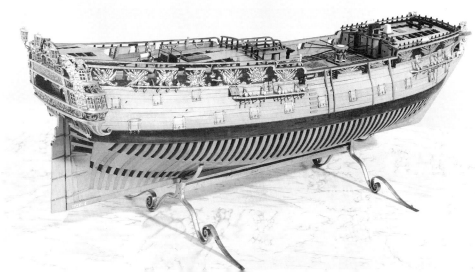

This Navy Board model of an unidentified 50-gun ship is ascribed to 1725, but although it has the beam of a 1719 Establishment ship, the gundeck is about 3ft too long at the most likely scale of 1/64. However, it accurately depicts many of the fittings of the time, including the prominent jeer capstan in the waist and the wheel on the quarterdeck. Under the break of the forecastle, the separate boatswain's cabin can be seen (its counterpart to starboard being for the carpenter). The upper deck gunports in the waist have no lids – a feature which seems to have become general during Queen Anne's reign. (NMM: B7633)

ship's boats or hoisting in the guns and other heavy items. The fore or jeer capstan, situated in the waist between the main hatch and the forecastle, was similar in construction but generally used for lighter work such as loading stores or getting up spars.

Steering

The traditional stern rudder, hinged vertically against the ship's sternpost by a series of pintles and gudgeons, had been in use from before the twelfth century. By the fifteenth century the tiller, fitted directly over the head of the rudder, was controlled directly by the helmsman who had to be located in the same vertical plane as the tiller, and thus on a large ship was stationed below decks and unable to see the movement of the sails or other indications of the ship's behaviour. Towards the end of the Tudor era, the introduction of the whipstaff, a vertical extension of the tiller which pivoted on a fixture on the upper deck, had allowed the helmsman to control the rudder's movement from the upper deck, but still restricted both physical control and operating efficiency of steering.

The main improvement came in during Queen Anne's reign, with the replacement of the whipstaff by steering ropes controlling the lateral motion of the tiller, and leading to a steering windlass stationed on the quarterdeck. The windlass was within a few years superseded by a fully-fledged steering wheel, while the refining of the system of steering ropes and blocks soon gave the helmsman more effective control over the tiller, which allowed the latter to be moved to the full sweep allowed by the internal width of the lower deck. The wheel was introduced later for Fourth Rates than for larger ships, where the disadvantages of the whipstaff were most obvious; the *Gloucester* of 1711, for example, still had a companion for its whipstaff, but by 1715 the wheel seems to have become standard.

The wheel was initially situated above the end of the tiller, and thus directly abaft the mizzen mast. In the 1730s the practice developed of moving it to the forward side of this mast, in order to improve the helmsman's view. This required a more sophisticated systems of blocks and tiller ropes, but the system was not perfected until 1771, when a new system of sweeps and rowles, designed by Pollard, Master Boatbuilder in the Portsmouth Dockyard, was approved by the Navy Board. The wheel until mid-century remained for most ships a single affair, fitted to the front of a metal spindle housed within a wooden cylindrical barrel over which the tiller ropes were wound as on a windlass; but by the 1750s most new Fourth Rates had a second wheel attached to the rear of the spindle, so that a second pair of helmsmen could apply their strength to the wheel when the weather necessitated greater leverage.

Navigation of the ship was the responsibility of the ship's master, the senior of the warrant officers, under the command of the captain. He, and all deck officers, were expected to provide their own charts and navigational equipment such as astrolabes and quadrants. However, heavier and more vital items such as compasses were supplied by the Navy Board. Each compass, with its magnetised needle able to pivot freely inside, was set into a brass bowl (confusingly called a 'box') which in turn was set into a brass ring on gimbals.

Two boxed compasses were carried just forwards of the helm of each vessel, protected from the elements by placing them within a wooden box – the binnacle or (more commonly) bittacle – which consisted of three compartments divided laterally. The central compartment contained a lantern or candle, and those on either side each contained a compass, placed low down so that at night the lantern's light would illuminate its surface through a rectangular glass plate set into the panel between the compartments.

The side compartments had room for storage above the compasses, and these were here fitted with drawers to hold sand-filled hour glasses, log and lead lines, and other navigational equipment. Each compartment had a vertically sliding shutter over an opening in the rear face of the bittacle (that side facing the wheel). One of the two side shutters would be open to allow the helmsman to look down onto the compass it guarded, while the central shutter remained closed (once the lantern was lit) to mask its direct light and protect the helmsman's night vision.

The bittacle was installed directly ahead of the helmsman and positioned so that the could look directly at one or other compass, depending upon which side of the wheel he stood. Seventeenth-century ships carried two bittacles, the second being placed on the quarterdeck where the officer of the watch could see the set of the sails at the same time as navigate by the compass; the introduction of the wheel (to supersede the whipstaff), and its later removal to the quarterdeck, removed the need for such duplication, but all Fourth Rates were issued a second (and larger ships sometimes a third) bittacle, each complete with its lantern and two compasses, which were presumably stored as spares below decks.

Pumps

Wooden-hulled ships are never dry. No matter how tightly constructed and well caulked with oakum, the seams of the hull allow some water to penetrate, and after a voyage of some months the joints of a large warship would be forced apart by the movement of the ship.

Much of the water on the upper deck could be disregarded, as it could drain through scuppers directly over the side of the ship; the scuppers were lead pipes let into the deck to carry water down and outboard, with a hinged leather flap at the outboard end to prevent seawater washing back in. But other water taken aboard had to be collected and returned to the sea. All the decks were accordingly cambered, so that water could drain to their sides rather than along the centreline where the hatches were collected (and water was discouraged from entering these by coamings built up around the hatchways). The sheer of the ship ensured that the decks also curved longitudinally, with their lowest point midships, and this also aided the drainage system.

A series of waterways then carried the water down through the various decks to the bottom of the hold, where it collected and had to be removed by pumps, whose wells (bottom ends) were situated at the lowest point, on the centreline in the hold, close to the heel of the main mast. Since the late sixteenth century British warships had been fitted with chain pumps to bring the water which collected in the pump wells up to the lower (gun) deck. There were two of these chain pumps, situated abreast just aft of the main mast; each

pump consisted of two wooden tubes or 'cases' bored longitudinally with holes of some 5in diameter. An endless chain passed up one tube and returned down the other, carrying at intervals a burr – a leather washer held in place with two wooden saucers, the washer forming a fairly close seal with the inside of the tube. In the seventeenth century the tubes were cut from elm, but about 1717 these were replaced by tubes bored from oak, with a round cross-section.

In addition, each ship also carried a pair of elm-tree pumps which were placed just forward of the main mast. These operated on the suction principle, and drew water directly from an inlet at the side of the ship (just below the waterline) up through holes bored through single trunks of elm. It was thus not to remove water from the bilges, but to draw water from the sea which was then delivered, under pressure, through outlets on the upper deck or the lower deck for use in fire-fighting or in washing down the decks.

Boats

From their earliest days English warships of any size were equipped with several boats for transferring men and stores between ship and shore, and for several ancillary roles such as when weighing anchors, or as an oared 'tug' when the parent ship was becalmed. Originally, each ship had a longboat, too large to be easily hoisted aboard so that it was usually towed at sea; in addition, a smaller boat or 'pinnace' was carried (the largest ships also carried a skiff, later a yawl), hoisted aboard by means of tackle stretched between the fore and main yards, and stowed on spars or booms stretching across the waist from the forecastle to the quarterdeck.

The boats had different roles. The longboat was designed for seagoing employment, while the pinnace was used primarily in sheltered waters, or in harbour. The obvious detrimental effects of the towed boat on the ship's sailing qualities led, by the middle of the seventeenth century, to the introduction of smaller longboats. As a less robust craft than the longboat, the pinnace was of much smaller cross-section than the longboat, although as the latter shrank in size it became little longer than the pinnace. The longboat could by now be hoisted aboard and stowed in the place of the pinnace, the latter then being stowed inside the longboat.

In 1701 a third boat was added to the Fourth Rate's Establishment – a six-oared Deal yawl (the term 'Deal' referring to the place of its development, not the material). The 1706 Establishment set out dimensions for the other two boats: the longboat was to be 30ft long and 9ft 2in broad, while the pinnace was to measure 29ft by 5ft 11in. The 1719 Establishment, as in other matters, laid down a more precise set of regulations for the boats aboard a 50-gun ship. The longboat was to be 30ft long, 8ft 8in broad, and 3ft 8in deep.

This fully rigged model represents a 1706 Establishment 50-gun ship, but the replacement of the sprit topmast with a jibboom suggests that it post-dates the introduction of the new Establishment of Masts in 1711 or that it was subsequently re-rigged. The model demonstrates the early method of stowing a boat (on the spare spars amidships), but while this was satisfactory for a barge or pinnace, the longboat was normally too heavy for this treatment and was usually towed at sea – as can be seen in the painting of the *Woolwich* in Chapter 10. (NMM: B1368)

The ten-oared pinnace was also 30ft long, with a breadth of 6ft 2in and depth of 2ft 6½in. The six-oared yawl was 23ft long, 5ft 7in across, and 2ft 5in deep.

In 1740 the pinnace was replaced by a larger version, 32ft long, while the yawl became 28ft long, with eight oars. In 1746 a fourth boat was added for ships built to the 1745 Establishment – a 25ft Deal cutter with six oars – and in 1781 another cutter – 18ft long with four oars – was added to bring up the complement to five boats. By the turn of the century, a second 25ft cutter had replaced the yawl.

Cooking facilities

The galley or cook-room for any British two-deck ship was positioned under the forecastle, forward on the upper deck, with its vent carried through the forecastle deck by a chimney, whose upper section carried the smoke some way above the deck, and was usually (but not always) topped by a cowl which could be turned to face away from the prevailing wind, so fumes and smoke would not be blown back into the galley. The galley formed a separate compartment inside the forecastle, positioned directly behind the forecastle bulkhead; this extra compartment reduced the risk of pilferage, and of damage under fire.

Within the cook-room, all Fourth Rates were equipped with two large copper cooking vessels or kettles, originally globular cauldrons but after about 1700 of cylindrical shape; they were known as the fish kettle and the small kettle, and were positioned side by side in the ash pit, surrounded until the middle of the century by a brick-built fireheath to contain the heat of the furnace; from then on the fire heaths were constructed of iron, while the two separate cooking vessels were replaced by a copper double kettle, a single vessel divided into two unequal parts with separate lids. There were two separate furnaces inside the fireheath, both vented to the chimney. These iron fittings were of tremendous weight; the fire hearth for the *Hannibal* (1780), for example, weighed 51⅞cwt, while the double kettle was another 8¾cwt; their combined

cost was £52-16-2d.[60]

The cook-room also contained preparation tables where the cook and his assistant could work, and a limited amount of food storage for day-to-day needs. The cook himself, usually a partially disabled former seaman, pensioned off from Greenwich Hospital, was also berthed within the forecastle, to be close to his galley.

Two contemporary models of the longboat from the 60-gun *Medway* of 1742, one showing the structure and the other fully rigged. At 1/48th scale the models measure 28ft by 8ft, which seems a little small for a 60's longboat, but the details are accurate enough. (NMM: B9575)

12. Armament

There are imperfect records of the ordnance carried by frigates during the Commonwealth era. The numbers certainly altered from time to time, and varied from ship to ship, but it is clear that few of the ships which later (usually following rebuilding) would emerge as 50-gun ships at this time carried many more than 40 guns. This is because much of the upper deck, and certainly in the waist, did not carry guns until late in the decade or even until after the Restoration. In fact, the vessels of this period that were built with 48 to 52 guns were the Third Rates – ships which would eventually develop into 60-gun ships.

A list of 1655 shows that the newly-built *Bristol*, *Portland* and *Dover*, clearly meant to typify the Commonwealth Fourth Rates, were established with 38 carriage guns – 24 culverins, 6 demi-culverins and 8 sakers.[61] Although no allocation to decks is quoted, and it is likely that at this date gun types were mixed on each deck, it seems probable that the culverins were intended as the gundeck armament; this was the only deck in 1655 to carry a full battery. Logically the demi-culverins were intended for the deck above, originally a half-deck but now a continuous upper deck even though not strengthened to take large carriage guns along the waist. Whether the sakers were intended for the forward part of this upper deck or for the quarterdeck is conjectural.

The same 'establishment' incidentally lists the munitions, stores and small arms for each of these Fourth Rates as 908 round shot, 462 double-headed shot, 100 barrels of powder, 60 muskets, 7 blunderbusses, 60 pikes and 40 hatchets. Earlier records show an armament when they were 34-gun ships of 2 demi-cannon, 10 culverins and 12 demi-culverins on the gundeck, plus 2 demi-culverins and 8 sakers on the upper deck.

The armament was being slowly standardised, although until well into the next century the weaponry actually carried by a warship could often differ considerably from the guns allocated to that vessel in its official 'Establishment'. Nevertheless, the lack of comprehensive records, as well as the frequent changes in many ships' actual weaponry, make a ship's Establishment of Guns a useful guide to relative firepower. The principal guns carried by Fourth Rates were the culverin, a gun throwing a shot of 18 pounds and at this time being of about 50cwts in weight and 11½ft length, and the demi-culverin, throwing a shot of 9 pounds and about 28cwt in weight and 10ft in length. The smaller saker fired a shot of some 5 or 6 pounds, although it must be stressed that there were

wide variations in the size and calibres of each class of gun. These variations were increased by the capture of Dutch weapons during the three wars of 1652 to 1674, which introduced 'intermediate' calibre guns of (nominally) 24-pound and 12-pound calibres.

As the contemporary portraits of the three ships mentioned show each to have twelve ports a side on the lower deck, a fair assumption is that the culverins were expected to fill all the lower deck ports (in practice, at least one pair of ports on the lower deck appears to have been unfilled on most occasions). As each of the three also show three or four ports a side on the quarterdeck, it seems logical that at least four of the sakers were mounted there, leaving six demi-culverins and four sakers for the upper deck ports. As this would only fill five ports a side, the implication is that at this date the upper deck had not been extended forward and remained a half-deck as the majority of the Fourth Rate frigates had been completed with.

This would appear to conflict with the portraits, which show the *Bristol* and *Portland* each with eleven, and the *Dover* with twelve, upper deck ports a side, and with the upper decks clearly running the length of the ships. However, the portraits date from a few years later, by which time this modification had seemingly been extended ('retro-fitted', in modern jargon) to virtually all the Fourth Rates built from 1647 onwards. By contrast, the same 1655 document shows the Third Rate frigates (those cited are the *Speaker* herself,

Table 108: Fourth Rates – Establishments of Guns and Men at Restoration in 1660

44 guns, 160 men: *Bristol*, *Leopard*, *Newcastle*, *Winsby*
    (renamed *Happy Return*), *Yarmouth*
40 guns, 150 men: *Centurion*, *Gainsborough* (renamed
    Swallow), *Indian*, *Kentish* (renamed *Kent*), *Portland*
40 guns, 140 men: *Advice*, *Assistance*, *Convertine*, *Diamond*,
    Dover, *Foresight*, *Jersey*, *Maidstone* (became *Mary Rose*),
    Mathias, *Nantwich* (renamed *Bredah*), *Preston* (renamed
    Antelope), *Reserve*, *Ruby*, *Taunton* (became *Crown*)
38 guns, 130 men: *Dragon*, *Elizabeth*, *Hampshire*, *Phoenix*,
    Portsmouth, *President* (now *Bonaventure*), *Sapphire*, *Tiger*
34 guns, 120 men: *Adventure*, *Nonsuch*
32 guns, 115 men: *Assurance*, *Constant Warwick*, *Marmaduke*
    (110 men only)
30 guns, 100 men: *Amity*, *Expedition*, *Guinny* (or *Guinea*)

The list also includes the *Princess* with 34 guns and 100 men;
however, this is presumably the anticipated position as she was not
yet completed, and she clearly was finally armed on completion
like the other 'broad-beamed' frigates.
Source: Pepys' Register, excluding some of the Dutch prizes with
non-standard weaponry.

HMS *Leopard* 1790

Drawings by John McKay

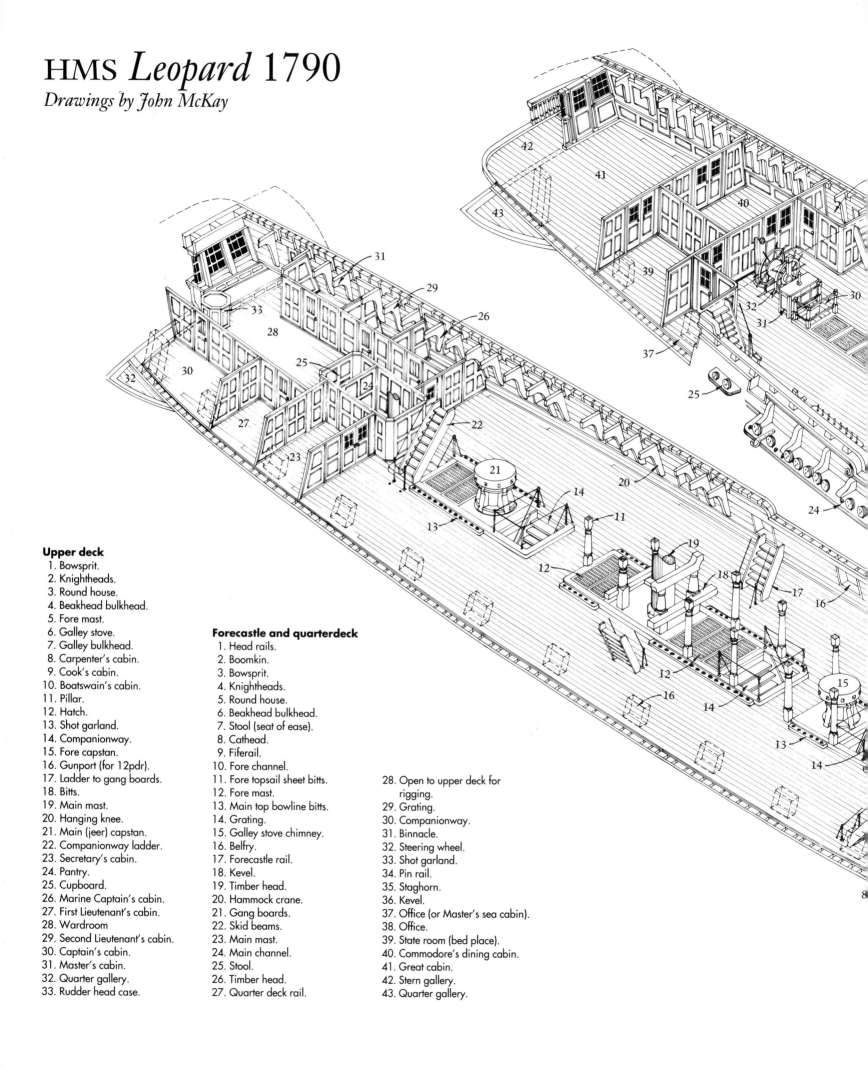

Upper deck

1. Bowsprit.
2. Knightheads.
3. Round house.
4. Beakhead bulkhead.
5. Fore mast.
6. Galley stove.
7. Galley bulkhead.
8. Carpenter's cabin.
9. Cook's cabin.
10. Boatswain's cabin.
11. Pillar.
12. Hatch.
13. Shot garland.
14. Companionway.
15. Fore capstan.
16. Gunport (for 12pdr).
17. Ladder to gang boards.
18. Bitts.
19. Main mast.
20. Hanging knee.
21. Main (jeer) capstan.
22. Companionway ladder.
23. Secretary's cabin.
24. Pantry.
25. Cupboard.
26. Marine Captain's cabin.
27. First Lieutenant's cabin.
28. Wardroom
29. Second Lieutenant's cabin.
30. Captain's cabin.
31. Master's cabin.
32. Quarter gallery.
33. Rudder head case.

Forecastle and quarterdeck

1. Head rails.
2. Boomkin.
3. Bowsprit.
4. Knightheads.
5. Round house.
6. Beakhead bulkhead.
7. Stool (seat of ease).
8. Cathead.
9. Fiferail.
10. Fore channel.
11. Fore topsail sheet bitts.
12. Fore mast.
13. Main top bowline bitts.
14. Grating.
15. Galley stove chimney.
16. Belfry.
17. Forecastle rail.
18. Kevel.
19. Timber head.
20. Hammock crane.
21. Gang boards.
22. Skid beams.
23. Main mast.
24. Main channel.
25. Stool.
26. Timber head.
27. Quarter deck rail.

28. Open to upper deck for rigging.
29. Grating.
30. Companionway.
31. Binnacle.
32. Steering wheel.
33. Shot garland.
34. Pin rail.
35. Staghorn.
36. Kevel.
37. Office (or Master's sea cabin).
38. Office.
39. State room (bed place).
40. Commodore's dining cabin.
41. Great cabin.
42. Stern gallery.
43. Quarter gallery.

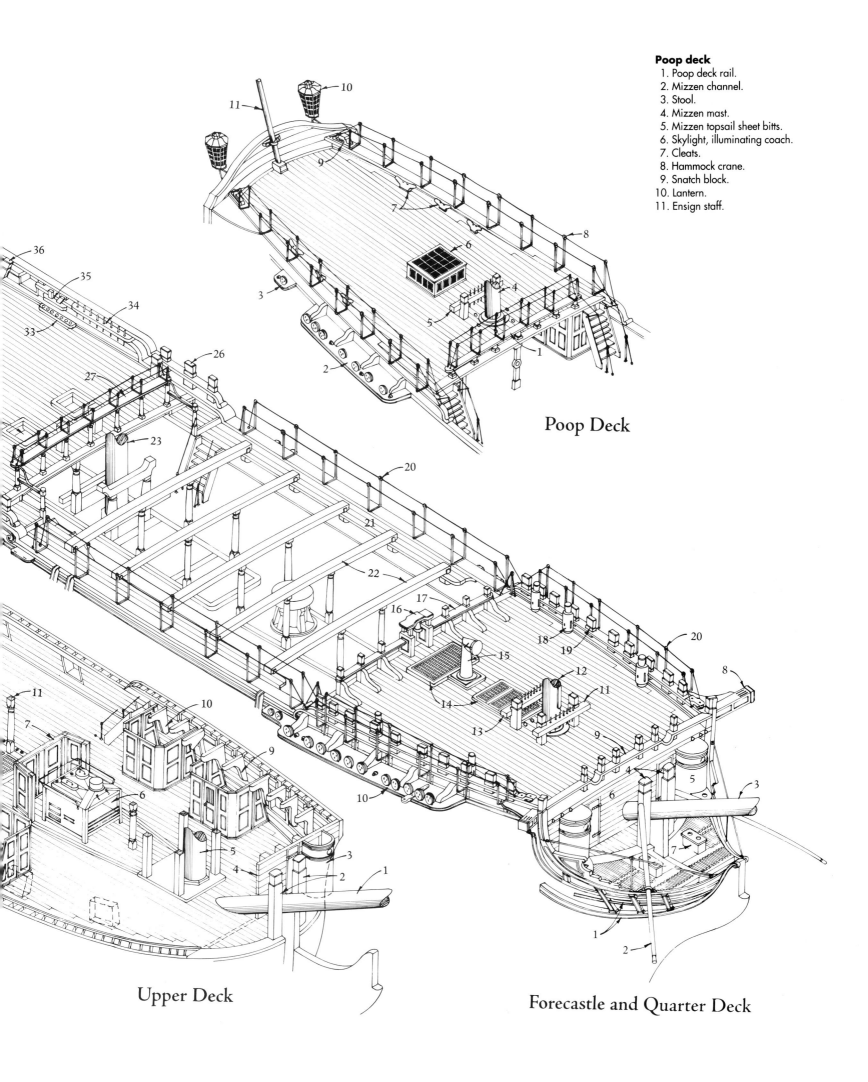

Poop deck
1. Poop deck rail.
2. Mizzen channel.
3. Stool.
4. Mizzen mast.
5. Mizzen topsail sheet bitts.
6. Skylight, illuminating coach.
7. Cleats.
8. Hammock crane.
9. Snatch block.
10. Lantern.
11. Ensign staff.

Poop Deck

Upper Deck

Forecastle and Quarter Deck

Fairfax (ii) and *Marston Moor*) with 4 demi-cannon, 22 culverins, 26 demi-culverins and 8 sakers – clearly complete two-deckers of 60 guns.

Pepys' Register of the 'force' (*ie* guns) carried by each ship at the Restoration shows that most Fourth Rates in 1660 were established with 38 or 40 guns. Exceptions were the *Bristol* and the 'broad-beam' ships – the *Leopard*, *Newcastle*, *Happy Return* (ex-*Winsby*) and *Yarmouth* – each with 44 guns (and 160 men). Most of the surviving pre-1650 vessels and smaller prizes also differed, having fewer guns. Thus the rapid growth by about ten additional guns which most Fourth Rates acquired was concentrated in the first few years of Charles II's reign, as the Establishment of 1666 shows that many of these ships were now close to or at the quantitative level that would become the 50-gun standard for these ships for the following century. The armament of the '50-gun' Fourth Rate was clearly becoming a 'norm' by this time, with 22 culverins being almost universally established on the gundeck, and a similar number of demi-culverins on the upper deck, leaving about a half-dozen sakers on the quarterdeck.

It is interesting to compare the 1666 Establishment with a list provided 'to the principal officer and commissioners provided to His Majesty's Navy', by the Ordnance Board on 18 May 1664 – the first list of all ordnance assigned to the fleet since the Commonwealth.[62] In 1664 four of the five 'broad-beamed' vessels (*Newcastle*, *Yarmouth*, *Leopard* and *Princess*) carried a mixed primary armament of demi-cannon and culverins – numbering 22 of these weapons on the *Newcastle* and 24 on each of the other three. It seems logical that all these weapons were carried on the gundeck, while the 20 demi-culverins attributed to each (22 on the *Leopard*) were mounted on the upper deck.

By 1666 the *Yarmouth*'s Establishment is given as 22 × 24pdrs and 2 culverins, presumably indicating that she had been substantially re-armed with captured Dutch guns on the gundeck (the 2 culverins being retained as bow-chase guns there). *Leopard* was now apportioned 22 demi-cannon and 2 culverins, indicating a policy decision to add to the firepower on at least two of these largest of the Fourth Rates. If so, it certainly was not consistently applied – the *Newcastle* and *Princess* retained the same mixture of demi-cannon and culverins, while the fifth of the type (*Happy Return*) still carried 22 culverins as her primary armament.

The tables set out within Deane's *Doctrine* in 1670 showed that most Fourth Rates were allocated about 125-135 barrels of powder and about 14½ tons of shot when stored for sea service. The *Greenwich* and *Leopard* were, as in other characteristics, significantly different; while still classed as Fourth Rates, they were established with 60 and 58 guns respectively, carried proportionately much more powder and shot, and were at this time closer to the Third Rates than to Fourth Rate ships.

Table 109: 1666 Establishment of Guns – Fourth Rates

Vessels	Guns	Lower deck	Upper deck and quarterdeck		Location uncertain
(A) With demi-cannon on the lower deck:					
Leopard	54	22	24 (demi-culv.)	6 (sakers)	2 (culverins)
Seven Oaks (prize)	54	22	24 (demi-culv.)	8 (sakers)	
(B) With demi-cannon and culverins on the lower deck:					
Princess	52	10 (demi-cannon)	4 (demi-culv.)	6 (sakers)	
		12 (culverins)	20 (8pdrs)		
Newcastle	50	10 (demi-cannon)	22 (demi-culv.)	6 (sakers)	
		12 (culverins)			
(C) With 24pdrs on the lower deck:					
Matthias (prize)	54	24	20 (demi-culv.)	10 (sakers)	
Yarmouth	52	22	20 (demi-culv.)	8 (sakers)	2 (culverins)
West Friesland (prize)	50	22	22 (demi-culv.)	6 (sakers)	
(D) With culverins on the lower deck:					
Charles V (prize)	54	22	24 (demi-culv.)	8 (sakers)	
Bristol	52	26	22 (demi-culv.)	4 (sakers)	
Mars (prize)	52	22	24 (demi-culv.)	6 (sakers)	
Happy Return	52	22	22 (demi-culv.)	8 (sakers)	
Antelope	52	22	20 (demi-culv.)	10 (sakers)	
Convertine	52	24	20 (8pdrs)	8 (sakers)	
Maria Sancta (prize)	50	22	22 (demi-culv.)	6 (sakers)	
Jersey, Mary Rose	50	22	20 (demi-culv.)	8 (sakers)	
Portland	48	22	24 (demi-culv.)	2 (sakers)	
Breda, Centurion, Diamond, Reserve, Swallow, Crown	48	22	20 (demi-culv.)	6 (sakers)	
Black Spread Eagle, Guilder de Ruyter (prizes)	48	22	18 (demi-culv.)	8 (sakers)	
Advice, Bonaventure	48	22	16 (demi-culv.)	10 (sakers)	
Assistance, Dover, Foresight, Kent, Ruby	46	22	20 (demi-culv.)	4 (sakers)	
Portsmouth	44	22	18 (demi-culv.)	4 (sakers)	
Saint Paul (prize)	40	22	18 (demi-culv.)		
Hope (prize)	40	22	18 (sakers)		
(E) With 12pdrs on the lower deck:					
Golden Lion (prize)	42	20	18 (6pdrs)	4 (sakers)	
Black Bull, Delfe, Zealand (prizes)	40	22	18 (sakers)		

(F) With culverins and smaller on the lower deck	Guns	Culverins:	Demi-culverins:	Sakers:	
Marmaduke	42	12	22	8	
Elizabeth	42	12	20	10	
Hampshire	42	12	16	14	
Dragon	40	12	20	8	
Tiger	40	12	16	12	
Sapphire	40	12	10	14	(does not add to total)
Amity	38	12	14	14	(does not add to total)
Assurance	38	10	24	4	
Adventure	38	10	14	14	
Guinea	38	10	10	18	
Constant Warwick	34	12	12	10	

Note this list excludes the new construction ships (*Greenwich*, *St David* and *St Patrick*) for which a breakdown is incomplete; it also excludes two prizes (the *Unity* and *Young Prince*) and the elderly *Welcome* (being disarmed), *Expedition* and *Providence*.

Source: Ordnance Establishment of April 1666 (Add 9302 in British Museum).

Table 110: Weight and cost (in £) of Ordnance and Gunner's stores, 1670

Vessel(s)	Guns (tons)	Shot (tons-cwt)	Powder (barrels)	Cost of guns (£)	Cost of shot (£)	Cost of powder (£)	Cost of stores (£-s)	Total cost (£-s)
Greenwich, Leopard	94	22-0	210	1692	329	630	578-19	3229-19
Newcastle	54	14-10	200	972	192	600	514-7	2278-7
Kent	56	14-10	135	1008	192	405	514-7	2119-7
Group B	54	14-10	135	972	192	405	514-7	2083-7
Bonaventure	54	14-10	131	972	192	393	514-7	2071-7
Group C	54	14-10	130	972	192	390	514-7	2068-7
Tiger	54	13-0	130	972	176	390	514-7	2052-7
Sapphire	50	14-10	130	900	192	390	514-7	1996-7
Assurance	50	13-0	130	900	176	390	514-7	1980-7
Warwick	44	14-10	125	792	192	375	488-10	1847-10
Dragon	44	13-0	130	792	176	390	488-10	1846-10
Adventure, Nonsuch	44	13-0	125	792	176	375	488-10	1831-10

Group B comprises the *Antelope, Bristol, Crown, Diamond, Happy Return, Jersey, Mary Rose, Portland, Princess, Reserve, Ruby* and *Yarmouth*. Group C comprises the *Advice, Assistance, Centurion, Dover, Foresight, Hampshire, Marmaduke, Portsmouth* and *Swallow*. The *Saint David* is not included in Deane's table, but would probably have fallen into Group B.
Note that the *Nonsuch*, launched in 1668, was actually classed as a Fifth Rate, unlike the previous ship of this name.
The guns (all iron) were priced at £18 per ton, and the powder at £3 per ton.
Source: Deane's *Doctrine of Naval Architecture*, 1670, pp80–81.

This model from Annapolis is one of the 123ft group of the 1690s, possibly the *Rochester* or *Anglesea*. There are 11 pairs of gunports on both the gundeck and upper deck; in the main the distance between the gunports is unusually wide (about 8½ – 8¾ft when scaled up), although the upper row seems particularly crowded towards the bow. Note there are no lids to the ports in the waist on this deck. (United States Naval Academy Museum, Annapolis model No 9)

The 1677 Establishment of Guns

With the close of the Dutch wars, the Admiralty successfully proposed a new building programme, comprising thirty ships of the First, Second and Third Rates. No new Fourth Rates were built under this plan, but the Navy Board did produce and introduce a new Establishment of Guns. While clearly conceived primarily as a guide for the arming of new ships as they were built, the Establishment set out a hypothetical set of weaponry for each vessel to which it was hoped that existing vessels would conform when they came to re-arm. Nevertheless, the longevity of iron guns, and the limited output of foundries, meant that the translation of a new Establishment to actual re-arming could take twenty years or more; in most cases, the re-arming actually took place when existing vessels were rebuilt.

The 1677 Establishment is the first to register a clear distinction between the larger (54-gun) Fourth Rates and the smaller vessel of 50 or fewer guns. Other than that the 54-gun ship carried 24 guns on its lower deck and 22 on the upper deck (with 8 sakers on the quarterdeck), the more marked distinction is that the lower deck guns on the 54 were 24pdrs, whereas the Fourth Rates of 46-50 guns had culverins, and the 42-44 gun vessels demi-culverins.

It seems clear that the determining factor was the ship's stability and hence its breadth – notably the 54s were all of 33ft breadth or more. Presumably the ill-fated *Saint Patrick* would have been similarly established as a 54-gun ship had she survived the Second Dutch War. This distinction between the 54-gun and 48-gun ships was to remain until the 1703 Establishment, notwithstanding the rebuilding of the four surviving 54s between 1692 and 1702.

The 1677 Establishment indicates that there was now a firm decision to strengthen the gundeck armament of the broad-beamed class. Along with the newer Fourth Rates built since the Restoration (the smaller *Kingfisher* being an exception, as of course were the new galley-frigates), they were now all established with 24 × 24pdrs (mainly Dutch) on the lower deck, with the upper deck carrying 22 × 6pdrs (likewise Dutch guns) instead of demi-culverins to compensate for the extra weight of the 24pdrs and to lower the ships' centres of gravity. Each was allocated 8 sakers on the quarterdeck to bring them each to 54 guns, their total weight or ordnance ranging from 72 to 77 tons. The new *Woolwich* was an exception; she had two fewer guns on the lower deck and two extra sakers on the quarterdeck, while her much heavier 8pdrs brought the total ordnance to 82 tons.

At the other end of the Fourth Rate, the vessels established to carry only demi-culverins on their lower decks likewise constituted a clearly distinct group among the Fourth Rates. It included almost all the surviving pre–1649 frigates – the *Constant Warwick*, *Tiger*, *Assurance* and *Adventure* – together with four newer vessels of a like size built as 36-gun Fifth Rates between 1666 and 1671, and re-rated as 42-gun Fourth Rates a few years later (they would revert to Fifth Rates in 1691). The *Dragon* is listed with 22 culverins, but these are described as averaging 30cwt, roughly the same weight as the average demi-culverin, so it is possible that this is an error by the clerk.

Virtually every other Fourth Rate was established with the 'standard' armament of 22 culverins on the gundeck, but like the larger vessels they had exchanged their upper deck demi-culverins for twenty 6pdrs, retaining six sakers on the quarterdeck to make them 48-gun ships. The 48-gun ship thus had sakers on both the upper deck and quarterdeck – in the former case twenty of the 6pdr variety (as this stage called 'ordinary' sakers) and in the latter case six of the 5pdr type (called 'light' sakers).

The 1685 Establishment (Table 112) reflects some disappearances. The *Princess* and *Yarmouth* have gone, as has the *Stavoreen*. Six ships have swapped their lower deck allowance of culverins for the new 12pdrs, also carried by the newly-purchased *Mordaunt*. The three smallest ships listed at the end of this table are now clearly separated from the rest, and equate with the four 40-gun ships temporarily raised from the Fifth Rate (to which they returned in 1691); of these the *Falcon* and *Sweepstakes* were established with twenty 12pdrs on their lower deck, and the *Phoenix* and *Nonsuch* twenty demi-culverins, and – like the small Algerine prizes also bearing 40 guns – are omitted.

In 1695 Colonel George Browne began a comprehensive survey on behalf of the Board of Ordnance of the precise weaponry carried aboard every British warship (as well as those in dockyards and ordnance depots around the country). The survey, usually referred to as the 1696 Survey although many of the ships were certainly inspected in 1695, continued at least until his death in 1702 and, although never finally completed, provides a full record of every piece of artillery carried aboard a vessel at the time of its inspection. It illustrates that the actual guns carried aboard a ship frequently differed in a radical manner from the 'Establishment' of Guns that vessel was allocated.

The results are reproduced in Table 113 and reflect the situation that existed in the period up to the 1703 Establishment, although the survey included none of the eight vessels launched in 1698 and 1699; it also omits several other Fourth Rates. Even within each class of gun, there were usually guns of different weights and lengths, even for the same vessel, and it should be noted that odd numbers of guns were not uncommon.

By the turn of the century all new 48s were

Table 111: 1677 Establishment of Guns (with weight of ordnance in tons in parenthesis)

Vessels	Guns	Lower deck		Upper deck		Quarterdeck		Total
(A) With 24pdrs on the lower deck:								
Woolwich	54	22	(47½)	22	(28½)	10	(6)	(82)
Oxford, Leopard	54	24	(50)	22	(23)	8	(4)	(77)
Greenwich	54	24	(48)	22	(23)	8	(4)	(75)
Saint David	54	24	(47)	22	(22)	8	(4)	(73)
Newcastle, Yarmouth,	54	24	(46)	22	(22)	8	(4)	(72)
* Happy Return, Princess*								
(B) With culverins on the lower deck:								
Portland	50	22	(44¾)	22	(20¾)	6	(3)	(68½)
Antelope, Kingfisher*	48	22	(42¼)	20	(20¼)	6	(3)	(65½)
Assistance, Swallow, Jersey,	48	22	(41¼)	20	(19¼)	6	(3)	(63½)
* Mary Rose, Diamond*								
Advice, Bristol, Dover,	48	22	(41)	20	(19)	6	(3)	(63)
* Stavoreen*								
Reserve, Foresight	48	22	(40½)	20	(18¼)	6	(3)	(61¾)
Crown	48	22	(40½)	20	(17¾)	6	(3)	(61¼)
Centurion, Ruby	48	22	(40½)	20	(17½)	6	(3)	(61)
Bonaventure	48	22	(37½)	20	(18)	6	(3)	(58½)
Hampshire	46	22	(34¼)	20	(16½)	4	(2)	(52¾)
Portsmouth	46	22	(34¼)	20	(16¼)	4	(2)	(52½)
Dragon	46	22	(33)	20	(15½)	4	(2)	(50½)
(C) With demi-culverins on the lower deck:								
Adventure	44	22	(32¼)	18	(15¾)	4	(2)	(50)
Tiger	44	22	(32½)	18	(15½)	4	(2)	(50)
Assurance, Constant Warwick	42	20	(27)	18	(13½)	4	(1½)	(42)

Note: on all vessels the upper deck guns are either 8pdrs or 6pdrs and the quarterdeck guns are sakers. This list excludes the four smaller ships which were temporarily re-rated as 42-gun Fourth Rates (*Sweepstakes*, *Falcon*, *Nonsuch* and *Phoenix*) with guns similar to the *Assurance* (although their tonnage of ordnance varied), but which belong to a study of 40-gun ships.
* the *Kingfisher* probably had only 20 lower deck culverins, but the 1677 list is confused (see Frank Fox, *The Great Ships*, Appendix IV).

supposed to mount 12pdr guns, so that it is probably that those ships completed in 1691–96 which were issued with culverins were among the last 48-gun ships to carry these old weapons. However, these guns probably remained aboard for several years after they were formally superseded by the 12pdr guns. The 8pdrs were almost certainly Dutch guns, as the British cast very few of this size, and these were later to be replaced on the upper deck by British 6pdrs.

On 3 June 1699, most of the Fourth Rates (excluding the new 60-gun ships and the 58-gun *Trident Prize*) were established with 48 guns (42 in peace) with the following exceptions:
54 guns (46 in peace):
Greenwich, Newcastle, Oxford, Woolwich.
46 guns (40 in peace):
Dragon, Kingfisher, Tiger.

The 1703 Establishment of Guns

The Ordnance Board in 1695 suggested that a new Establishment of Guns was needed, not only to provide for the new types of ships which had been added to the fleet, but because improvements in gun design had made some of the older types obsolete. The Admiralty turned down this initiative,[63] but in 1699 the Navy Board made a similar proposal, pointing out that

Table 112: 1685 Wartime Establishment of Guns

Vessels	Guns	Lower deck	Upper deck, quarterdeck and forecastle	
(A) With 24pdrs on the lower deck:				
Woolwich	54	22	22 (8pdrs)	10 (sakers and saker cutts)
Oxford	54	22	26 (8pdrs)	6 (demi drakes)
Greenwich	60	24[1]	26 (demi)	10 (sakers)
Saint David	54[2]	24	22 (8pdrs) +2 (demi)	6 (saker cutts) +2 (sakers)
Three ships newly ordered 1682-83	54	22	22 (demi)	10 (demi drakes)
(B) With culverins on the lower deck:				
Leopard	54	24	24 (demi drakes)	6 (demi cutts)
Newcastle	52	24 (drakes)	22 (demi drakes)	6 (saker cutts)
Dover	54	22 (drakes)	24 (demi)	8 (saker cutts)
Foresight	52	22 (drakes)	22 (demi drakes)	8 (saker cutts and minions)
Swallow	50	22	22 (8pdrs)[3]	6 (saker cutts and falconets)
Portland	50	22	22 (8pdrs)	6 (saker cutts and 3pdrs)
Centurion	50	22 (drakes)	22 (8pdrs)	6 (saker cutts)
Crown	50	22 (drakes)	22 (demi drakes)	6 (saker cutts)
Assistance	48[2]	22 (drakes)	22 (demi)	6 (saker cutts)
Advice	50	22	20 (8pdrs)	8 (saker cutts)
Happy Return	48	22	20 (demi)	6 (demi cutts)
Jersey	48	22	22 (6pdrs)	4 (saker cutts)
Mary Rose	48	22	20 (8pdrs)	6 (demi cutts)
Reserve	48	22	22 (demi)	4 (saker cutts)
Ruby	48	22 (drakes)	22 (demi drakes)	4 (saker cutts)
Portsmouth	48	22 (drakes)	20 (6pdrs)	6 (saker cutts)
Dragon	44	16 (incl 11 drake)	20 (demi drakes)	8 (saker cutts & drakes)
(C) With 12pdrs on the lower deck:				
Bonaventure	52	22	22 (8pdrs)	8 (saker drakes and 3pdrs)
Bristol	48	22	22 (8pdrs)	4 (3pdrs)
Diamond	48	22	20 (demi)	6 (saker cutts)
Antelope	46	22	20 (demi drakes)	4 (saker cutts)
Hampshire	46	20	20 (6pdrs)	6 (minions and 3pdrs)
Kingfisher	46	20	20 (6pdrs)	6 (3pdrs)
Mordaunt	46	20	18 (8pdrs)	8 (sakers)
(D) With demi-culverins on the lower deck:				
Tiger	46	20 (drakes)	18 (sakers)	8 (saker cutts)
Tiger Prize	46	20 (drakes)	26 (sakers)	
Golden Horse	40	20 (drakes)	16 (6pdrs)	4 (minions)
Constant Warwick	40	18	18 (6pdrs)	4 (3pdrs)
(E) With mixed armament on the lower deck:				
Adventure	40	12 (culverin) +6 (demi)	16 (6pdrs)	6 (saker cutts)
Assurance	42	10 (culverin) +12 (demi)	16 (6pdrs)	4 (3pdrs)
(F) With 8pdrs on the lower deck:				
Half Moon, Two Lions (prizes)	40	18	18 (6pdrs)	4 (minions)

Notes: the 1685 Establishment was prepared on Admiralty instructions, but seemingly did not receive official approval. Nevertheless, it conformed more precisely than in 1677 to what was actually carried, and there is some evidence that attempts were made to follow it conscientiously. The guns are not allocated to specific deck levels, but by this date most guns of one type were confined to the same deck, with the heaviest guns on the lower deck; their allocation can thus be deduced with reasonable certainty. The above table excludes the *Sweepstakes, Falcon, Phoenix* and *Nonsuch*, temporarily re-classed as Fourth Rates; each of these was established with 40 guns. Note that in the table above (only), 'demi' stands for demi-culverin.
[1] including two culverins. [2] total does not tally with sum of individual types. [3] including two demi-culverin.

the long years of war had revealed many ships to be severely over-gunned.[64] In 1702 the Navy Board met a committee of flag officers and together produced a series of proposals for greater uniformity in the arming of future vessels, and for a reduction in the excessive weights of metal carried by many vessels. The 50-gun ships, many carrying a lower deck armament of heavy 24pdrs or culverins, were in future to carry nothing larger than 12pdrs.[65]

The new Establishment was approved by Order in Council on 7 January 1703.[66] It implied tremendous changes; for example, the traditional saker was in effect to be everywhere replaced by a 6pdr gun of various calibres. However, it again transpired that the Ordnance Department had not been consulted over the manufacture of the new guns required by the Establishment. For many years the Establishment remained an objective of what the Navy wished each class of ship to carry (in many of them, after enlargement through rebuilding). Many of the older vessels never received their new armament until after 1716, when yet another Establishment had been introduced.

While standardising (at least, in theory) the lower deck guns of the 50s as 12pdrs, the quantity of guns carried was to rise for most of these ships, with 54 guns becoming the established level for the majority in wartime.

The archives of the Ordnance Storekeeper at Priddy's Hard, the magazine of the Portsmouth Dockyard, usefully show the 'remains' of guns aboard most of the ships calling there in the early eighteenth century (although the records are incomplete). It shows that few ships were fitted exactly according to the Establishment during the War of the Spanish Succession. Several ships are shown before the outbreak of war in 1702, and before the new Establishment was promulgated, still in what is a presumably a peacetime condition.

The 1716 Establishment of Guns

Following the death of Queen Anne and the close of the war, another committee of flag officers was appointed in 1715 to look at the Establishment. It decided to continue the standardisation beyond that demanded in 1703. Now all 50-gun ships were to have the same armament, although again it was realised that some ships would not be able to do so until the programme of re-building reached them in a few years' time. It was simultaneously decided that the 1703 Establishment had gone too far in reducing the firepower of the guns carried on Fourth Rates, and the new 50-gun armament was now to comprise 18pdrs on the lower deck and 9pdrs on the upper deck.

As this would mean considerably heavier weapons, it was decided that there would be four fewer guns on the quarterdeck, so that the 50-gun ship would actually carry fifty guns rather than fifty-four (wartime

Establishment). Even so, the weight of ordnance rose by 10 tons, and as a consequence a new Establishment of dimensions was authorised three years later to provide larger ships to carry the extra weight.

Unlike the 1703 Establishments, which had served as a guide for future re-arming rather than as a programme for implementation, the 1716 Establishment was put into effect over the following decade and by the end of the 1720s most 50-gun ships were actually armed in accordance with it. The Navy was helped in this regard by a quarter-century of relative peace, which enabled the implementation to be carried out fairly methodically.

By 1733 the Admiralty was becoming aware that French and Spanish vessels of the same nominal number of guns as British warships were progressively becoming larger and more powerful. Seeking to improve the firepower of its own vessels, it proposed a new Establishment of Guns which would, among other things, replace the 18pdrs of future 50-gun ships by 24pdrs.[67] But this time the objections of the Ordnance Board that it would find it impossible to produce so many new guns rapidly won the argument, and the Privy Council ruled that the 1716 Establishment be re-instated. Not until a new Establishment of dimensions was introduced in 1741 to increase the size of ships was further consideration given to the 1733 proposals, which were finally introduced in 1743.

The 1743 Establishment of Guns

The 1743 Establishment provided the new 50-gun ship with twenty-two 24pdrs on the lower deck (in lieu of 18pdrs) and the same number of 12pdrs on the upper deck (replacing 9pdrs). Unlike the 24pdrs which had formerly been carried by 60-gun ships, and which had a length of 9½ft, the new 24pdrs allocated to the 50-gun ship were 9ft weapons, weighing 46cwt and with a calibre of 5.84in.[68] The 12pdrs were also shorter weapons than the 9ft guns carried as the principal

Table 113: 1696 Survey of guns

Vessels	Guns	Lower deck	Upper deck, Quarterdeck and forecastle	
(A) With 24pdrs on the lower deck:				
Greenwich	60	24*	26 (demi-culverin)	10 (sakers)
Woolwich	54	22	20 (8pdrs)	12 (sakers)
Oxford	52	22	22 (8pdrs)	8 (sakers)
(B) With culverins on the lower deck:				
Romney	52	22	20 (demi-culverin)	10 (sakers)
Newcastle	52	24	22 (8pdrs)	6 (sakers)
Blackwall, Guernsey, Southampton	50	20	22 (8pdrs)	8 (minions)
Chester	50	22	22 (6pdrs)	6 (minions)
Chatham	49	21	18 (8pdrs)	10 (minions)
Nonsuch	46	20	20 (demi-culverin)	6 (minions)
Pendennis	46	18	22 (demi-culverin)	8 (sakers)
Assistance	46	17	21 (demi-culverin)	8 (sakers)
Falkland	46	18	20 (8pdrs)	8 (minions)
Crown	44	18 (drakes)	20 (demi-culverin)	6 (sakers)
Deptford	43	16	19 (6pdrs)	8 (minions)
Bristol	38	18	20 (8pdrs)	
(C) With 12pdrs on the lower deck:				
Colchester	50	22	20 (8pdrs)	8 (sakers)
Burlington	50	20	22 (demi-culverin)	8 (minions)
Dragon	47	19	20 (8pdrs)	8 (sakers)
Lincoln, Warwick	44	20	22 (demi-culverin)	2 (minions)
Ruby	41	22	19 (demi-culverin)	
Kingfisher	40	20	16 (6pdrs)	4 (3pdrs)
Bonaventure	40	18	20 (6pdrs)	2 (minions)
(D) With demi-culverins on the lower deck:				
Tiger	42	18	18 (sakers)	6 (saker cutts)

Note that there are various vessels not included in the above table, for which no returns were shown. The guns are not allocated to specific deck levels, but by this date most guns of one type were confined to the same deck, with the heaviest guns on the lower deck; the allocation can thus be deduced with reasonable certainty.
* including two culverins

The framing plan for the *Experiment*, made seven weeks after the sheer draught (1372A) reproduced in Chapter 6, shows that the gunport widths on the gundeck have been reduced to the same as on the upper deck, reflecting the decision reached in the interim to mount 12pdrs on both decks. The framing plan shows how relatively lightly built this class was, reinforcing the idea that they were intended as an alternative to the new single-decked frigates. (NMM: DR1373)

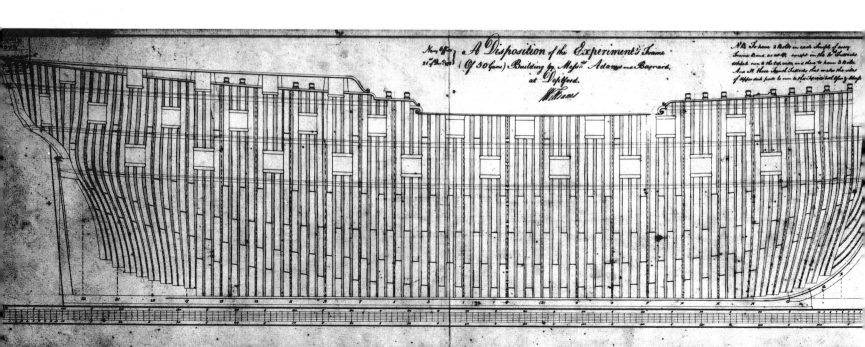

Table 114: Establishments of Guns for Fourth Rates (excluding 60s), 1703

		Length of gun	Weight of gun	Total weight of guns	Total weight of shot
(A) Pre-Establishment (*Bristol*, 1693 RB):					
Lower deck	22 × culverin cutts	9ft 4in	36cwt	792cwt	396lbs
Upper deck	20 × 8pdrs	8ft 4in	26cwt	520cwt	160lbs
Quarterdeck	10 × minion (4pdr)	7ft 0in	11cwt	110cwt	40lbs
Total				1422cwt (71.1 tons)	596lbs
(B) 1703 Establishment, war at home levels:					
(54-gun ship)					
Lower deck	22 × 12pdrs	9ft 0in	31cwt	682cwt	264lbs
Upper deck	22 × 6pdrs	8ft 6in	22cwt	484cwt	132lbs
Quarterdeck	8 × 6pdrs	7ft 0in	18cwt	144cwt	48lbs
Forecastle	2 × 6pdrs	9ft 6in	24cwt	48cwt	12lbs
Total				1358cwt (67.9 tons)	456lbs
(50-gun ship)					
Lower deck	20 × 12pdrs	9ft 0 in	31cwt	620cwt	240lbs
Upper deck	22 × 6pdrs	8ft 0 in	20cwt	440cwt	132lbs
Quarterdeck	6 × 6pdrs	7ft 0 in	18cwt	108cwt	36lbs
Forecastle	2 × 6pdrs	8ft 6 in	22cwt	44cwt	12lbs
Total				1212cwt (60.6 tons)	420lbs
(48-gun ship)					
Lower deck	20 × 12pdrs	8ft 6 in	29cwt	580cwt	240lbs
Upper deck	20 × 6pdrs	8ft 0 in	20cwt	400cwt	120lbs
Quarterdeck	6 × 6pdrs	7ft 0 in	18cwt	108cwt	36lbs
Forecastle	2 × 6pdrs	8ft 6 in	22cwt	44cwt	12lbs
Total				1132cwt (56.6 tons)	408lbs
(C) 1703 Establishment, peacetime (and war abroad) levels:					
(54-gun ship)					
Lower deck	20 × 12pdrs	9ft 0 in	31cwt	620cwt	240lbs
Upper deck	18 × 6pdrs	8ft 6 in	22cwt	396cwt	108lbs
Quarterdeck	6 × 6pdrs	7ft 0 in	18cwt	108cwt	36lbs
Forecastle	2 × 6pdrs	9ft 6 in	24cwt	48cwt	12lbs
Total				1172cwt (58.6 tons)	396lbs
(50-gun ship)					
Lower deck	18 × 12pdrs	9ft 0 in	31cwt	558cwt	216lbs
Upper deck	20 × 6pdrs	8ft 0 in	20cwt	400cwt	120lbs
Quarterdeck	4 × 6pdrs	7ft 0 in	18cwt	72cwt	
Forecastle	2 × 6pdrs	8ft 6 in	22cwt	44cwt	12lbs
Total				1074cwt (53.7 tons)	372lbs
(48-gun ship)					
Lower deck	18 × 12pdrs	8ft 6 in	29cwt	522cwt	216lbs
Upper deck	18 × 6pdrs	8ft 0 in	20cwt	360cwt	108lbs
Quarterdeck	4 × 6pdrs	7ft 0 in	18cwt	72cwt	24lbs
Forecastle	2 × 6pdrs	8ft 6 in	22cwt	44cwt	12lbs
Total				998cwt (49.9 tons)	360lbs

The 50-gun group comprised the *Assistance*, *Bonaventure*, *Crown*, *Dover*, *Kingfisher*, *Reserve* and *Ruby* (all rebuilds).
The 48-gun group comprised the *Advice*, *Dragon* and *Tiger* (all rebuilds), plus the *Triton Prize*.
These two groups were short-lived, and they were up-rated to 54-gun ships after 1½ years (Admiralty Order of 9 August 1704).
The pre-Establishment ship quoted is a sample but it should be remembered that the guns established for each ship differed widely (and the weapons actually carried even more widely) with guns of various 'natures', diameters of shot and lengths being carried, even on the same deck. It cannot be over-stressed that the lengths and weights of guns were design figures, and that casting methods meant that individual weapons varied considerably in both length and weight. For example, lengths were rounded off to the nearest 6in, and a design weight attached to that length.

weapon under the 1703 Establishment; the new upper deck guns, specially introduced for the 50-gun ship, were 8½ft long, with a weight of 31cwt and a calibre of 4.64in.

The six guns on the quarterdeck and forecastle were to remain 6pdr weapons under the new Establishment, but even here the actual weapons were changed. The old 50-gun ship had carried 8ft guns of 20cwt on the quarterdeck and 9ft guns of 24cwt on the forecastle, but these were superseded by 7ft (23cwt) guns and 8ft (26cwt) guns respectively, both with a calibre of 3.67in.

The heavier but shorter-barrelled weapons reflected improvements in both casting methods and in powder production during the previous three decades. The new guns were much less prone to bursting than earlier models, and were capable of taking increased charges of powder to increase their range. This charge in normal service amounted to 11 pounds of powder for the 24pdr shot, 6 pounds for the 12pdr shot, and 3 pounds for the 6pdrs. As the quality of powder and the preparation of charges continued to improve, the amounts required continued to fall and by the start of the French Revolutionary War were about two-thirds of the 1745 requirements.

The allowances of lighter weapons were also revised when the 1745 Establishment was introduced. The 50-gun ship was allocated 150 muskets, each with its sling, bayonet and cartouch- (or cartridge-) box, and the same number of cutlasses with their belts and bayonet-frogs; there were 120 hand *granadoes* (grenades), 60 pairs of pistols with hooks, 40 boarding-axes ('pole axes well steeled'), 100 pikes, 50 iron crow(bar)s, and a drum. These revised amounts of small arms took into account the increased complement of 350 men and boys provided to work the larger carriage guns.

The carronade

No further major alterations in the firepower of the carriage weapons carried by 50-gun ships were to take place before the final disappearance of the traditional Fourth Rate at the close of the Napoleonic struggle, other than the gradual improvement in casting techniques and in the preparation of (powder) charges. From the late 1780s new British guns designed to the new patterns of Blomefield were cast with a breeching ring above the button. Moreover the new casting increased the proportion of metal that lay at the breech end of the gun and reduced the proportion at the muzzle end. Improved accuracy also saw a reduction in the 'windage' allowed between the diameter of the shot and the bore of the gun, thus increasing the effective use of the explosion and improving accuracy of shot.

It was among the smaller weapons mounted by British warships that changes were to take place. The swivel-mounted ½pdr guns on the upperworks, and other basically anti-personnel weapons employed up to the time of the American Revolutionary War, were replaced by new short-range weapons by the close of that conflict, as the Navy Board promoted the introduction of the carronade on the superstructure of most British warships. Although the early experimentation with carronades saw weapons of up to 68pdr shot being constructed on conventional gun carriages, manufacture was soon concentrated on smaller types, optimised for short-range operation against the crews and rigging of enemy vessels; a slide mounting was introduced which enabled these weapons to be operated by a minimum-sized gun crew.

For the 50-gun ship, the first carronade establishment of July 1779 witnessed the allocation of six carronades to the top of the roundhouse, and a further pair to the forecastle; as for all the larger ships in the fleet, these first carronades were to be 12pdrs, but the 50-gun ship was also allocated two 24pdr carronades to be mounted on the quarterdeck, the only ships to be provided with this calibre weapon.[69] By 1782 most remaining 50-gun ships carried carronades, although they often varied from the 1779 Establishment.

In 1794, with the renewal of war, the Admiralty Board looked at the carronade armaments of all ships. Since the end of the American War, most carronades mounted during that conflict had been landed in an attempt to reduce peacetime stress on vessels' upperworks, and frankly because most captains did not relish their use. At the start of 1793, only four Fourth Rates had orders to carry any carronades, and among those that did (all *Portland* class 50s lying in ordinary), none matched exactly the 1779 Establishment; the *Isis* had only the six 12pdrs on the poop, the *Leander* mounted the same plus two 24pdrs on the quarterdeck, the *Jupiter* carried only two 18pdrs on the quarterdeck, while the *Adamant* had four 18pdrs (two quarterdeck, two forecastle) plus eight 12pdrs on the poop.

A new scale was brought in at the end of November 1794 and made compulsory although, like the revised manning scale brought in seven months before, it was only translated into practice as and when individual ships came into port for refitting. The change from the 1779 Establishment was minimal for the 50-gun ship, with the addition of a second pair of 24pdr carronades on the quarterdeck.[70]

Table 115: Re-armament of 50-gun ships before and after issuance of 1703 Establishment (only ships re-gunned at Portsmouth shown – from the Priddy's Hard archive)

Pre-Establishment:

Hampshire	28.7.1701	18 × 12pdr	20 × 6pdr	6 × minion	(44 guns)[1]
Deptford	13.8.1701	20 × culverin	22 × 6pdr	8 × minion	(50 guns)
Assistance	22.5.1702	20 × 12pdr	22 × demi-culv	8 × minion	(50 guns)

Post-Establishment:

Dragon	29.6.1703	18 × 12pdr	28 × saker		(46 guns)
Lichfield	29.6.1703	22 × 12pdr	20 × demi-culv	8 × minion	(50 guns)
Nonsuch	10.7.1703	20 × culverin	22 × demi-culv	8 × minion	(50 guns)
Antelope	19.7.1703	20 × 12pdr	30 × 6pdr		(50 guns)
Hampshire	19.12.1704	20 × 12pdr	22 × 6pdr	8 × minion	(50 guns)
Hazardous	11.8.1705	22 × culverin	22 × 12pdr	10 × 6pdr	(54 guns)
Colchester	12.1.1708	22 × 12pdr	32 × 6pdr		(54 guns)
Weymouth	4.2.1708 [2]	20 × 12pdr	20 × 6pdr	8 × minion	(48 guns)
Falmouth	30.4.1713	22 × 12pdr	32 × 6pdr		(54 guns)

[1] presumable the same as she carried in 1704 but with two fewer guns on each deck (*ie* a peacetime complement).
[2] the *Weymouth* also appears on 27 November 1707, with exactly the same composition of ordnance.

Table 116: Establishments of Guns for a 50-gun ship, 1716–82

		Length of gun	Weight of gun	Total weight of guns	Total weight of shot
(A) 1716 Establishment (50-gun ship)					
Lower deck	22 × 18pdrs	9ft 0in	39cwt	858cwt	396lbs
Upper deck	22 × 9pdrs	8ft 6in	26cwt	572cwt	198lbs
Quarterdeck	4 × 6pdrs	8ft 0in	20cwt	80cwt	24lbs
Forecastle	2 × 6pdrs	9ft 0in	24cwt	48cwt	12lbs
Total				1558cwt (77.9 tons)	630lbs
(B) 1743 Establishment					
(50-gun ship)					
Lower deck	22 × 24pdrs	9ft 0in	48cwt	1056cwt	528lbs
Upper deck	22 × 12pdrs	8ft 6in	31½cwt	693cwt	264lbs
Quarterdeck	4 × 6pdrs	7ft 0in	19cwt	76cwt	24lbs
Forecastle	2 × 6pdrs	8ft 0in	22cwt	44cwt	12lbs
Total				1869cwt (93.45 tons)	828lbs
(58-gun ship)					
Lower deck	24 × 24pdrs	9ft 6in	49cwt	1176cwt	576lbs
Upper deck	24 × 12pdrs	9ft 0in	32½cwt	780cwt	288lbs
Quarterdeck	8 × 6pdrs	8ft 0in	22cwt	176cwt	48lbs
Forecastle	2 × 6pdrs	9ft 0in	24cwt	48cwt	12lbs
Total				2180cwt (109 tons)	924lbs
(C) 1782					
Lower deck	22 × 24pdrs	9ft 0in	47cwt	1034cwt	528lbs
Upper deck	22 × 12pdrs	9ft 0in	32cwt	704cwt	264lbs
Quarterdeck	4 × 6pdrs	7ft 0in	19cwt	76cwt	24lbs
Forecastle	2 × 6pdrs	7ft 6in	20½cwt	41cwt	12lbs
Total				1855cwt (92¾ tons)	828lbs

Note: The 1743 Establishment '58-gun ship' was in effect a reduced 60-gun ship.

Table 117: Carronades supplied to 50-gun ships by 16 July 1782 (NMM MID/9/2 of 22 July 1782)

	Forecastle	Quarterdeck	Roundhouse	Upper deck	Station at 20.1.1783
Portland class					
Portland	2 × 18				Newfoundland (flagship)
Bristol	2 × 12	2 × 24	6 × 18		East Indies
Renown		4 × 18	6 × 12	2 × 32	North America
Isis			6 × 12		East Indies
Leander		2 × 24	6 × 12		Leeward Islands
Adamant	2 × 18	2 × 18	8 × 12		(in Ordinary)
Assistance	2 × 24	2 × 12	6 × 12	2 × 32	(in Ordinary)
Older types					
Chatham	2 × 12		6 × 12		North America (flagship)
Warwick	2 × 12	2 × 24	4 × 12		North America

The *Preston, Romney, Salisbury, Centurion* and *Jupiter* were not shown as issued with carronades; nor were the captured *Princess Caroline* and *Rotterdam*. The newly-launched *Cato* and the *Grampus* and *Trusty* were not completed until later in 1782.

Table 118: Armament carried by 50-gun ships, Napoleonic War

	Lower deck	Upper deck	Quarterdeck		Forecastle	
	Guns	Guns	Carronades	Guns	Carronades	Guns
Chatham (1758)	22 × 24	22 × 12		4 × 6		2 × 6
Portland (1770)	22 × 24	22 × 12		4 × 6		2 × 6
Centurion (1774)	nil	4 × 12	10 × 24		4 × 24	
Isis (1774)	22 × 24	22 × 12		4 × 6		2 × 6
Bristol (1775)	22 × 24	22 × 12		4 × 6		2 × 6
Jupiter (1778)	22 × 24	22 × 12	4 × 24	4 × 6	2 × 24	2 × 6
Adamant (1780)	22 × 24	22 × 12	10 × 24	2 × 12	2 × 24	2 × 12
Leander (1780)	22 × 24	22 × 12	10 × 24		2 × 24	
Trusty (1782)*	22 × 32pdr carr.	18 × 12		6 × 6		
Europa (1783)	nil	18 × 12		6 × 6		6 × 6
Leopard (1790)	22 × 24	22 × 12		4 × 6		2 × 6
Diomede (1798)	22 × 24	22 × 12		4 × 6		2 × 6
Grampus (1802)	22 × 24	22 × 12		4 × 6		2 × 6
Antelope (1802)	22 × 24	22 × 12	8 × 24	2 × 12	4 × 24	2 × 12
Hindostan (1804)	26 × 24		28 × 24*			
New Jupiter class	22 × 24	24 × 12	8 × 24		2 × 24	2 × 6

Note the *Chatham* was renamed *Tilbury* in 1810, and the *Leander* was renamed *Hygeia* in 1813.
* as troopship.
Source: NMM RUSI/64.

Table 119: Amount of powder (in lbs) required per ignition for sea service, 50-gun ships, c1795

Type of use:		Proof	Service	Saluting	Scaling
Long guns:	24pdr	18	8	6	2
	12pdr	12	4	3	1
	6pdr	6	2	2	½
Carronades:	42pdr	9	4½	4½	1½
	32pdr	8	4	4	1¼
	24pdr	6	3	3	1
	18pdr	4	2	2	1
	12pdr	3	1½	1½	¾
Swivels	½pdr	½	3 oz	3 oz	1 oz

This table is based on assumption that powder is dry and in good condition, and applies about 1795.
Source: NMM SPB/15 (Notebook of Captain Edward Rotheram), p78.

13. Stores

In the very bottom of the hold, iron ballast was stowed longitudinally between the riders – the heavy beams which began just outboard of the keelson and rose to just below the orlop deck. Shingle ballast was laid on top of this, and this served to prevent from shifting the casks and other containers that held the provisions. The total amount of ballast, about 200 tons in a typical late eighteenth-century Fourth Rate, was calculated when the ship was designed, and established by the Navy Board. The positioning of the ballast, and of the provisions stowed on top of it, determined the trim of the ship and thus its performance under sail; as a consequence this storage was the responsibility of the ship's Master.

The stores and provisions for use during a ship's deployment were under the control of one or other of the warrant officers. Provisions and clothing were the responsibility of the purser. Apart from day-to-day needs, these were all kept in the hold, or in one or other of the purser's storerooms below the orlop deck. Most provisions were issued from casks brought up from the hold as required to the steward's room, a compartment off the cockpit, and the ship's steward (the purser's assistant) was also allowed a small bedplace here; he oversaw the daily issue of food from here for the day's meals, and measured out the quantities from his stores here.

The gunner was responsible for all the ordnance on the ship, and for supplies of powder and shot.

Shot was stored in two specially-constructed wooden lockers, rectangular boxes with hinged lids, fitted in the lower hold just forward of the pump well; the main projectiles stored here were iron round shot, but the gunner also needed to store grape, double-headed, langridge and cannister shot, for which there were separate compartments within the lockers; from the mid-eighteenth century, a third shot locker was fitted further forward, just aft of the magazine. Powder was stored in the main magazine, built in the forward part of the hold; by 1716 most Fourth Rates (and larger ships) had a second, smaller powder store below the after part of the cockpit, around the base of the mizzen mast.

The gunner also had charge for many other munitions, including paper and flannel or canvas to construct cartridges, wads and tompions for the guns, the armourer's tools, and the ship's small arms – as well as spares for almost everything from trunnion axles to the blocks and tackles for the guns. His storeroom for most of this was forward on the orlop deck, and next to this a separate narrow passage gave access to a small scuttle leading down into the light-room, which was rigidly separated from the magazine it illuminated.

Just aft of this, along the starboard side of the orlop deck, the carpenter stored his supplies of timbers and tools, as well as paints and oils to preserve and colour the wood. On the larboard (port) side opposite, the boatswain's stores were more varied than those of his

The inboard profile for the *Romney* of 1762 shows the increasing compartmentalisation of the hold. (NMM: DR1426)

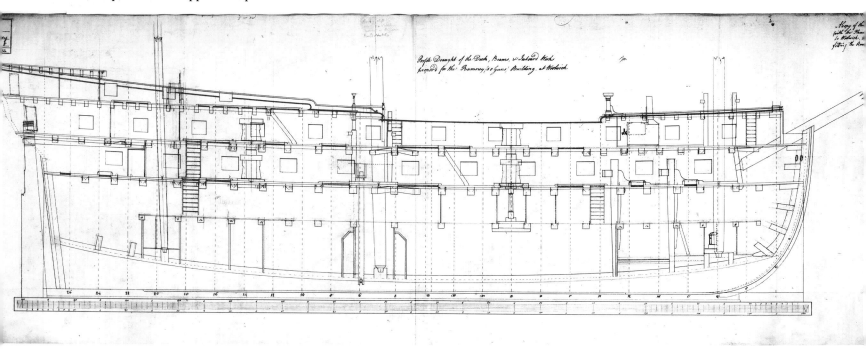

Table 120: Dimensions and capacity of casks and other containers used by the Royal Navy (late eighteenth century)

Container	Length ft in	Bilge ft in	Chine ft in	Capacity gallons	Pieces of: beef	pork	Flour lbs	Pease gallons	Oatmeal gallons
Leaguer	4 6	3 0	2 5	150					
Butt	4 4	3 0	2 2	108					
Puncheon	3 5	2 6½	2 1	72	170	310	672	76	
Hogshead	3 0	2 3	1 11	54	124	220	448	64	84
Barrel	2 7	2 0	1 11	36	86	154	336	48	72
Half hogshead	2 4	1 11	1 7	28	64	120	224	32	48
Rundlet or rumlett	5 1	3 0 deep							
Vats (for sails)	4 7	2 9 deep							
Leaguer for water	4 10	3 3	2 6½	189	(used in ground tier)				

French leaguers of 4 *barriques* are 250 wine gallons; they have some of 3 and some of 2 *barriques* (a *barrique* is 60 wine gallons).
Source: NMM SPB/15, p69.

Table 121: Account of HMS *Rochester*'s weight of provisions, draught of water, height of ports, etc, on sailing September 1757

Provisions		Tons	Cwt	Lbs
Water in the Ground Tier		56	0	0
in other casks		35	0	0
Beer		58	10	0

Beef (17 puncheons)   Pease (20 hogsheads)
Pork (18 puncheons)   Bread (340 bags)
Suet (6 barrels)   Butter (60 firkins)
Vinegar (7 barrels)   Cheeses (53 in number)
Flour (27½ barrels)   Goats (15 chaldron)
Oatmeal (18½ barrels)   Wood (18 cords)
(the above were complete provisions for 350 men for 4 months)

			Tons	Cwt	Lbs
Iron ballast			55	0	0
Shingle ballast			174	0	0
Masts and yards of estimation			34	18	34
Ordnance: LD	22 × 24pdr guns		51	12	63
UD	22 × 12pdr guns		32	15	24
QD	4 × 6pdr guns		4	2	42
Fc	2 × 6pdr guns		1	18	41
Round shot		3280 rounds	25	1	24
Grape shot		334 rounds	2	7	40
Double-headed shot		132 rounds	1	1	24
Gun carriages			15	3	64
Powder		(200 barrels)	10*	0	0
all other Gunner's stores in gross			5	0	0
Seamen with their chests and bedding			27	0	0
GRAND TOTAL (excluding provisions' weight*)			589	10	20

Draught of water	fwd	18ft 3in	Height of the upper sides of the lower sills of the GD ports from the water		
	abaft	19ft 4in			
			fwd	4ft 8in	
			midships	4ft 3in	
			abaft	5ft 8½in	

Source: PRO ADM/95/65. *estimated (tonnage not quoted in documents)

fellow warrant officers. All the unused rigging, as well as spare blocks and tackle, were under his supervision, while all the spare sails and canvas were in a separate sail room just forwards; he also had charge of the anchor cables and other equipment stored on the cable tiers further aft, with an additional sail room on the centreline between the latter.

In 1670 the value of the boatswain's stores (including cordage) costed for a Fourth Rate was £244, while the carpenter's stores were £32; the exceptions were the more heavily gunned *Greenwich* and *Leopard*, where the equivalent amounts were £300 and £40 respectively. The cost of victualling a ship for six months' service was estimated at 8d per day per man, or about £1031-6-8d for a complement of 170 including the officers, as it was calculated on 182 days.[71]

The final storeroom in the cockpit was the surgeon's store or dispensary. Originally tiny, described as an 'overgrown sea chest' by Ned Ward in 1707, it grew as the supply of medical equipment and remedies improved, and by the end of the eighteenth century was a sizeable storeroom.[72] There was, throughout this period, no established location for a sick berth, but in general it was allotted to the cockpit as the location most protected from enemy shot during battle. In 1809 a permanent operating table was issued which was fitted in the centre of the cockpit, adjacent to the dispensary, but around the same date the sick room was relocated to the starboard side of the forecastle, where it could be properly fitted out as a hospital.

All these storerooms were carefully outfitted with lockers and racks so that the warrant officers' stores and equipment could be carefully organised for rapid access and for stock-taking. Each of the standing officers had a yeoman, an experienced and trusted rating who was responsible to him for the security and tidiness of the storeroom.

A somewhat incomplete record of the ordnance, stores and ballast aboard a 50-gun ship under wartime conditions, stored for a four-month voyage for a complement of 350 men, is shown for the *Rochester* in 1757 (Table 121). A more complete report for the *Salisbury* made in 1770 when sailing stored for three months in peacetime conditions (*ie* with an established complement of only 280) shows that the full weight of items stored aboard amounted to over 831 tons (Table 122). The two Tables taken together illustrate virtually complete breakdown of the actual contents of a fully laden 50-gun ship; a somewhat later Establishment gives the theoretical amounts and values of all goods laden in a standard 50-gun ship.

Table 122: Weights of fittings, ordnance, naval and victualling stores on HMS *Salisbury* on sailing from Blackstakes 14 July 1770

Provisions	Tons	Cwt	Lbs
Water in the Ground Tier (150 butts, 23 puncheons, 20 hogsheads)	87	13	0
Water and beer in the Second Tier (28 butts, 42 puncheons, 36 hogsheads, 24 half-hogsheads)	40	0	0
Beer in the Third Tier (127 butts)	63	10	0
All species of dry and wet provisions	37	12	59
Coals, wood and candles	28	15	0
Subtotal	257	10	59
(the above were complete provisions for 280 men for 3 months)			
Iron ballast	50	0	0
Shingle ballast	150	0	0
Masts and yards complete	50	5	76
Rigging and fittings for same: cordage	29	12	12
blocks, deadeyes, thimbles, hooks, etc	8	0	63
other stores expended about the rigging	0	12	56
Boatswain's sea stores for 8 months: cables, and other cordage	34	4	8
anchors	10	16	0
sails	7	18	56
boats	6	0	0
all other sea stores	8	13	46
Carpenter's sea stores for 8 months: iron fire hearth and double kettle	2	10	20
all other sea stores	17	3	12
Ordnance: LD 22 × 24pdr guns	53	18	106
UD 22 × 12pdr guns	35	15	60
QD 2 × 6pdr guns	2	4	34
Fc 4 × 6pdr guns	4	6	93
Round shot for 24, 12, 6 and ½pdr guns	24	9	62
Grape shot for 24, 12, 6 and ½pdr guns	1	16	108
Double-headed shot for 24 and 12pdr guns	0	12	68
Gun carriages on all the decks	12	9	37
Powder in the whole (200 barrels)	10	0	0
all other for the Gunner in gross	11	16	90
Seamen with their chests and bedding	39	9	0
GRAND TOTAL	831	4	42

Draught of water fwd 18ft 8in
abaft 19ft 7in

Height of the upper sides of the lower sills of the GD ports from the water

fwd 5ft 3in
midships 4ft 7½in
abaft 5ft 7in

Source: PRO ADM/95/66.

The plan of the orlop deck of the *Salisbury* shows the final arrangements for the 50-gun ships. The orlop now extends the full length of the ship. The cabins for the boatswain and carpenter are now forwards on this deck, adjoining their respective storerooms, and the gunner's cabin has moved forwards to sit in front of the sailroom in similar proximity to his stores and the main magazine. All storerooms are now fitted with racking and other aids to organising their contents. Aft, the accommodation around the cockpit has been extended forward to provide cabins for midshipmen. (NMM: DR1438)

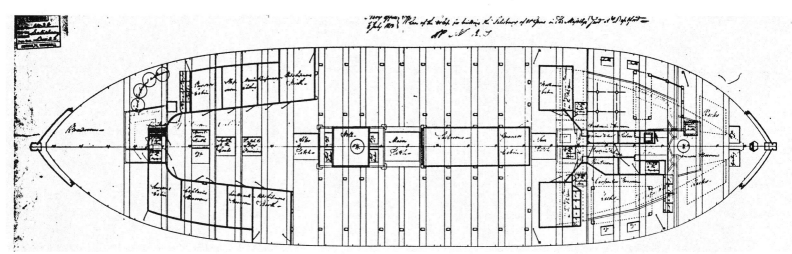

14. Costs and Funding

The cost-effectiveness of the 50-gun ship must take into account many factors. First among these would be the outlay involved in constructing and outfitting a new Fourth Rate compared with other Rates, and its operational costs in terms of manpower and supplies.

Deane provides costs for the Fourth Rates (among other ships) in service in 1670 (Table 123). Note that the Portsmouth built ships were most expensive at £8 or £8½ a ton.

For the period of the Establishments, the Navy Board Regulations produced estimates of the costs of building and equipping each class of ship, and of storing them for eight months service with boatswain's and carpenter's stores. For the 50-gun ship under the 1719 Establishment this amounted to £10,192 for hull, masts and yards, plus £3020 for rigging and stores for a total of £13,212, compared with £17,831 for a 60-gun ship.[73] Since the broadside of the 50-gun totalled 315 pounds compared with 435 pounds for the 60-gun ship under the 1716 Establishment of Guns, a crude 'bangs per buck' assessment would mean that the 60-gun vessel was about 2.3 per cent more effective to build and equip than its smaller compatriot.

In practice, all ships entering service at this time were technically rebuilds of former ships rather than new construction, although increasingly the old ships were taken completely to pieces and only a proportion of the materials taken from the dismantling used in the 'rebuilt' vessel. Other ships unfit for further service underwent a 'Great Repair', the highest of several categories into which the Navy Board graded the amount of work requiring to be done. Often such Great Repairs amounted to almost as much work as an approved rebuilding. The *Falmouth*, for example, which had been newly built in 1708, underwent a Great Repair at Portsmouth from July 1714 to March 1715 at a cost of £7521; for comparison, the rebuilding of the *Guernsey* at Woolwich in 1717 cost £8501. Similarly the *Falkland*, rebuilt at Deptford in 1720 at a cost of £8435, had a further £8241 expended on her in a Great Repair at Portsmouth from May 1726 to December 1727.[74]

Estimates of the costs of operating are more unreliable, given the widely varying attitudes (financial and social) of individual pursers, as well as variations in other departments, but as it may be assumed that expenditure on provisions and other consumables would roughly speaking be proportional to the manpower being maintained aboard ship, the 30 per cent increase in complement required by the 60-gun ship would indicate a similar small saving of around 6 per cent

Table 123: Prices of Fourth Rates, 1646–70 (all in £ and shillings or £-s-d in last two columns)

Vessel [1]	Hull complete[1] £-s	Cordage £-s	Cables £-s	Anchors £-s	Blocks, Tops, and Pumps	Sails £-s-d	Total[2] £-s-d
1646 Group:							
Assurance	2352-0	292-10	468-0	180-14	79-0	217-12-0	3589-6-0
Adventure	2618-0	292-0	452-5	175-17	79-0	212-10-0	3830-2-0
£6½ a ton Group:							
Constant W'wick	1982-10	315-10	465-15	180-14	79-0	255-0-0	3278-9-0
Dragon	2743-0	292-10	450-0	180-0	79-0	231-4-0	3975-14-0
Tiger	2912-0	310-10	495-0	196-4	79-0	271-0-2	4263-14-2
Sapphire	2873-0	315-0	495-0	196-4	79-0	271-0-2	4229-4-2
Reserve	3334-10	322-17	497-5	196-4	79-0	271-0-2	4700-16-2
Advice	3334-10	322-17	497-5	196-4	79-0	231-4-0	4661-0-0
Foresight	3393-0	322-17	495-0	198-8	79-0	271-0-2	4759-5-2
Assistance	3386-10	321-3	495-0	193-4	79-0	231-4-0	4706-1-0
Centurion	3451-10	322-17	495-0	210-0	79-0	288-8-8	4846-15-8
Dover	3604-5	322-17	495-0	210-0	79-0	271-0-2	4982-2-2
Gainsborough	3529-10	322-17	495-0	196-4	79-0	271-0-2	4893-11-2
Jersey	3640-0	322-17	495-0	196-4	79-0	271-0-2	5004-1-2
Kentish	3906-10	322-17	495-0	196-4	79-0	271-0-2	5270-11-2
Maidstone	3432-0	322-17	495-0	196-4	79-0	271-0-2	4796-1-2
Marmaduke	2600-0[3]	321-15	495-0	196-4	79-0	271-0-2	3962-19-2
Newcastle	4101-10	360-0	495-0	196-4	79-0	271-0-2	5502-14-2
Portland	3932-10	322-17	495-0	196-4	79-0	271-0-2	5296-11-2
Preston	3142-15	322-17	495-0	196-4	79-0	271-0-2	4506-16-2
Taunton	3484-0	322-17	497-5	196-4	79-0	283-6-2	4862-12-8
Winsby	3932-0	322-17	495-0	196-4	79-0	288-7-8	5313-8-8
Yarmouth	3952-0	322-17	495-0	196-4	79-0	269-3-4	5314-4-4
£7½ a ton Group:							
President	3378-15	322-17	495-0	196-4	79-0	271-0-2	4742-16-2
Ruby	4175-12½	322-17	497-5	210-0	79-0	271-0-2	5555-14-8
Hampshire	3592-10	322-17	495-0	196-4	79-0	271-0-2	4956-11-2
£8 a ton Group:							
Diamond	4360-0	322-17	495-0	210-0	79-0	288-8-8	5755-5-8
Bristol	4256-0	322-17	513-0	210-0	79-0	288-8-8	5669-5-8
£8½ a ton Group:							
Portsmouth	3587-0	322-17	495-0	196-4	79-0	271-0-2	4951-1-2
Princess	4726-0	322-17	495-0	196-4	79-0	271-0-2	6090-1-2
Leopard	5482-10	405-0	654-15	251-0	85-0	372-8-10	7250-13-10
Greenwich	5491-0	405-0	654-15	251-0	85-0	372-8-10	7259-3-10

The price of hulls was calculated from a price per ton to the builder – £7 per the 1646 Group, and the rest as shown grouped above.
The cordage (rigged) was priced at £45 per ton, the cables at £45 per ton, the anchors at 43/- per ton (for 4th Rates) and the sails at 17d per square yard. [1] from Builder, including masts and spars. [2] excluding ordnance (see Table 108) and stores. [3] based on nominal 400 tons.
Source: Deane's *Doctrine of Naval Architecture*, 1670.

over the 50-gun in terms of operating costs per pound of firepower.

By the time of the proposed 1733 Establishment, the estimated cost of producing and equipping a 50-gun ship had risen by some 14.6 per cent to £15,140, and for a 60-gun ship by about 13.8 per cent to £20,292. As the increases in firepower and complement originally propounded for the various classes was not introduced at this time, the sole deduction that can be made is that the savings to be secured by building 60-gun ships instead of 50-gun ships had grown by an insignificant 0.7 per cent.

The 1741 Establishment calculated again the costs of constructing the various classes. The costs of the 50-gun ship grew by a further 13.4 per cent to £17,185, while for the 60-gun ship they grew by only 5.2 per cent to £21,350. Given no change in firepower, this signified that the procurement costs relative to broadside weight now gave a 10 per cent advantage to the 60-gun ship. It is against this background that the gradual move towards the larger Fourth Rate during the 1726 to 1733 period should be viewed.

Enemy prizes constituted a fairly low-cost, as well as rapid, means of augmenting the fleet. Captured enemy 50s were added to the fleet wherever found fit to be bought for the Navy; naturally, most had suffered damage before surrendering, so that time and money had to be expended in repair, and in altering features of the ship to convert them to the standard required by the Navy. This last was not a consequence of poor design or workmanship by competitive navies, but a feature of the different strategic needs for which each country outfitted its fleet.

The Prize Courts determined the value of ships to be taken into the British Navy on the basis of a fixed rate per ton, with an estimate of the value of stores and fitting aboard. For example, the 1745 prize *L'Auguste* was valued at £6¼ per ton, or £5415-16-5¾d, plus £901-7-6½d for her stores, on 18 March 1745 before being received into the Navy on the following day;[75] two years later, *Le Diamant* was valued at £6 per ton, or £6081-2-6½d, with another £854-3-10½d for her stores.[76] The dockyard's estimate of the cost of repairs needed to put the ship into fit condition for the Service was then deducted before the balance was then paid to the Agents for dispersal to the officers and crew of the capturing vessel or vessels as 'prize money'. In the two examples given, *L'Auguste* was judged fit to be taken into the Navy, while *Le Diamant* was estimated to required £2700 laid out on her before becoming fit.

With the abandonment of the system of Establishments, no estimated cost for a whole type of ship

Table 124: Total costs of sample 50-gun ships (including fitting out) 1740s – 1800s

1741 Estab.	£	*Romney* class	£	*Portland* class	£	*Grampus* class	£
Chester (1744)	24,246	*Romney* (1762)	31,142	*Bristol* (1775)	27,016	*Cato* (1782)	28,037
				Hannibal (1779)	25,890		
Bristol class	£	*Warwick* class	£	*Adamant* (1780)	27,497		
Bristol (1746)	24,288	*Warwick* (1767)	23,853	*Leander* (1780)	26,831	*Antelope* class	£
				Europa (1783)	29,352	*Antelope* (1802)	38,369
Mod 1745 Estab	£	*Salisbury* class	£	*Leopard* (1790)	28,814*	*Diomede* (1798)	43,804
Chatham (1758)	24,580	*Centurion* (1774)	24,744				

* excludes £992 spent at Portsmouth prior to ceasing work there.

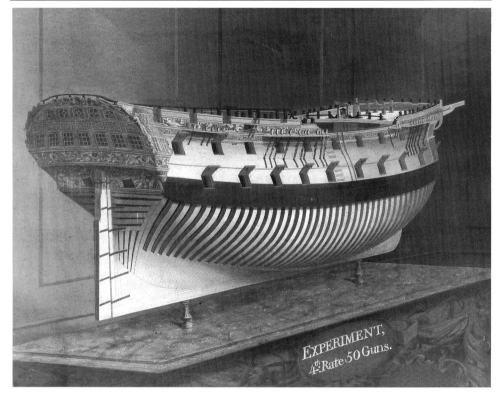

EXPERIMENT, 4th Rate 50 Guns.

became applicable, but estimates of the costs for individual ships during the remainder of the eighteenth century show a gradual increase in both the 50s and in the 60s. While no comprehensive costing exists, empirical evidence suggests that the cost of the 50-gun ship by mid-century was about £24,500 but by the time of the American Revolution had risen to about £27,500 (see Table 124).

Equivalent sample figures for 60-gun ships show no indication that the procurement costs for these exceeded those for the 50s by Anson's day, although logic dictates that on average they must have done so; the 64s which superseded them cost around £38,000 apiece by the American War, but of course the relative strength and firepower was by now much greater. Following this war, the cost of building and fitting an average 50 was estimated in 1788 at just under £32,000, while by the close of the century the final 50s to be built were costing £40,000 or more.

Among the series of oil paintings of a models presented to George III the 50-gun ship is the only type represented by more than one vessel: the standard *Portland* and the lightweight *Experiment*, clearly indicating that the latter was regarded as an entirely different type and, as the prototype's name suggested, a new concept. Only two were built, which almost certainly indicates that they were found to be less cost-effective than the conventional single-decked frigate they were compared with. This painting shows *Experiment* with circular lights on the quarterdeck instead of the rectangular ones included on her draught; in any event, all the lights on this level were fakes, as she had no superstructure on the quarterdeck. (Science Museum photo B560638)

15. Aspects of Service

The most glamorous role for any warship was in battle – particularly in fleet actions where lines of opposing vessels poured fire into their opposite numbers. This was the role for which the line of battle ship had been created, and initially it was one shared fully by the 50-gun ship, as the history of fleet action described in Part I of this book has set out. Indeed, in the second half of the seventeenth century it was the Fourth Rate ship which numerically dominated fleet actions.

As we have seen, from the first half of the century the relatively low firepower and strength of construction of the smaller two-deckers gradually saw their removal from fleet service, where the strongest and most powerfully-armed ships – the three-deckers and the larger two-deckers – were both more effective and better able to withstand the punishment of enemy fire. From the onset of the Seven Years War, the 50-gun ship was technically removed from the line of battle – although individual ships continued to find employment in this service for another half-century.

However crucial, fleet actions were rare occurrences. Often, the Royal Navy's command of the high seas meant that enemy fleets were discouraged from leaving harbour. Even when control of the oceans was actively disputed, it was on infrequent occasions that battlefleets actually met, and quite often even such encounters were inconclusive. The larger ship of the line, being too expensive to deploy on other duties, consequently spent much of its time in port, or on fruitless patrols.

The 50-gun ship, and smaller warships or every size, generally led a more varied existence. Throughout their period of service, they found employment in many roles, and even when reduced in numbers they were relatively less often laid up out of commission. Their duties were not the sort to attract the headlines, but were equally essential to the survival of the country, and to the eventual success of the Navy in a long-drawn-out war.

Convoys and cruising

The practice of marshalling lightly protected merchant shipping in wartime into groups, and deploying warships to escort such groups along the major shipping lanes to protect them against enemy warships and privateers, goes back to medieval times. Originally, when differences between merchant vessels and warships were minimal, any form of warship was likely to

Four of the Commonwealth Fourth Rates comprised Commodore Richard Beach's squadron which on 17 August 1670, in rare co-operation with a Dutch squadron under Van Ghent, destroyed six Algerine pirates in the Western Mediterranean, a more active method of commerce protection than convoys and cruising. The four ships, shown in this Van de Velde drawing of Beach's Action, were (left to right): the *Centurion*, *Jersey*, *Portsmouth* and *Hampshire*. (NMM: VV532)

be used. As the warship became more distinctive, the employment of warships became more selective.

With the creation of the Commonwealth in 1649, the Rump Parliament had moved swiftly to increase the size of the Navy. While England and France were officially at peace, an undeclared war was in progress, while royalist privateers and the residual Stuart warships preyed on English shipping. Two Convoy Acts in 1650 set up a system of convoys, a measure which proved its worth when war broke out in 1652.[77]

During the Dutch Wars of 1652 to 1674, both England and the Netherlands were economically dependent for their survival on seaborne trade. Indeed, their rivalry for trade was the very essence of the three wars. Yet realisation of their mutual vulnerability deterred both countries from concerted attempts to destroy each other's shipping. The Dutch attempted various fleet attacks on English homebound convoys, but these attempts were not extensive and met with limited success.

The Anglo-French wars which commenced in 1688 were more dangerous in that Britain (and the Dutch who were now in alliance) was far more vulnerable than France to all-out war against merchant shipping. After 1692, the inability of the French fleet to overcome their opponents in fleet action led to the adoption of a strategy of economic blockade in which attacks on shipping formed the main weapon. The English response was to detail a proportion of the Navy to serve as cruisers for trade protection; the 1694 Supply Act stipulated the numbers and types of such vessels, notably the largest group (16 out of 44 vessels) were required to be Fourth Rates.

Relatively few vessels could be provided for such purposes. The larger ships of the line were too expensive to use regularly in this role, although they were certainly so employed when available. A Navy composed substantially of three-deckers and large two-deckers had to expand rapidly to provide relatively cheap convoy escorts of all sorts. The building of large numbers of 123ft and 130ft Fourth Rates, as well as smaller vessels, was designed primarily to fill this gap. While over the following century 50-gun ships would regularly find themselves in the line of battle, even after the 1750s, the convoy escort function became their prime wartime activity.

A logical corollary to this role was the hunting of enemy raiders. Rather than await attacks on shipping convoys, individual ships of small squadrons were dispatched by the Admiralty with the task (often combined with others) of patrolling areas of the globe where hostile warships threatened merchantmen, and intercepting such enemies. Some British warships were deployed to patrol specific areas of ocean or coastal waters, between certain limits of latitude and longitude. Others were to cruise off enemy ports, to catch raiders entering or leaving their bases, while yet others were stationed at specific points along the trade lanes, particularly those used regularly by British shipping. Freed of their fleet responsibilities, these duties were particularly suitable for 50-gun ships with their capacities for extended voyages.

The system was renewed with every war that England – and then Britain – subsequently faced. In 1708 Parliament again legislated for cruisers – this time 43 – to be deployed in the specific role of trade protection. In 1744, 1756 and 1778, the renewal of war found France more concerned with protecting her own growing trade routes, and the emphasis on the *guerre de course* was less. But renewed hostilities after the French Revolution saw a return to depredations upon British shipping. The 1793 Convoy Act and the 1798 Compulsory Convoy Act, the English response to these measures, were effective in regulating shipping and preventing unescorted sailings for all but a few licensed 'runners', but required a massive increase in the quantity of escort vessels that had to be provided by the Navy.[78]

Minor Station flagships

As most 50-gun ships were built with a roundhouse on the quarterdeck – or could be fitted with one fairly easily – they proved popular for use as Admirals' commands on overseas stations, although usually only the minor ones in wartime. The flag officer could take over the captain's accommodation, with the captain having to seek space among the other commissioned officers (which in practice meant that the captain took over the first lieutenant's berth, with subsequent

An unidentified 50-gun ship moored off Malta about 1770 (the lateen mizzen yard has been retained with half-mizzen sail). The ship, which has the full-length roundhouse usually required for a flag role, wears a commodore's broad pendant at the main truck. The neat harbour stow of the topsails and line of marines on the gangways implies the kind of ceremonial 'showing the flag' which was so often the peacetime lot of the 50-gun ship. (NMM: PW8514)

displacement all down the line). At the same time, the 50-gun ship was the smallest ship (and thus with the lowest running costs) with which this could be done. We have seen in Part I of this book that this was a frequent employment for the smaller Fourth Rates.

The precise suitability of a 50-gun ship for this role was appraised on the basis of the accommodation available for the flag officer. The *Chatham*, for example, was in February 1772 reported to the Admiralty Secretary by the Navy Office as 'fitted with her Great Cabin under the Roundhouse, has a Walk in the Stern, and is a proper ship for an Admiral going to the Leeward Islands'. The reply next day from Philip Stephens was that the ship was 'to be sheathed and fitted for Foreign Service, and for the support of a Flag Officer, and to be reported when fit for such done.'[79]

Troopships

The original role of the warship, before the introduction of sea artillery transformed it, was the transport of soldiers across the sea. Even after the arrival of the heavy gun, this function remained an important if subsidiary task for the Navy, whose command of the sea throughout most of the eighteenth century meant that British military power could be projected to any corner of the world; and the growth of empire meant that substantial units of the British Army had to be carried to distant areas of the globe. Apart from the simple carriage of troops, the warship was often required to play a direct role in landing troops on hostile shores – amphibious operations as they came to be called – and in the support of British troops in coastal areas by bombardment from the sea.

The great majority of troop movements were made by merchantmen hired by the Navy Board and given modifications to allow them to house a body of troops for a sea voyage. The British Navy – like its rivals, particularly the French – also owned several purpose-built troop vessels of its own. In 1798 the Navy Board set up a separate subsidiary, the Transport Board, to manage both owned and hired vessels. Normally such vessels were able to carry troops in the ratio of one man for every two tons burthen, although in the early part of the century this was about one man for every 1½ tons.

However, on various occasions warships were themselves fitted to carry troops. For this purpose the lower deck of a two-decker, with its guns taken out and gunports stopped up, provided an effective floating barracks-room. With their perceived effectiveness as colonial flagships and having established their use in amphibious operations in North America, the older 50-gun ships were frequently used for trooping, although other classes of warship including frigates were also often used.

To operate *en flûte* in this way for anything except a temporary mission, the two-decker required considerable modification. Its main battery of guns was taken out or stored in the bottom of the hold, where it was used as ballast until such time as the ship's transport role was complete and it could revert to its more usual operations. The resultant large space along each side of the lower deck was divided up into a series of cabins, each for three or four soldiers who strung up hammacoes in them every night. Since speed was not a prime requirement of the troopship (which usually sailed in convoy), they were masted and rigged to a lesser Establishment than that they had formerly met, which with their reduction in firepower meant that a smaller crew would be required. The lighter spars occasionally caused a problem, as they were still expected to serve a ship of 1100 tons:

> The *Leopard*, as a troopship, was not fitted with the rigging allowed to a 50-gun ship, but with that of a frigate of 28 guns, and a crew suitable to that class. However, we had the (usual) allowance of boats, the launch being a very heavy one. The lower yards, not being of sufficient strength for that weight, was sprung in hoisting her out. I had therefore to represent this to the Powers above, who ordered stronger yards to be supplied.[80]

The masts and spars, as well as the rigging and sails, were clearly in line with the usual Establishment of a 28-gun frigate instead of being that normally supplied for a 50. Their dimensions were significantly less.[81]

The conversion was usually carried out in a dockyard, and frequently the ship was docked for a month or two while the work was done, although this was partly explained by the requirement for most such vessels to be re-coppered at the same time, since troop deployments were frequently to tropical areas. However, some conversions were done outside the dockyards (*eg Brakel* at the Nore – see Table 125) while any re-masting done was accomplished with the aid of a sheer hulk. The *Trusty* was converted twice, having reverted to a 50-gun ship at Portsmouth in 1800 after her first employment as a troopship.

This role was taken up by some of the last 50-gun two-deckers after the end of the Napoleonic War; the last to serve was the *Jupiter*, which operated as a troopship during the Opium War with China from 1839 to 1842.

Table 125: 50-gun ships fitted as troopships, 1793 to 1815

Vessel	Fitted at	Arrived	Docked	Undocked	Sailed
Europa	Portsmouth				Apr 1798
Brakel	The Nore				June 1799
Trusty	Woolwich	22 Dec 1798	7 May 1799	20 July 1799	3 Aug 1799
Trusty	Chatham	9 Apr 1802	16 Nov 1703	17 Dec 1803	22 Feb 1804
Leopard	Chatham	7 Sep 1810	28 Dec 1810	11 Feb 1811	28 Apr 1811
Diomede	Chatham	8 Sep 1811	10 June 1812	7 Aug 1812	17 Sep 1812

In addition to the above, the *Medusa* in 1796 and the Dutch prizes *Tromp* and *Alkmaar* in 1798 were employed as troopships. After the Napoleonic Era, the *Antelope* in 1817, the *Romney* in 1822 and the *Jupiter* in 1837 were converted to troopships, but these fall outside this study.

The GRAMPUS. *Hospital Ship lying off Deptford.*

Harbour service

Increasingly from the time of the wars of 1739 to 1748, obsolete warships of any size whose hulls remained sound were able to find a new role as harbour hulks to extend their life. This practice coincided with the end of the tradition of rebuilding, as it was no longer a requirement to take elderly vessels to pieces to incorporate any sound timbers into building their replacement.

A variety of roles were undertaken by harbour hulks, but by far the most common was as a 'receiving' ship, as temporary accommodation for large numbers of sailors awaiting assignment to other warships. These floating barracks provided several advantages over land-based facilities. They were cheap in that they offered reasonably weather-proof quarters for substantial numbers of men without the expense of constructing or hiring buildings. Their isolation from the shore – in an age when few sailors could swim – discouraged the ever-present risk of desertion. Finally they were reasonably flexible, as the hulks could be towed from one port to another to meet alterations in demand, whereas space for facilities ashore was restricted within the confines as a dockyard.

In 1759 the *Chester* found employment at Milford Haven as a *floating battery*, serving there until 1762. Her condition meant that she was no longer an effective sea-going vessel, but in the restricted waters of the Haven she could provide heavy guns as a defence against attacking squadrons. This was a role more often fulfilled by smaller vessels or mercantile conversions, although during the French Revolutionary War several small two-deckers were so employed. Three Dutch 56-gun ships were among those converted to the role in 1801 and 1803 (see Part I).

In July 1823, the *Antelope* was hulked to be sent to Bermuda as a static accommodation ship for convicts. She was fitted for her new role from 25 August to 22 September, sailing for Bermuda on 14 November. In late 1827 she was joined at Bermuda by the *Coromandel*, which served in the same role.

The *Grampus* was one of several 50-gun ships which ended their days as hospital hulks, commencing with the *Chester* (of 1708 vintage) in August 1743. The *Medusa* became a seagoing hospital ship in 1797 but was lost the following year. The Dutch prize *Alkmaar* served as a hospital ship from 1801 until 1805, when she was replaced by the *Jupiter* (herself lost in 1808). The *Grampus* served as a hospital hulk moored off Deptford for the Committee for Distressed Seamen from 1820 to 1832. (NMM: A536)

Appendix A: Rebuilds, 1680 to 1750

Decade:	1680–97	1698–1709	1710–19	1720–29	1730–39	1740–49	1750–59+
(A) The 'core' 46 ships of 50 guns from 1720 to 1727:							
Advice (1650)		RB 1698	NB* 1712			NB 1746	BU 1756
Antelope (1653#)	BU 1693	NB 1703			BU 1738	RB 1742	BU 1783
Assistance (1650)		RB 1699	RB 1712	RB 1725		NB 1747	BU 1773
Bonaventure (1650#)	RB 1683		RB 1711 ¹	RB 1722		sunk 1748	
Bristol (1653)	RB 1693		NB* 1711			RB 1746	BU 1768
Burlington	NB 1695				BU 1733		
Centurion (1650)	NB* 1691			BU 1729	NB as 60		NB as 50
Chatham	NB 1691			RB 1721		sunk 1749	NB 1758
Chester	NB 1691	NB* 1708				NB 1744	BU 1767
Colchester	NB 1694	RB* 1707		RB 1721		NB 1744	BU 1773
Dartmouth		NB 1698*	RB 1716			RB 1741 (lost 1747)	
Deptford (1687)		RB 1700	RB 1719	BU 1726	NB as 60		50 in 1752
Dover (1654)	RB 1695		RB 1716		BU 1730	NB as 44	
Dragon (1647)	RB 1690	RB 1707	RB# 1711		NB as 60		Sunk 1757
Falkland	NB 1690	RB 1702		RB 1720		RB 1744	Sold 1768
Falmouth	NB 1693	NB* 1708		RB 1729		BU 1747	NB 1752
Gloucester	NB as 60	NB as 60	NB* as 50	BU 1724	NB 1737	NB* 1745	BU 1764
Greenwich (1666)		RB 1699		BU 1724	RB 1731	NB* 1747	Lost 1757
Guernsey	NB 1696		RB 1717		BU 1737	RB 1740	BU 1786
Hampshire (1653)		NB* 1698			BU 1739	NB 1741	BU 1766
Jersey		NB* 1698			NB as 60		Hulk 1771
Leopard (1659)		NB 1703		RB 1721	BU 1739	NB 1741	BU 1761
Litchfield	NB 1694				RB 1730	NB 1746	Lost 1758
Newcastle (1653)	RB 1692	NB* 1704			RB 1733		NB 1750
Nonsuch (1668)	NB* 1696		RB 1717			NB 1741	BU 1766
Norwich	NB 1693		RB 1718			NB 1745	BU 1768
Oxford (1674)		RB 1702		RB 1727			BU 1758
Panther		NB 1703	RB 1716			NB 1746	BU 1756
Pembroke	NB as 60	Lost 1709	NB* as 50	BU 1726	NB as 60	Lost 1749	NB as 60
Portland (1652)	NB* 1693			RB 1723		NB 1744	BU 1763
Preston ²	NB 1698		²			RB 1742	NB 1757
Reserve (1650)		NB* 1704	³			NB 1741	BU 1770
Rochester	NB 1693		RB 1715			NB 1749	BU 1770
Romney	NB 1694	NB* 1708		RB 1726		44 in 1745	NB 1762
Ruby (1652)	RB 1687	RB 1706				NB 1745	BU 1765
St Albans (1687)	Lost 1693	NB 1706	RB 1718			NB as 60	BU 1765
Salisbury	NB 1693	NB* 1707		RB 1726		NB 1745	NB 1769
Severn	NB 1695				RB 1739	NB* 1747	BU 1759
Southampton	NB 1693	RB 1700		Hulk 1728			BU 1771
Strafford		NB 1714			NB as 60		Sunk 1756
Swallow (1653#)	Lost 1692	NB 1703	RB 1719	BU 1728	NB as 60	BU 1742	
Tiger (1647)	RB 1681	RB 1701		RB 1722		NB 1743 ⁴	Lost 1760
Tilbury		NB 1699		BU 1726	NB as 60	NB as 58	Lost 1757
Warwick	NB 1696		RB 1710	BU 1726	NB as 60		NB as 50
Weymouth	NB 1693		RB 1718		NB as 60	Lost 1745	NB as 60
Winchester		NB 1698	RB 1717			NB 1744	BU 1769
Woolwich (1675)		RB 1702			BU 1736	RB 1741	(BU 1747)
Worcester		NB 1698	RB 1714		NB as 60		BU 1765
(B) the other 50s (excluding prizes):							
Anglesea	NB 1694		BU 1719	NB as 40			
Coventry	NB 1695	Lost 1704					
Crown (1654#)		RB 1704	Lost 1719				
Maidstone						NB 1744	(lost 1747)

In the above table, 'NB' stands for Newbuilt, 'RB' for Rebuilt, 'BU' for broken up. The date in parenthesis following each ship's name is the date of *original* launch (if before 1680). Since building (or rebuilding) took several years, the date used throughout is that of launch (or re-launch). * = after loss of former ship of this name. # = originally different name.
¹ renamed *Argyll* 1715. ² built 1698 as original *Salisbury*, and did not receive new name until 1716. ³ renamed *Sutherland* 1716. ⁴ renamed *Harwich* 1743.

Bibliography

As well as the primary sources listed in the Notes, a large amount of both nineteenth and twentieth century material is available for wider reading on this subject. What follows is not a complete listing of the works I have used or which proved useful, but only an indication as to what the reader may consult; further titles may be found in the endnotes.

Edward Archibald, *The Wooden Fighting Ship in the Royal Navy* (London 1968)

James Colledge, *Ships of the Royal Navy, Vol 1* (London 1969; second edition 1987)

John Charnock, *History of Marine Architecture*, 3 vols (London 1800–02)

Charles Derrick, *Memoirs of the Rise and Progress of the Royal Navy* (London, 1806)

John Fincham, *Treatise on Masting Ships and Mastmaking* (London 1829; final edition 1854 reprinted 1982)

John Franklin, *Navy Ship Board Models 1650–1750* (London 1989)

Robert Gardiner (ed), *The Line of Battle: The Sailing Warship 1650–1840* (London 1992; a volume in the comprehensive *Conway's History of the Ship* series)

David Hepper, *British Warship Losses in the Age of Sail 1650–1859* (Rotherfield 1994)

AJ Holland, *Ships of British Oak* (Newton Abbot 1971)

Frank Howard, *Sailing Ships of War 1400–1860* (London 1979)

Brian Lavery, *Deane's Doctrine of Naval Architecture 1670* (London 1981); *The Arming and Fitting of English Ships of War 1600–1815* (London 1987)

Frank Lecalvé, *Liste de la Flotte de Guerre Française* (Toulon 1993)

James Lees, *The Masting and Rigging of English Ships of War 1625–1860* (London 1979; second edition 1990)

Michael Oppenheim, *A History of the Administration of the Royal Navy and of merchant shipping in relation to the Royal Navy, Vol. 1, 1509–1660* (London 1896 – planned later volumes never published)

Andrew Thrush, 'In Pursuit of the Frigate, 1603–40', *Bulletin of the Institute of Historical Research* Vol 64, No 153 (1991).

Appendix B: French 50-gun ships, 1688–1750

The seventeenth-century French *vaisseaux* were divided into five rates, rather than six as in England. Like the English Navy, the number of guns increased over the second half of the century, with the average *vaisseau de 3me rang* being of 50 guns in the 1660s and varying from 50 to 60 guns in the 1690s, with 24pdrs on the lower deck; the *vaisseau de 4me rang* was on 40 guns in 1660 and between 40 and 50 guns in the 1690s. Thus the French Third Rate was generally equated with the British Fourth, and on a simple count of guns this seems valid. However, the French ordnance was on balance of greater weight, with fewer guns on the upperworks and more concentrated on the lower and upper decks. Moreover, the greater weight of the French *livre* meant that a French 12pdr shot measured the equivalent of almost 13 English pounds (12 pounds, 15¼ ounces: Wm James, *Naval History of Great Britain*, Vol 1, p45).

Prior to 1689, the French 40-gun ship was supposed to carry a mixed battery of ten 12pdrs and ten 8pdrs on the lower deck, eighteen 6pdrs on the upper deck, and two 4pdrs on the quarterdeck. Ideally, the 1689 (French) Establishment raised this to four 18pdrs and sixteen 12pdrs on the lower deck, twenty 8pdrs on the upper deck, and four 4pdrs on the quarterdeck. To carry the extra weight, the ships were to be 30 *pouces* (32in) broader. As in England, however, this *règlement* was seen as a desirable target rather than strictly interpreted.

The typical turn-of-the-century French *4me Rang*, therefore, carried twenty or twenty-two '12pdrs' on the lower deck and the same number of 6pdrs on its upper deck, in a similar manner to the British 50-gun ship. Only perhaps a third had any carriage guns on the quarterdeck, and these were usually four 4pdrs. The total weight of shot was thus between 360 and 412 *livres* (or 388 and 445 English pounds). The *Renommée*, to select an example, was 126 (French) feet in gundeck length (equivalent to 134ft 4in) and was 31 French feet in beam (33ft 0½in), with twenty-two 12pdrs, twenty 8pdrs and six 4pdrs – a total weight of shot of 448 livres (484 pounds). In the eighteenth century the upper deck guns generally became 8pdrs rather than 6pdrs. Moreover, several of the alleged 'frégates-vaisseaux' were built to carry 18pdrs on the lower deck in lieu of 12pdrs. Thus in practice there were few differences between the *vaisseau* of 50 guns and the *1ère Ordre frègate* with guns on two decks.

The *3me Rang* ships actually comprises two fairly distinct types. Those ships of 50 to 56 guns usually carried twenty-four 18pdrs on the lower deck, twenty-six 8pdrs or 12pdrs on the upper deck, and sometimes about four 4pdrs or 6pdrs on the upperworks; few were built after 1710, and none after 1750 except for *Le Sagittaire*, actually built to carry 64 guns and completed with 24pdrs on the lower deck as was the earlier *L'Amphion* (1749). The other type, vessels built with 24pdrs, were much closer to British 60s (later 64s) without all the latter's quarterdeck weapons, so do not fall within the present study. The last 50-gun ships built for the French navy were those of 1748–50. Additions after that were converted (*Sagittaire*), purchased (*Dauphin*) or donated in wartime service (the three Bordeaux vessels).

Vessel	Built		Fate
Group 1: 44- to 50-gun type (generally *4me Rang* with 12pdrs on lower deck)			
Trident	Toulon	(1688)	Taken by HMS *Plymouth* 27.6.1695 (became HMS *Trident*).
Maure	Toulon	(1687–88)	Taken by HMS *Bredah* and *Warspite* 13.12.1710 (became HMS *Moor*).
François	Le Havre	(1688)	Deleted 1722.
Adroit	Le Havre	(1690–91)	Sunk by the English 1703.
Volontaire	Toulon	(1695)	Taken and destroyed by the English at Vigo 12.10.1702.
Adélaïde	Toulon	(1698)	Wrecked 1714.
Renommée	Bayonne	(1699)	Deleted 1723.
Protée	Dunkirk	(1700–05)	Ordered as the *Amphytrite*, renamed at launch. Deleted 1722.
Griffon	Lorient	(1705)	Taken by Hardy's squadron 19.8.1712 (not added to RN).
Argonaute	Brest	(1722)	Became pontoon 1747.
Parfaite	Brest	(1722–23)	Burnt by accident 1746.
Néréide	Rochefort	(1722)	Deleted 1743.
Jason	Le Havre	(1723–24)	Rebuilt 1744–45; taken 14.5.1747 by Anson (became HMS *Jason*).
Gloire	Le Havre	(1726–27)	Rebuilt 1740–42; taken 14.5.1747 by Anson (became HMS *Glory*).
Rubis	Le Havre	(1728)	Taken by the British 14.5.1747 by Anson (became HMS *Rubis*).
Aquilon	Toulon	(1731–33)	Destroyed 14.5.1757 by HMS *Antelope*.
Auguste	Brest	(1738–39)	Taken by HMS *Portland* on 9.2.1746 (became HMS *Portland's Prize*).
Aurore	Rochefort	(1744)	Deleted 1753.
Group 2: 50- to 56-gun ships built for the French Navy or purchased into service (generally *3me Rang* with 18pdrs on lower deck)			
Fleuron	Toulon	(1688)	Hulked 1719.
Fortuné	Toulon	(1688–89)	Burnt 1707 at Velez Malaga 24.8.1704.
Perle	Dunkirk	(1690)	Lost 1709.
Entendu	Dunkirk	(1690–91)	Deleted 1701.
Indien	Lorient	(1692)	Lost 1699.
Capable	Dunkirk	(1692–93)	Deleted 1706.
Bon	Brest	(1693)	Deleted 1703.
Gaillard	Bayonne	(1694)	Taken (as a privateer) by HMS *Suffolk* 14.5.1710.

Fougueux	Brest	(1694–95)	Taken by HMS *Weymouth* and *Dover* 12.1696 (then foundered).
Téméraire	Brest	(1694–95)	Rebuilt 1706; deleted 1723.
Solide	Brest	(1695)	Taken and destroyed by the English at Vigo 12.10.1702.
Mercure	Brest	(1696)	Hulked as hospital ship; in this role taken by HMS *Namur* 15.8.1746.
Hasard	Lorient	(1698)	Taken by HMS *Orford* and others 11.1703 (became HMS *Hazardous*).
Toulouse	Toulon	(1703)	Taken by HMS *Stirling Castle* and *Hampton Court* 2.12.1811; became HMS *Thoulouse*).
Triton	Bayonne	(1702–03)	Deleted 1720.
Bourbon	Lorient	(1706)	Taken by the Dutch 24.3.1707.
Content	Lorient	(1716–17)	Sold 1747 (to French East India Company).
Tigre	Toulon	(1722–24)	Condemned 1754.
Alcyon	Toulon	(1724–26)	Burnt 12.11.1757 by HMS *Hussar* and *Dolphin*.
Diamant	Toulon	(1729–33)	Taken by Anson on 14.5.1747 (became HMS *Isis*).
Apollon	Rochefort	(1738)	Destroyed at Louisbourg 17.7.1758.
Caribou	Quebec	(1743)	Breakwater 1749; deleted 1757.
Oriflamme	Toulon	(1743–44)	Taken (*en flûte*) by HMS *Isis* 1.4.1761.
Ferme			Taken by HMS *Pembroke* 4.8.1746.
Arc-en-Ciel	Bayonne	(1745)	Taken by HMS *Torbay* 12.6.1756.
Fier	Toulon	(1745)	Rebuilt 1764; deleted 1780.
Amphion	Brest	(1748–49)	Rebuilt 1764; deleted 1787.
Aigle	Rochefort	(1748–50)	Stranded 1765.
Hyppopotame	Toulon	(1749)	Sold 1776 as *Fier Rodrigue*.
Sagittaire	Toulon	(1759–61)	Former 64-gun; deleted 1787.
Bordelais	Bordeaux	(1762–63)	Deleted 1778.
Ferme	Bordeaux	(1762–63)	Deleted 1774.
Utile	Bordeaux	(1762–64)	Deleted 1771 or 1780?
Dauphin	Lorient	(1770)	Purchased French East Indiaman; sold 1773.

Group 3: Captured British 48- to 56-gun ships (original names in parenthesis where renamed by the French):

–	(*Portsmouth*)	In French hands 9.8.1689 (sunk shortly after?)
Vaillant	(*Mary Rose*)	In French hands 22.7.1691 (deleted 1699).
Heureux Retour	(*Happy Return*)	In French hands 14.11.1691 to 4.1708 (retaken by RN).
Jersey		In French hands 28.12.1691 (deleted 1717).
–	(*Diamond*)	In French hands 30.9.1693 (fate unknown).
Dartmouth		In French hands 14.2.1695 to 22.10.1702 (retaken at Vigo Bay).
Salisbury		In French hands 21.4.1703 to 23.3.1708 (retaken).
Coventry		In French hands 3.8.1704 to 17.3.1709 (retaken)
Falmouth		In French hands 15.8.1704 (sold 1705).
Blackwall		In French hands 31.10.1705 (deleted 1719).
Pendennis		In French hands 31.10.1705 (sold 1706).
Chester		In French hands 21.10.1707 (sold 1709).
Rubis	(*Ruby*)	In French hands 21.10.1707 (sold 1708).
–	(*Bristol*)	In French hands 4.5.1709 (sunk next day during recapture).
Severne	(*Severn*)	In French hands 29.10.1746 to 25.10.1747.
Greenwich		In French hands 17.3.1757 to 14.1.1758 (wrecked).
Expérimente	(*Experiment*)	In French hands 24.9.1779; razéed 1794 and deleted 1795.
Annibal	(*Hannibal*)	In French hands 21.1.1782 (deleted later in 1782).
Leander		In French hands 18.8.1798 to 3.3.1799 (taken by Russians).
Calcutta		In French hands 26.9.1805 to 12.4.1809 (sunk by Cochrane at the Basque Roads).

The above table is not a complete list of French *3me* and *4me Rangs*, but only of those comparable with the RN's smaller Fourth Rates. Prizes taken from the Dutch and other allies in 1688–1713 are excluded, and British prizes listed separately. Dates are French dates (*ie* 'New Style' or Augustinian calendar) and so differ from British dates ('Old Style') before 1752. Where more than one year is quoted for building, the first is the start of construction (*mise en chantier*) and the last is that of launch (*mise á l'eau*). For more complete information, readers are referred to Jean Boudriot's superb study on French 64-gun and 50-gun ships.

Razéed 74s: A number of French 74-gun ships were cut down and became 54-gun ships and served in this capacity during the French Revolutionary War; they are excluded from the above table.

Notes

Draughts of 50-gun ships

1. John Franklin, in *Navy Board Ship Models*, suggests it may be the 1646-built *Adventure*.
2. The four 36-gun vessels are not covered in this volume, as they properly belong to a study of the 40-gun Fifth Rate.
3. PRO – WO/55/1718.
4. The *Ruby* in 1666 was established with only 46 guns and 170 men, but it is clear that the shortfall was in the quarterdeck sakers.
5. These are 'war at home' figures; in war abroad or in peace each had forty-two guns and 200 (150 in peace) men.
6. PRO – ADM 106/3069; this rebuilding seems to have been overlooked in the Dimensions Book.
7. I am indebted to David Hepper for this information.
8. PRO – D (W) 1778-V–1371.
9. Some sources record the *Anglesea* as built in the new Plymouth Dockyard; however, this was not ready until late 1694, *after* this ship was built, and other evidence shows her to be privately built by a Mr Flint.
10. Michael Oppenheim, *The Maritime History of Devon*, p76.
11. PRO – ADM 3/9 and ADM 9/3; see also Ehrman; PRO – ADM 3/8.
12. See the Sergison Papers.
13. Admiralty Order of 20 November 1695.
14. PRO – ADM 106/3120; I am grateful to David Hepper for pointing this out to me.
15. ADM 1/3599.
16. See the Sergison Papers.
17. Admiralty Order of 23 May 1744.
18. PRO – ADM 95/89, 6 December 1718.
19. PRO – ADM 95/12, 27 January 1719.
20. PRO – ADM 95/12, 11 June and 29 June 1723.
21. PRO – ADM 95/12, 31 May 1728; and PRO – ADM 95/12, 7 January and 17 February 1729.
22. NMM – ADM/A/2176, 7 June 1729.
23. PRO – ADM 7/339, 28 April 1733.
24. PRO – ADM 7/340, 25 March 1733.
25. NMM – ADM/B/120, 3 December 1742.
26. PRO – ADM 7/340, dated 11 October 1752.
27. PRO – ADM 95/94 Warrant Book.
28. NMM – ADM/B/187, letter of 3 November 1772.
29. NMM – ADM/B/187, letter of 10 January 1773.
30. PRO – ADM 95/38.
31. NMM – ADM/B/193, letter of 27 May 1776.
32. Captain Andrew Snape Hammond to Hans Stanley, 29 September 1776, quoted in *Naval Documents of the American Revolution*, Vol 6, p975.
33. PRO – ADM 766/106.
34. According to Campbell's *Lives of the Admirals*, reprinted in Fincham, p102.
35. PRO – ADM 106/3564, Sheerness Letter Book.
36. PRO – ADM 106/1843, letter to Navy Board, 24 July 1797.
37. William James, *Naval History of Great Britain*, Vol 5, p427.
38. Personal communication, Grant Walker, USN Academy Museum, Annapolis.
39. PRO Adm 106/2509, 10 June 1787.
40. L G Carr Laughton, *Old Ship Figure-heads and Sterns* (London 1925).
41. PRO Adm 106/2507, no 150, quoted in *Mariners' Mirror* Vol 3 (1913), pp20–1.
42. R J B Knight, 'The Introduction of Copper Sheathing into the Royal Navy 1779–1786', *Mariners' Mirror* Vol 59 (1973), pp 299–309.
43. PRO Adm 106 of 24 September 1781 and Adm 106/2508 of 2 October 1781.
44. NMM SPB/15, p70.
45. Establishment proposed 30 July 1673, presented to the Admiralty on 15 August, adopted 16 October 1673.

(continued opposite)

(Dansk = Danish Rigsarkivet, Copenhagen; Science = Science Museum, London):

12pdr (130ft) types

1457	*Litchfield*		1694-1720	NMM	Stigant	Lines & profile (pre-1720).
1580	*Antelope*		1703-1738	Dansk		Lines (1727).
1366	*Dragon* (ex-*Ormonde*)		1711-1733	NMM	Acworth	Lines.
4823	*Strafford*	(1706 Estab.)	1714-1726	Science	Phillips	Lines and profile.

18pdr type

4824	*Winchester*	(1706 Estab.)	1717-1744	Science	Phillips	Lines and profile.
4825	*Deptford*	(")	1719-1726	Science	Phillips	Lines and profile.
1359	*Falkland*	(1719 Estab.)	1720-1743	NMM	Stacey	Lines and profile.
1362	*Chatham*	(")	1721-1749	Dansk	Stacey	Lines.
1335	*Colchester*	(")	1721-1742	NMM	Rosewell	Lines and profile.
6196	*Oxford*	(")	1727-1758	NMM	Allin	Lines and profile.
1458	*Litchfield*	(")	1730-1744	NMM	Lock	Lines and profile.
1417-1418	*Saint Albans*	(1733 Est.)	1737-1744	NMM	Lock	Lines/Lines and profile.
1421	*Severn*	(")	1739-1746	NMM	Lock	Lines.
1363	*Guernsey*	(")	1740-1769	NMM	Ward	Lines/And as hulk (1769).
1356	*Dartmouth*	(")	1741-1747	NMM	Hayward	Lines.
1520	*Woolwich*	(")	1741-1747	NMM	Stacey	Lines.
1399	*Antelope*	(")	1742-1783	NMM	Hayward	Lines.
1472-1473	*Preston*	(")	1742-1748	NMM	Fellowes	Lines.
1484 {	*Leopard*	(")	1741-1761	Dansk		Lines and profile.
	Sutherland	(")	1741-1770	NMM		Lines
	Nonsuch	(")	1741-1766	NMM		Lines.
	Hampshire group	(")	1741-1770	NMM	misc.	Lines.

24pdr type

1485-1489	1741 Establishment contract-built			NMM	Allin?	Lines & profile/decks.
?	*Harwich*	(")	1743-1760	NMM	Barnard	Lines and profile.
?	*Colchester*	(")	1744-1744	NMM	"	"
1360	*Falkland*	(")	1744-1768	NMM	Ewer	"
1443	*Panther*	(")	1746-1756	NMM	Fellowes	Lines.
?	*Litchfield*	(")	1746-1758	NMM	Barnard	Lines and profile.
?	*Colchester*	(")	1746-1773	NMM	Carter	"
1415	*Bristol*	(Mod.1741 Est.)	1746-1768	NMM	Holland	Lines (incomplete).
1416	*Rochester*	(")	1749-1770	NMM	Holland	Lines and profile.
1394	1745 Establishment contract-built			NMM	Allin?	Lines and profile.
?	*Assistance*	(")	1747-1770	NMM		Lines & profile/decks.
1394	*Greenwich*	(")	1747-1757	NMM		Lines & profile.
8022a	unnamed		1756	NMM		Deck plans.
1474	*Preston*		1757-1785	NMM	Allin	Lines/stern.
1361	*Chatham*		1758-1793	NMM	Allin	Lines.
1571	*Warwick*		1767-1783	NMM	Bately	Lines & profile.
1425-6	*Romney*		1762-1804	NMM	Slade	Lines & profile/spec.
1427-8	*Salisbury*		1769-1796	NMM	Slade	As built (full set)
1368-9	*Centurion*		1774-1808	NMM	Slade	As built (lines & pr/decks).
?	*Portland* class		1770 on	NMM	Williams	Lines & profile/decks/framing.